Understanding Realities Now: Nina's travelogues

Nina van Gorkom

2020

2

Published in 2020 by:
Zolag
www.zolag.co.uk

ISBN 9781897633380
Copyright Nina van Gorkom

Contents

Editors Foreword

This book has a single aim: to help the reader understand the true nature of the reality of the present moment. This moment.

It consists of 9 travelogues, discussions with Acharn Sujin Boriharnwanaket, the good friend in Dhamma, a Thai Buddhist lay follower. They have taken place over the last seven years in a variety of places, mostly Thailand, South Vietnam and Sri Lanka. The various situations are used to show the relevance of the teachings to daily life. The book starts with an interview with the author about her book *Abhidhamma in Daily Life*. She has also written and has published 4 other books on Abhidhamma topics.

Nina's writing is straight, uncluttered, she uses simple words to disseminate and embellish the deep meaning of Sujin's dhamma talks. She draws on her detailed knowledge of Abhidhamma texts and for precision uses some Pāli words. Quotes are used from the original Theravāda Suttas to show that the meaning of these words is consistent with the teachings of the Buddha. Her writing and Sujin's conversation help the reader understand the depth and subtlety of the teachings. They help the reader understand the realities of daily life. The reality which 'appears' now.

The book is suitable for the beginner, but with a caveat. It is difficult and takes great patience over a long period to appreciate. It is an impressive piece of work but only for those who have persevered with its meaning.

I would like to thank Acharn Sujin Boriharnwanaket, Nina van Gorkom, Sarah and Jonothan Abbott and the Dhamma and Support Foundation who have helped me glimpse the depth and subtlety of this great teaching.

   With much gratitude and appreciation, I share this work with a
wider audience.
   Alan Weller

1

Mijn Interview

An interview with Nina van Gorkom about the Abhidhamma. The original interview was in Dutch and has been translted into English. Nina van Gorkom is the author of the book Abhidhamma in Daily Life.

Question: Can you say in short what is the Abhidhamma?

Nina: The Abhidhamma explains what life is. Before hearing the Buddha's teachings we had different ideas about life. Life is only one moment and it changes all the time, it falls away immediately. At the moment of seeing, life is seeing, at the moment of hearing, life is hearing. The Buddha explained about all that can be experienced through the senses and the mind. We always thought that life is permanent, and that there is a self coordinating all experiences. The Buddha explained that there is no self, only momentary realities that change all the time. What we take for a person are different mental moments and physical moments. None of these moments can stay and they cannot be controlled, and they cannot be caused to arise.

Question: How did you come into contact with the Abhidhamma?

1

Nina: I came to Thailand and met Acharn Sujin. I was looking for something but did not know what. I thought that there must be something else apart from parties and all the things that keep us busy in daily life. She explained that vipassana, insight into what is real, can be developed in daily life. Since I had a very busy life I thought that I could not retire and stay in a quiet place. She took me to the provinces, outside Bangkok, and explained to me simple things in the situation of daily life. For example, when we worry or have problems, these are only moments of thinking. She did not wait explaining to me about nama, mental phenomena , and rupa, physical phenomena. She explained that these are different kinds of reality. Nama can experience something and rupa cannot experience anything, but it can be experienced. She explained realities as they occur in different situations. Situations are not realities. We think of people and things but actually there are only nama and rupa. We can think of situations, ideas, concepts, and thinking itself is a reality. But what we think is not real in the absolute sense.

Question: How did you begin studying the Abhidhamma?

Nina: By reading suttas and listening to Acharn's radio programs. I listened each morning during breakfast. In this program she explained about citta, a moment of consciousness, that arises within a process or series of cittas. She enumerated each of these moments of citta that succeed one another, explaining this each day again and again. In this way one could learn about the processes of citta. Asking questions I found important. Every time I visited Acharn I had a whole list of questions. She also made me work, writing about Dhamma. She had an English program and every fortnight there had to be a new program. I had to think it over and write down what I had reflected on. That was very helpful for the development of understanding.

Question: It was a favorable condition that there was a teacher near you. What advice do you have for others who want to begin with the study and do not have a teacher near them?

Nina: The Buddha said all the time that one should listen to the Dhamma and consider what one hears. This can also be done by reading of the texts, but that is not sufficient. Discussion helps, such as we do at our online meetings, asking questions, discussing and reflecting on what one has heard. There are no other means than these.

Question: The Abhidhamma often deals with consciousness, and what is the meaning of consciousness, citta?

Nina: Before coming into contact with the Buddha's teachings we always thought of a self who coordinates all experiences, such as I see, I think, and also the brain plays its part. The Buddha's teaching is quite different. There are specific conditions for each moment of citta. The visual object and eyesense are conditions for seeing, they associate so that seeing can arise. At the same time is seeing result of a former deed or kamma. There are many types of citta. Seeing and hearing are results of kamma, deeds committed in the past. We see and hear agreeable objects or disagreeable objects, seeing and hearing are results of good deeds and evil deeds. Then there are reactions to these experiences, these are more the active side of our life. We can react with wholesome consciousness or unwholesome consciousness, and this is also conditioned. It is conditioned by accumulations of former experiences. Because of our education, what our parents taught us, there may be wholesome moments of generosity, moments of assisting others, and such good qualities fall away immediately together with consciousness. But each moment of consciousness conditions the following consciousness and that is why good and bad qualities can be passed on. They are never lost, they are passed on from one moment of consciousness to the next one, from one life to the next life. That can be called accumulation, accumulation of good and bad qualities in consciousness. Such accumulations are among others a condition for the way we react to sense impressions.

Question: The book you wrote about the Abhidhamma is called *Abhidhamma in Daily Life*. Can you elaborate more on what the Abhidhamma means in daily life?

Nina: The Abhidhamma helps one to know oneself, but what we call self are actually the changing moments of consciousness. The aim of the Buddha's teaching is not having more wholesomeness and less unwholesomeness. The aim is understanding, understanding that whatever arises is conditioned. It cannot be controlled, but it can be understood. One reacts to whatever occurs with attachment or with aversion, and these have arisen already. It is not possible to make them disappear, but they can be understood as conditioned elements, thus, as non-self.

Question: Can you say more about feelings and emotions?

Nina: We find feelings about our different experiences so important. We think of my feelings, my problems. It means that we are engaged with ourselves.

Feeling in the Buddha's teachings is different from emotions as we see them in the conventional meaning. Feeling is only a mental factor, cetasika, which accompanies each citta. Its function is tasting the object that is experienced by citta. There are not only pleasant feeling and unpleasant feeling, but also indifferent or neutral feeling. Seeing now is accompanied by indifferent feeling. We believe that there is at that moment no feeling, but there is indifferent feeeling and it falls away immediately. Feeling is a reality that is quite different from what we consider feeling in conventional sense. We are very attached to feeling and our ideas about feeling, but actually it is only a cetasika that falls away immediately. When we have problems in life we find them very important, but in fact these are only moments of thinking with different cetasikas such as aversion which falls away immediately. We believe that we can control them but in the end they are solved in a way that is totally different from what we expected. I experienced that during my journey. I was worried but my traveling which I find so difficult. I was reminded by a friend that in that way I was occupied with myself. I could not have any control. They were always solved in a way beyond expectation. I was worried how I could manage without a walker when arriving in Thailand and Vietnam. But there were walkers when I arrived, people had given them to me. I could not have known this ahead of time.

Sarah had given me very good reminders about worry, she had just had an accident, an electrical shock because of touching an electric device. She was flung from one side of the room to the other side. Shortly afterwards she spoke very helpful words to me to remind me of the truth while I was worrying, but she could not remember what she had said. Those were kusala cittas that conditioned her speaking. It was beyond control.

Question: We always want to experience agreeable emotions. Can you add something about that?

Nina: When we do not have them as expected we are disappointed. One cannot control anything and one has to accept that.

I heard during our sessions about people who awoke during the night because of fear, but that is not in accordance with the Buddha's teachings. There should be a removal of a burden when one follows his teachings. One cannot control whatever happens, but one can come to have more understanding. The Path of the Buddha does not have anxiety as effect.

Question: But we all have fears. How should we see these in according with the Abhidhamma?

Nina: By not taking them for self or mine. Only a mental reality, not self. One can never know the next moment.

Question: Alertness or paying attention is a very important factor.

Nina: This word may be misleading. We need a word that is a translation of sati but alertness could suggest a self who is alert and notices whether a reality is wholesome or unwholesome. It may give an idea of a self who notices this. Sati is a cetasika that can only arise with a wholesome citta. It is non-forgetful of what is wholesome. There are many levels of sati, such as sati that is non-forgetful of generosity. Or we have an opportunity to help someone else, but we are lazy and do not move. But when sati arises because of conditions, it remembers that helping is wholesome and then we will help others. That is only one level. There is also sati of a higher level. There are many different realities such as seeing, thinking of what is seen, attachment, and then there is the realization that understanding of these realities is beneficial. It is not self that realizes this, it is sati. Sati is mindful, non-forgetful, of whatever reality appears. Sati may arise or may not arise, we do not know ahead of time, we cannot arrange for it.

Question: Which were the four points that were mentioned by a friend during your journey as conditions for understanding?

Nina: Listening to the teachings, and this can be by means of discussion or reading. Considering what one heard, thus, not merely passively listening. One does not have to do this deliberately, but later on during the day, for example, there may be conditions to recall what one heard or what one read and reflect upon this. These are two points. The third point is that considering the Buddha's words is to be in daily life. It is not necessary to go to a specific place. It has to be in daily life. While we are talking or in the kitchen we can consider the Dhamma we heard. The fourth point is confidence, confidence that this the Buddha's word, and that we can develop understanding of what he taught.

Question: Are these four points helpful to establish sati?

Nina: We should not have an idea that it is necessary to establish sati. It depends on conditions whether or not sati arises. What is most important is not alertness, but understanding, the understanding of the different moments of consciousness and the physical phenomena, nama and rupa. This is the aim and it can condition later on direct understanding of realities through satipatthana. We should not have expectations. When we have expectations there is already attachment. Whatever attachment there may be, it is counterproductive.

Part I

The Meaning of Dhamma

2

The Meaning of Dhamma

The Dhamma Study group in Vietnam had organised Dhamma sessions
in June, 2019, in Nha Trang and Hoi An. Acharn Sujin could not come
this time since she was recovering in hospital after a journey in India but
Sarah and Jonothan were going to lead the discussions. Much of what
I am reporting from these has been taken from their inspiring remarks.

Ann from Canada and Roti from Mexico also joined the sessions.
The Vietamese Dhamma Study Group is very active and Dhamma books
are printed all the time. They had just finished printing Acharn's book
on Metta, Loving Kindness, which I had translated from Thai into English. They had designed a beautiful cover with a hand of the Buddha.

Before leaving Bangkok for Vietnam Sarah had asked Acharn whether
she had any message for the listeners at the sessions. She said: "One
word: dhamma." Sarah elaborated: "What is the meaning of dhamma?
Dhamma is the meaning of life at this moment. Usually there is no
understanding of life. We follow our daily routine without any understanding of life."

Sarah explained that in whatever situation we are, there are just

9

passing dhammas, each arising because of their own conditions and impermanent. We can learn to see life in a different way, for example, when we lose dear persons through death. Wherever we traveled, there was time and again a case of someone who had lost a dear person. This time I met someone who was depressed because of the loss of her husband ten years ago. She often went to the movies to forget about her loss.

We all cling to persons, but we can learn from the Buddha that what we take for a person are only citta, consciousness, cetasikas, mental factors accompanying consciousness, and rūpa, physical phenomena. They arise for an instant and then fall away immediately. What we used to find so important, the different feelings, our experiences through the senses and our thinking, are just passing dhammas.

The Buddha taught what life is. Before hearing the Buddha's teachings we had ideas about life different from his teaching. In reality, life is only one moment of consciousness, citta, and it changes all the time; it falls away immediately. At the moment of seeing, life is seeing, at the moment of hearing, life is hearing. The Buddha taught what can be directly experienced one at a time, through the sense-doors and the mind-door. He taught that each reality arises because of its own conditions and that there is not any person who can make it arise. Each reality arises just for a moment and then it is gone immediately, never to return.

At each moment in life there is the loss of an object we hold dear, there is a kind of death. We may experience a pleasant sound or a delicious flavour, but it is gone immediately. We are attached to all objects appearing through the senses and the mind, but actually we cing to nothing and are misleading ourselves with regard to what is real. When we lose a dear person through death we feel sorrow because of our clinging to pleasant sights, sounds and other objects experienced through the senses. We no longer see or hear the beloved person, but we are really thinking of ourselves, we mourn ourselves.

We always thought that life could last for some time, and that there is a self coordinating all our experiences in life. We thought of a self who sees and thinks about what is seen, who hears and thinks about what is heard, all at the same time. The Buddha explained that there is no self, only momentary realities that change all the time. None of these moments can stay and they cannot be controlled, they cannot be caused to arise. We usually live in the fantasy world of "I", thinking of "I see, I hear, I touch". They are only different dhammas.

One of the listeners realized that he often confused thinking of stories and concepts with realities. He realized this while he was thinking of the problems that arose within his family. That shows how useful discussion about this subject is. In this way understanding of the level of pariyatti can grow.

Because of the experiences through the senses and the mind-door different feelings arise: pleasant feeling, unpleasant feeling and indifferent feeling. We find feeling so important and take it for "my feeling". We wish to experience only pleasant things and when there is an unpleasant object such as a loud sound, unpleasant feeling arises. Whatever is experienced, also feeling, are passing dhammas that cannot be controlled. We wish to control what will happen in our life, but we never know what the next moment will bring and during my journey I was reminded of this fact several times.

When we have problems in life we find them very important, and we worry. In fact, these are only moments of thinking with different cetasikas such as aversion which falls away immediately. We believe that we can control the events of life but in the end problems are solved in a way that is totally different from what we expected. I was worried about my traveling I find so difficult.

Sarah gave me very good reminders about worry. She had just had an accident, an electrical shock because of touching an electric device in the hotel room. She was flung from one side of the room to the other side. Shortly afterwards she spoke very helpful words to me to remind me of the truth while I was worrying, but she could not remember what she had said since she still had to recover from the shock. Kusala cittas conditioned her speaking. This was beyond control but it happened because of conditions. She explained that when one is worried one is occupied with oneself and one forgets that whatever reality appears is beyond control. We can make useful plans, believing that we can determine the outcome and then we are thinking of situations instead of understanding the reality which appears now, such as seeing, hearing, attachment or aversion. When we are just thinking of situations we usually do this with an idea of self and this will not lead to the understanding of realities.

I was worried how I could manage to go around without a walker when arriving in Thailand and Vietnam. But there were walkers when I arrived, people had given them to me with great generosity. I could not have known this ahead of time. Problems are solved beyond expectation.

Hang and I wanted to eat some noodles and we went to the restaurant of the hotel. The owner of the hotel had offered food to monks who were visiting from Myanmar and since there was much food left she invited us for luncheon. At the table we were sitting together with her family members and friends. We had not expected to enjoy a meal together with such a delightful company when we went out for some noodles. It happened all because of conditions. During the meal I met Jotamoi from Myanmar who had studied the Abhidhamma for many years and given lectures on this subject. Hang and I spoke to him about the Dhamma Study Group and invited him to join our sessions. He had no more time since he had to accompany the group of monks from Myanmar, but the next day he sent us a few useful questions.

One of his questions was about the difference in teaching as we find it in the Suttanta, the Abhidhamma and the Vinaya. It seems that we read in the suttas about things that should be done whereas in the Abhidhamma there is reference to realities. It seems that the Vinaya mainly deals with the establishment of rules, with sīla.

The Buddha taught about the reality appearing at the present moment and the way to develop understanding in order to eliminate ignorance. He taught that whatever reality appears is non-self. The teachings contained in the three parts of the Tipiṭaka are actually the same. In the Suttanta he would speak about persons and situations, but also at those moments he was referring to realities arising because of conditions. He spoke time and again about all realities of daily life as they are experienced through the six doors and he asked the listeners whether these realities are permanent or impermanent and whether they can be taken for self. He would speak about making an effort for the arising of kusala, and the elimination of akusala, but then he was referring to the sobhana cetasika (wholesome mental factor) right effort which is a factor of the eightfold Path and which is always arising together with right understanding of realities. Right effort does not belong to a person. It arises because of wholesome accumulations. Each wholesome or unwhwolesome quality that arises with the citta falls away immediately with the citta, but it is not lost, it is accumulated in the citta. Since each citta is succeeded by a following citta wholesome and unwholesome qualities are carried on from one citta to the following citta, from moment to moment, from life to life.

Not only in the Abhidhamma but also in the suttas we read about the ultimate realities of the five aggregates khandhas), the elements (dhātus), the sense-fields (āyatanas), about all realities which are classified in different ways as nāma and rūpa.

As to the Vinaya, this deals among others with akusala sīla. Sīla comprises kusala dhamma, akusala dhamma, and for the arahat avyākata (indeterminate) dhamma which is neither kusala not akusala[1] People are inclined to think that sīla are just rules to be followed, but sīla is the behaviour of the citta at this moment. Kusala sīla develops through right understanding of the citta at this moment. Any reality which appears now can be investigated and considered in order to understand its true nature. The development of understanding is the highest kind of sīla.

We read in the teachings about sīla (morality), samādhi, (calm) and paññā (understanding) and people are inclined to think that there is a certain order of developing these qualities. There is no rule that they should be developed in a certain order. The factors of the eightfold Path can be classified in this threefold way, but all factors develop together with right understanding of the eightfold Path[2]

Kusala sīla comprises all levels of sīla and the highest sīla is the development of right understanding of realities. As to samādhi, calm, this arises with every sobhana (beautiful) citta. When a moment of right understanding of a reality arises, there are sīla and samādhi as well.

There are several ways by which sīla, samādhi and paññā have been classified. They can be considered under various aspects. One way is the classificication of the ariyans who have reached the perfection of sīla, of the ariyans who have rached the perfection of samādhi and of

---

[1] He does not commit kamma that can bring a result in the future. For him there are no conditions for rebirth.

[2] The three abstinences, right speech, right action and right livelihood, are the sīla of the eightfold Path, right mindfulness and right concentration the calm, samādhi, of the eightfold Path, right thinking and right understanding the wisdom of the eightfold Path.

the ariyans who have reached the perfection of paññā. The sotāpanna who has eradicated the wrong view of self has no more conditions to violate the five precepts, he has perfected sīla. He has no more conditions to commit the kinds of akusala kamma that lead to an unhappy rebirth. The non-returner (anāgāmī) who has realized the third stage of enlightenment, has perfected calm, samādhi. He has eradicated all attachment to sense objects, he is no longer absorbed by them. The arahat who has eradicated all ignorance and other kinds of defilements has perfected paññā.

It is because of the development of right understanding of the reality appearing at the present moment that the different stages of enlightenment can be attained and defilements are eradicated stage by stage. Not because one should develop sīla first, then calm and then paññā.

Right understanding of what is reality should be developed and this is different from knowing conventional notions such as a table, a tree or a person. Acharn Sujin reminded us of what dhamma is by her message to Sarah about dhamma. Dhamma is what can be directly experienced through one of the senses or the mind-door. Sound is a dhamma that can be directly experienced through the earsense, without having to think about it. We believe that we hear the sound of a barking dog, but then there is thinking of a concept, a story. There is no barking dog in the sound.

Before coming into contact with the Buddha's teachings we ony knew conventional truth. But the Buddha taught what can be directly experienced one at a time, through the sense-doors and the mind-door. He taught that it only lasts for one moment and then it is gone, never to return. He taught that each reality arises because of its own conditions and that there is not any person who can make it arise.

We can lead our daily life as usual, thinking of our friends, of persons, of food, of our house, but we can learn the difference between thinking of concepts of persons and things and understanding of what can be directly experienced at the present moment.

It is beneficial to understand the difference because in that way we can learn how much ignorance there is of the truth of life. We do not try to change anything that arises because of conditions, but understanding can grow. Understanding the truth of life is more precious than anything else.

3

Understanding Ultimate Realities

Understanding of our life now can be developed. We usually follow our daily activities with attachment and ignorance, but any reality that appears can be the object of understanding. One of our friends liked playing the guitar and spent much time on this. Time and again he was wondering whether he should spend more time on studying Dhamma instead of playing guitar. Whatever arises in life happens by conditions. One person likes music, another person painting or sports. It is not useful to think of how little awareness and understanding there is and what one will do to have more. Then one is concerned about oneself and this will not be helpful to have more understanding of the truth of non-self. Satipaṭṭhāna is not "doing something" but the arising of mindfulnes and understanding by conditions whereby direct understanding of nāma and rūpa is developed. We were often reminded by Acharn with the words: "Let understanding work its way".

No one can stop attachment from arising right now. One of our friends remarked that conditions can be created for the non-arising of attachment. However, if one tries to make things happen in a specific way one fails to see the truth of anattā.

When people spoke about their different defilements Jonothan kept on saying: "It does not matter, it does not matter." When asked to explain what he meant by this, he said:

"What has arisen, has arisen. It can be understood. It is of no use to analyse it, finding out whether it is kusala or akusala. Then we are choosing a specific object and it is not understanding the present moment. There is no understanding of any reality that is appearing now."

We can lead our life naturally, swimming, playing guitar, doing our job. It is of no use to try to change our life style. Understanding can be developed in any situation. If one just thinks of being in favorable situations there will never be understanding of what dhamma is that just arises because of its own conditions.

When one thinks that the development of the Path is too difficult, there is again the idea of self, an idea of "I who cannot do it". When one thinks about what one shall do, thus, about the future, there is forgetfulness of the present moment. One does not understand that there are only conditioned dhammas which are beyond control, non-self. Thinking arises now, and then it is gone immediately. If there is no understanding of the present moment yet, it does not matter. When understanding has been accumulated more the present moment can be known naturally, without any expectation.

What can be directly experienced now, without having to think about it, is just dhamma. Usually realities such as hardness, heat or cold are directly experienced through the bodysense but they are not known as dhammas. Right understanding has to grow so that they can be understood as realities appearing through the bodysense that arise for a moment and then fall away immediately.

Each reality arises and falls away very rapidly. Seeing is immediately followed by other cittas. Then seeing arises again and again in other processes. We could not know a single moment of seeing, only a sign, in Pali: nimitta, remains. Of each reality that arises a nimitta is experienced. This can remind us that realities arise and fall away extremely fast.

At the end of the Dhamma sessions, in Nha Trang, the monk who followed the sessions asked Jonothan to resume in a few points the contents of the sessions.

Jonothan mentioned four points: Listen carefully, consider carefully, remember this while going about one's daily life, and have confidence. He elaborated on these points in the following way: As to listening carefully, this means hearing an explanation of the Buddha's teaching and every opportunity to hear that can be taken when understanding is being developed. One needs to hear everything more than once, from different aspects and different parts of the teachings.

As to the second point: just hearing is not enough, there need to be some reflection as one goes about one's daily life. The meaning is deep and subtle. It cannot be comprehended just on a single hearing without reading, turning it over in one's mind, considering how it relates to the present moment.

This has to be done while going about one's daily life and that means that there is no need for a special kind of place, special circumstances or environment for this to happen. One can hear Dhamma from an unexpected source, consider it during unlikely activities. Anything other is not the Path of the Buddha.

There should be confidence that the first and second points are sufficient if properly understood, and that they can condition awareness to arise. It may seem that there must be more that can be done, but there should be confidence that those factors mentioned by the Buddha are sufficient for awareness to arise, in time, when the conditions are there. Be patient also.

These are precious points. As to confidence, one should not be disheartened that the development of understanding of the present reality takes a long, long time. Jonothan also said about confidence: "Confidence in the Dhamma, confidence in the development of kusala, regardless of the situation." We may be disappointed when things do not work out the way we expected, but we should not forget that whatever reality presents itself is conditioned already.

At the end of the sessions in Nha Trang one of the children who listened to the Dhamma conversations made a touching speech, showing her gratefulness for all she had learnt those days. She spoke with great confidence. It was inspiring to notice people's enthusiasm. The mother of someone who regularly attended the sessions was listening to recordings during the time she worked in the rice field. This is heavy work in a hot climate but it did not prevent her from listening and considering the truth of Dhamma with confidence. Different families sponsored our lunches each day and they walked with their children past our tables so that we had an opportunity to meet them and to express our appreciation.

After Nha Trang we had a short flight to Hoi An where some of us stayed in Anicca Villa. Those were happy days when we enjoyed the hospitality of Sun and Mai. Every day a delicious Vietnamese meal was prepared and before, during and after the meal we had Dhamma conversations. Nam and his younger brother Nguying joined our discussions and Nam, who has a great musical talent, played the piano for us. The two French architects who had designed this villa and several other resorts came along and they had basic questions which were useful for everybody. We discussed how one is inclined to wish to control whatever occurs and if things do not work out according to one's wish one may vex oneself and believe that this is one's own fault. Sarah explained that right understanding that whatever occurs is because of the appropriate conditions is like the removal of a heavy burden. There will be less clinging to an idea of self one used to find very important, and no feelings of guilt.

Again we have to remember the true meaning of dhamma; whatever arises is dhamma and this means that nobody can make good qualities arise, that there is no person. It is natural to think of persons, of our friends, but in order to understand the truth we have to consider the present reality. There is no reality to be known that is a person, a friend. Visible object is experienced through the eyesense and in visible object there is no person, in sound that is heard there is no person. We tend to forget that what we take for a person is only citta, cetasika and rūpa that do not last, even for a splitsecond. When someone speaks unkindly to us we have aversion or anger and we keep on thinking of "that terrible person". We forget that the real problem is always the attachment, aversion and ignorance that arise within ourselves. In reality no person is heard, only sound is heard and there is no one who acts or speaks. It is important to know what is real in the ultimate sense and what is only imagination. I have heard this often but we can hear it again and again in order to be reminded of the truth. It is not wrong view to think by way of conventional notions such as this or that person or situation.

It is necessary for leading our daily life naturally and to communicate with others. At the same time we can develop understanding of what is real in the ultimate sense. There is wrong view when we believe that a person or self really exists.

If we have a problem we tend to think about it with attachment or aversion and we take our thinking for self. Sarah explained that the aim of the study of Dhamma is not to stop such thinking, but that this is the time for understanding Dhamma. Whatever occurs can be understood as just passing dhammas. Sarah said: "When confidence develops there will be less thinking of 'how can I have more understanding.' There can be understanding just now of what appears."

If we wonder about the way to have more understanding, it takes us away from the present moment. We should not try to focus on particular realities, because realities appear naturally, just when there are conditions for them to arise and appear. We should not forget that life is in a moment, just in this moment. Very gradually we can come to understand the difference between life in conventional sense, life as different situations, and life just in a moment, such as seeing appearing now or thinking appearing now. We think of many stories in a day, but they are just fantasy, not reality.

When we wonder whether we should or should not do this or that, we are inclined to control the situation we are in or we think that another situation, not the present one, is more favorable for the development of understanding.

Some people believe that the development of samatha is necessary for the understanding of realities. One may wonder whether the Buddha taught samatha. During the sessions people asked questions about samatha. Also before the Buddha's time samatha was developed. The Buddha taught about all kinds of kusala, and these can be developed with right understanding. Samatha should not be developed without understanding of what true calm is. Some people believe that when they close their eyes and think of a wholesome subject such as metta, that they develop calm. One should have right understanding of calm. Calm is a sobhana cetasika that arises with each wholesome citta[1] At the moment of calm there are no attachment, aversion or ignorance. If

---

[1] There are actually calm of citta and calm of cetasikas.

one has accumulated the inclination to develop higher degrees of calm, even to the degree of jhāna, one should see the danger of clinging to sense objects. If one does not see this, calm cannot be developed. Right understanding of the characteristic of calm and of the way to develop it with an appropriate subject is indispensable.

There can be wise reflection at any time and at any place. There is no need to wait for a favorable time or to go to a quiet place. Some people believe that they have to be calm first before they can develop understanding of realities. Or they think that when there are less defilements there is more opportunity for the arising of awarenes and understanding. Akusala has been accumulated and it will continue to arise. Only direct understanding that has reached the level of lokuttara can eradicate stage by stage the latent tendencies of attachment and other accumulated defilements.

We often hear that the development of understanding begins at the present moment. We can listen more and consider the reality appearing now, be it seeing, sound or attachment, even for a few moments. Life will never be as we think or plan. It cannot be known what hearing hears the next moment or what thinking thinks the next moment.

There is no self who is listening and considering the Dhamma. These are only moments of citta arising because of conditions. Someone may hear for the first time that there is no "I" who sees or hears. It is only the seeing that sees, the hearing that hears. There can be a beginning of understanding the truth. Considering the realities that appear are wholesome moments that do not last, that fall away immediately. Each moment of citta falls away immediately but it conditions the following moment. In this way understanding can be accumulated from moment to moment. At a following moment there may be a little more understanding of realities. Then we listen and consider again and gradually understanding can grow. This helps us to see that it is not "I" who understands.

Intellectual understanding, pariyatti, can condition direct understanding, paṭipatti. Pariyatti does not mean theoretical knowledge of the teachings, it is always related to the present moment, to what appears now.

Seeing appears time and again and we can consider its nature. We can begin to understand that it is a conditioned reality, conditioned by kamma, by eyesense and visible object, and that it only experiences visible object, no persons or things. Thinking about persons and things is another citta, and it follows so closely after seeing, that it seems to arise at the same time as seeing. But there can be only one citta at a time experiencing one object.

Before realities can be understood as non-self, it should be known what appears now. Understanding of the level of pariyatti does not experience realities directly, it experiences concepts of realities. It should be emphasized that the objects are concepts of reality, not concepts in the sense of stories, situations or imagination, such as a person, a building or a table. Seeing, hearing, sound or feeling may appear, and understanding can investigate these realities so that they will be known as only dhammas. When understanding of the level of pariyatti has become very firm, it can condition direct understanding of them. There should be no expectation when there will be direct understanding of realities, but there can be confidence that the truth of Dhamma can be penetrated little by little. Otherwise the Buddha would not have taught it.

4

Sati of Vipassanā

Sati is a wholesome cetasika that is non-forgetful of what is wholesome. Sati can be of different levels, of dāna, of sīla, of samatha and of vipassanā. When there is an opportunity to be generous in giving or assisting someone else, we may be lazy and forgetful so that it is impossible for us to be generous or to help. When sati arises it uses the opportunity for kusala and it is non-forgetful of generosity and mettā. At such moments it guards the six doorways: whatever object is experienced through one of the six doorways is experienced without attachment, aversion or ignorance.

Sati is not awareness or mindfulness as we use these words in conventional sense. It is not: knowing what one is doing, like walking, or focussing on an object. One should know what the object of sati is: any object that appears at the present moment by conditions. It is not a situation or a concept but a reality like sound, hardness, attachment or thinking. There should not be any selection of specific objects; also unpleasant objects and unwholesome objects can be known one at a time when they appear. That is the only way to understand that whatever

23

appears is anattā; it is not in one's power to have any control. If one
believes that the situation is not favorable for sati or that one should
create conditions for sati one is on the wrong Path leading one further
away from the truth.

Anger or attachment can be object of mindfulness. They may arise
because these realities also arose in the past. They arose and fell away
with the citta but they are accumulated from one moment of citta to
the succeeding moment of citta, from life to life. Kusala and akusala lie
dormant in each citta and when there are conditions they can arise.

When we remember that kusala cittas and akusala cittas arise in
processes in a certain order that cannot be altered it will be clearer
that they are beyond control. Seeing arises within a process and after it
has fallen away three more moments of cittas arise before kusala cittas
or akusala cittas performing the function of javana arise. They are all
gone before one can think about them. Nobody can prevent them from
arising. Who knows what seeing will see the next moment or what
thinking will think of. Whatever arises because of conditions can be
object of mindfulness.

It is important to know what is real and what is only imagination.
We believe that we can hear a dog barking. Sound is real, but a barking
dog does not exist in the ultimate sense. What we take for a dog is
only citta, cetasika and rūpa which do not last for a moment. Sati
can only be mindful of the present reality, not of a conventional notion.
When sati is mindful of a reality like sound there can be understanding
of that reality as anattā. It was explained time and again that when
there is more understanding of the level of pariyatti, thus, intellectual
understanding of this moment, it will lead to realizing that there are
only passing dhammas which are beyond control. Even when one has
heard this many times, it is beneficial to be reminded of the truth.
There is usually absorption in stories, in a fantasy world, instead of
understanding the present reality.

When one does not know the difference, misunderstandings of what
the Buddha taught may arise. An illustration of this fact is the way some
people understand the Buddha's teaching about kamma and the result,
vipāka, produced by kamma. Some people think of this truth by way
of a situation. When they have an unpleasant experience they say: "It
is my kamma." In reality kusala kamma or akusala kamma produces a

pleasant object or unpleasant object at the moment of rebirth or during life through one of the senses, such as seeing or hearing. A moment of vipāka is gone immediately but one may think of it as a long lasting event. The difference should be remembered between thinking of a whole situation, of concepts or ideas, and understanding the truth of the reality appearing at the present moment.

During the discussions Sarah and Jon pointed out very often that when we cling to the idea of a person, of a self and believe that a person or self really exists, we live in a fantasy world and do not understand realities. It is natural to think of persons and situations, but they are not real in the ultimate sense. They are not realities that can be directly experienced one at a time as they appear at the present moment.

Jonothan said: "The ignorance, misunderstanding, that needs to be overcome is not the thinking of the concept of a being, a person, but the ignorance or misunderstanding of the reality appearing at the present moment." Thus, we need not avoid thinking of this or that person, but at the same time understanding can be developed that in reality what we take for a person are only citta, cetasika and rūpa that arise and fall away, that do not stay on. In that way we shall know the difference between the fantasy world of stories and concepts and the real world.

People had questions about attaining nibbāna. Sarah and Jon pointed out again and again: the development of awareness and understanding begins now in daily life, that is the only Path to nibbāna. The reality appearing now can be understood and thinking of attaining nibbāna is speculation that is not helpful.

All we find so important in life such as a pleasant place to stay, good friends, is just a moment of thinking. Life exists only in one moment. At the moment of seeing, life is seeing, at the moment of thinking, life is thinking. Gradually we can learn to attach less importance to the stories we think of and which are only fantasy. Thinking is real. It arises because of the appropriate conditions, but the object we are thinking of is mostly a story, a concept, and thus not real. While listening and considering more we learn that the way we used to consider the events of life is quite different from what the Buddha taught and what we can verify at this moment. Before we had no idea of what the present moment is. Gradually it becomes clearer what the meaning is of "just passing dhammas".

Acharn asked time and again: "Why do you listen?" Is it because we want to be a better person with less ignorance and less akusala, we want to have more calm? Then we are thinking of a self who wants to improve his life. When we are in a difficult situation we usually think about a self who wants to solve problems and we cling to the idea of a change of situation. In reality there are only seeing, hearing, visible object or hardness. On account of such experiences we think of stories, pleasant or unpleasant. Seeing or hearing which arise now are vipākacittas, results of kamma committed long ago. After the vipākacittas have fallen away, kusala cittas or akusala cittas arise which react with wholesomeness or unwholesomeness towards what is experienced.

The Buddha said: "Avoid evil, do good and purify the mind." These words are not a prescription to be followed without any understanding of realities. When there is more understanding of anattā, of reality arising because of conditions, we can take his words in the right way. When people are told to have mettā all day there is an idea of "I" who can do something. Mettā is adosa cetasika, (non-aversion) and it can only arise when there are the right conditions. When one has kindness towards people one likes there may be moments of metta, but there are also likely to be moments with attachment. Kusala cittas and akusala cittas alternate and one may take for mettā what is attachment. Without paññā that knows the characteristic of the reality which arises we are likely to confuse mettā and attachment.

Before we went to Vietnam we visited Acharn a few times in Teptharin Hospital. One topic we discussed was the development of the perfections (paramis)[1] We should not try to know whether or not there is at this moment development of the perfections. She said: "Daily life is the proof how much the perfections are developed." There must be the firm understanding of non-self. Several times Acharn emphasized that the development of understanding is much more difficult and deeper than anyone can think about. Acharn remarked: "Understanding does not mind how much it develops. It is self who thinks about this."

I said that it is very important to remember that it is more difficult than you would think. Acharn remarked that otherwise akusala cannot

---

[1]These are the excellent qualities the Bodhisatta developed in order to attain Buddhahood: liberality, morality, renunciation, wisdom, energy, forbearance, truthfulness, resolution, loving kindness and equanimity.

be eradicated. Ignorance and attachment continue on, from life to life, for aeons. We are just reading and talking about realities, but there must be the understanding of non-self at any time. "It is harder and harder" she said. She emphasized the difficulty of eradication of ignorance to show how deeply ignorance and wrong view are accumulated. Acharn said: "Lobha is making its way all the time and this is so very difficult." We do not realize it that we cling to an idea of "self that should have understanding". We take akusala citta with clinging for kusala citta and that takes us further away from the truth. We may underestimate the power of the latent tendencies that can condition the arising of wrong view at any time.

The different levels of akusala were brought up by Sarah and Jon during the discussions. There are three levels: the anusaya kilesa (latent tendencies), the pariyuṭṭhāna kilesa (arising with the akusala citta) and the vītikkama kilesa (transgression, misconduct). The latent tendencies do not arise with the citta but they lie dormant in each citta, they are subtle defilements that can condition the arising of akusala citta. The medium defilements (pariyuṭṭhāna kilesa) arise with akusala citta but they are not of the degree of unwholesome courses of action. The vītikkama kilesa are transgressions or misconduct.

The latent tendencies are called subtle defilements, but they are very powerful and tenacious. They can only be eradicated by the magga-citta of the different stages of enlightenment. Since they are latent and do not arise, they cannot be known.

We talked about the intoxicants, the āsavas, subtle defilements that arise. After seeing which is vipākacitta there are just a few more cittas and then during the moment of cittas performing the function of javana, the āsavas often arise with the akusala citta: the intoxicant of clinging to sense objects (kāmāsava), of clinging to existence (bhavāsava), of wrong view (diṭṭhāsava) and of ignorance (avijjāsava). The āsavas arise time and again, even right now, immediately after seeing, hearing and the other sense-cognitions, but they are unknown. Cittas succeed one another extremely rapidly and they have already gone in a flash.

Seeing arises now and then the āsavas of ignorance and wrong view are likely to follow. They pass very quickly but they can condition the arising of ignorance and wrong view again and again. Acharn said: "Even when you do not say 'I see', the 'I' is there. Only paññā can understand it. The way to eradicate is so far away. Only paññā can understand better and deeper, it can see what appears now as it is. There is no need to say that it appears as not self, that is thinking again."

Acharn reminded us that it is very difficult not to cling to the idea of self: "No matter when, it comes in instantly as long as one forgets it's not self. Even right now, whatever arises passes away never to return. This moment is the test, any time!"

Jonothan remarked that it is wrong to wish for more understanding. Acharn answered: "One is trapped by ignorance and cinging, having expectations about sati."

Acharn explained about letting go of the object that is experienced. When paññā begins to understand a characteristic of a reality, there may be the inclination to hold on to that object and then there is no opportunity to investigate other realities that follow. One does not let go of the object. At the moment of understanding there is no thought of "I know". If there is no letting go there is clinging to an idea of self who thinks about realities. I remarked that it is difficult to kow the difference between the moments with wrong view and without wrong view. Sarah asked me: "Does it matter to know? Otherwise there is clinging again. When it is time it is known naturally, and we are not trying to work it out."

Seeing now is not the same as seeing a moment ago. Seeing arises and then it falls away never to return and this is life. We have heard this often but we did not consider this enough. We still have an idea that seeing can stay, that it is always there. There are actually six worlds, the world appearing through the eyes, through the ears and through the other senses and the mind-door. Acharn was speaking about the world during a session at the Foundation. She spoke about the first stage of insight when there is clear understanding of nāma as nāma and of rūpa as rūpa, of only one reality at a time: "Where is the world? The world is lost. It is amazing, no one, no world; only one characteristic as it is. Hardness is hardness, where are the arms and the legs, the whole world? They are all gone."

She said several times that it is so amazing that only one reality appears, no self. We think of our whole body but this is only an idea. When the body is touched hardness may appear and hardness is a reality that can be directly experienced. At such a moment there is not clinging to our whole body. We talk about nāma and rūpa but they do not appear clearly as is the case when moments of insight-knowledge arise. There has to be firm understanding of the level of pariyatti and it can condition later on direct understanding.

What is the first noble truth of dukkha, was a question that was raised. The noble truth of dukkha is dukkha of all conditioned realities, saṅkhāra dukkha. It is the unsatifactoriness of conditioned realities that arise and fall away and can, therefore, not be a refuge. When paññā is of the level of pariyatti, it is understood intellectually that nāma and rūpa are dukkha, but the arising and falling away of realities can only be penetrated when paññā is of the level of paṭipatti, direct understanding. After the third stage of insight knowledge it is really understood what dukkha is. In one of the sessions at the foundation Acharn said about dukkha: "What is the use of what arises and falls away? To understand this is to understand dukkha. There is nothing, and that is dukkha... Whatever has arisen must have conditions for its arising and whatever arises falls away rapidly. It is no more, never to return in the cycle of birth and death." It cannot return and be something that one likes. We cling actually to what is nothing.

The second noble truth is the cause of dukkha and that is lobha, clinging. It hinders the understanding of the truth of dukkha, that is why it is the second noble Truth. It is opposed to wisdom. When we cling to a reality we think that it is there all the time, that it does not arise and fall away.

Because of lobha there is clinging to what cannot last and we go on to think of people and things as being lasting and real. This leads to more clinging and craving throughout many successive lives. So long as there is clinging there are conditions for rebirth and we shall continue to be subject to the unsatisfactoriness inherent in the impermanence of conditioned realities. The third noble truth is the ceasing of dukkha. When there is no more clinging there will not be rebirth. The fourth noble truth is the Path leading to the ceasing of dukkha. This is the development of understanding of all realities appearing at the present moment.

Acharn often repeated that one has to study each word of the teachings, one word at a time. She said: "Study with respect, great respect to each word. Otherwise one takes it that's very easy, very simple; it cannot be like that at all." This reminds us not to underestimate the subtlety of dhamma.

We should remember Acharn's message to the listeners of the Dhamma session, her message of one word: dhamma. We have to consider the meaning of dhamma as it appears now, in our daily life. It has no owner and it cannot be controlled.

When someone asked Acharn to speak some encouraging words, she answered: "All are dhammas". One may be upset by troubles in life, by problems, but there are only dhammas, conditioned realities.

Part II

My Time with Acharn Sujin

5

First Meeting

Suzaki wrote:

"What I am curious first is to know your vivid, or perhaps inspiring moment you had at the earlier years with Acharn Sujin. I read some comment from the book 'Buddhism in Daily Life.' But more specifically, how was your impression from the first meeting?"

Nina: I met Acharn Sujin for the first time in the Wat Mahathaat temple where a foreign monk was teaching about the jhāna-factors (to be developed in tranquil meditation) and also helped us to read suttas. We read the "Parinibbāna sutta" and the "Kesaputta sutta" (mostly called Kalama sutta). I was impressed by the realization that you do not have to accept anything from others, but have to find out the truth for yourself. Acharn Sujin kept rather to the background in this temple. I approached her and said that I wanted to learn about meditation that you can apply in daily life. My life was very busy, being in the diplomatic service. (In Japan the teachers at the language school called me "Mrs Party".) I felt that there must be something else in life, apart from just being engaged with parties. Acharn Sujin said, "Yes, vipassanā can be developed in daily life", and she invited me to her house. From then on I came to her several times a week with many questions. I asked her about belief in God and how to find out the truth. She answered: "What is truth will appear". She also helped me to see what clinging is, clinging to a belief. I had never considered this before. She said from the beginning that in the teaching of Dhamma, the person who teaches is not important; it is not the person but it is the Dhamma that matters.

This was new also for Thais; in Asian countries there is a great respect for teachers and people tend to follow what teachers say. When teachers wrote about Dhamma in olden times they would not mention the source of their quotes. Acharn Sujin greatly contributed to a change in this mentality, always encouraging to looking up the texts oneself, verifying the truth for oneself. She started interest in the translations of Commentaries and promoted this. I remember our visits to the library of Wat Bovornives and our conversations with monks. A friend made notes and gradually Commentaries in Thai were printed.

Acharn Sujin gave lectures in a temple every Sunday and quoted suttas. She asked a monk in advance about the Commentary to the relevant text. I tried to look up the suttas in my English editions

6

Abhidhamma in Daily Life

Suzaki wrote:

"How skilfully did she bring the technical matter, Abidhamma? If I may say so into the living, daily practice? Any specific event that you can highlight?"

Nina: When I was at her house, she explained about nāma and rūpa, about kusala citta and akusala citta. She answered my questions and very soon made me work for an English radio program. The first chapters that you find in 'Buddhism in Daily Life' are from notes with my conversations with Acharn Sujin. Every two weeks I had to finish a new chapter. It was a busy, but happy time. She helped me to see that all those different cittas (consciousness), cetasikas (mental factors arising with consciousness) and rūpas (physical phenomena) occur in daily life. I learnt that whatever occurs is conditioned; that good and bad inclinations are accumulated from moment to moment and that these condition our behaviour. Everything I learnt was relevant to daily life.

An example: we visited a bhikkhu who smiled when I told him about my interest in the teachings. Acharn Sujin asked me whether I knew why he smiled. She explained that this was because of happy feeling, somanassa. This sounds very simple, but it made me realize that feeling conditions our outward appearance.

She reminded me of how conditions affect our daily life under various circumstances. We were waiting near a kuti, a bhikkhu's dwelling, for a certain monk. He was not there and I suggested that we would find out about him. She said, "Let us sit at this stone and just wait and see what happens because of conditions". We sat quietly for quite some time. What a good lesson! I am so grateful for all those reminders I received in the situation of my daily life. It is true: we think of people we want to meet, but in fact, there are only different experiences, such as seeing, hearing and thinking, and they are all conditioned.

I was used to taking notice only of the outward appearance of people, but now I learnt about different cittas which condition our behaviour. People may look very pleasant and peaceful, but what do we know about their cittas which change from moment to moment?"

When crossing a street she said: "Elements on elements", and it is so true: hardness appears, and it is only an element. We think of feet and street, but let us consider what can be directly experienced. However, it took many years before all these lessons were absorbed, and I needed later on during different journeys many explanations about the difference between thinking and awareness, before I understood a little more. (Later on I come back to this).

Acharn Sujin used to go in retreat in a center but one day she realized that actually daily realities are the objects of vipassanā. From then on she did not go anymore in retreat, and this happened not so long before I met her. Since most people were not used to this approach, they had many questions about vipassanā in daily life. I found this approach the only reasonable one and did not doubt about its value. We have to know our own accumulations, our inclinations we take for self. They appear, and thus, they can be objects of insight.

Acharn Sujin always stressed that there is no rule about how one should develop understanding and that one cannot direct what object appears at a particular moment. I find this most reasonable, because whatever is experienced by citta is conditioned.

We went to different temples, also in the province. People asked questions about vipassanā and concentration. Although I was just learning Thai, Acharn Sujin made me talk as well. I enjoyed simple life in the province, without any fringes. People treated me as one of them, and that is what made me happy.

People asked whether slowing down one's movements would be helpful for the development of vipassanā. Acharn Sujin asked one person to run and to find out whether there is any difference as to what realities are appearing. The conclusion was: it is all the same. True, seeing is always seeing, no matter we run or sit. Seeing is a citta, an ultimate reality that should be known as it is, non-self. I heard a dog barking and asked whether hearing a dog is an object of insight. She explained that hearing just sound is different from thinking of a dog. I listened, but only many years later I understood the point.

People also asked: "Is this kusala (wholesome), is that akusala (unwholesome)". Her answer was: "You can only know for yourself. Nobody else can tell you". She also explained that it would be very easy if someone else were to tell you: "Do first this, then that, and you will make progress". Her advice always was : "There are no rules, there is no specific order of the objects insight can be developed of". In the whole of the Tipiṭaka we learn about realities that arise because of conditions and are non-self. Now, also in the practice we have to be consistent, how can we force ourselves to be aware of specific objects. She kept on warning us of subtle clinging to progress, to result. Expectations are lobha, attachment. She repeated many times: "Don't expect anything". We should not expect anything from ourselves nor from others. Expectations bring sorrow. I am grateful for her example in this matter, and her example of patience and equanimity. Some people heavily criticized her, but she was always patient and calmly explained about cause and effect: what cause will bring what effect. We should be clear about this. Do we want only calm or is our aim understanding?

7

The glimpse of Dhamma

Suzaki wrote:
"You said before: 'I became used to the different types of citta, consciousness.' What were the few specific incidents in your early days that made you find the glimpse of dhamma?"

Nina: At breakfast I listened to Acharn Sujin's radio program and heard time and again the terms denoting the different cittas arising in sense-door processes and mind-door processes. Thai and Pāli are very close, and in this way I could learn all these terms. But becoming used to these terms does not mean experiencing all the different cittas. Acharn Sujin explained that intellectual understanding is a foundation for awareness and right understanding that can arise later on. She stressed the importance of foundation knowledge: knowledge of the details of cittas, of their different characteristics, of cetasikas (mental factors), such as feeling, akusala cetasikas, beautiful cetasikas and rūpas. Indeed, as we read in the suttas, listening, considering are most important conditions for the arising of satipaṭṭhāna, sati (awareness) and paññā (understanding) that directly realize characteristics of nāma and rūpa.

We begin to recognize attachment, lobha, and aversion, dosa, in our lives, and this is useful, but we should not take this for awareness. For many years I thought that thinking was awareness. We may think without words, recognize realities very quickly, but, when we are very sincere, there is still an idea of self who does so. It is not paññā of satipaṭṭhāna.

I began to know that laughing is conditioned by lobha, and this made me feel somewhat uneasy when laughing. I had an idea of wanting to suppress laughing. Lobha again! Acharn Sujin explained that we should behave very naturally, and not force ourselves not to laugh: "Just do everything that you are used to doing, but in between right understanding can be developed". "We have to know our good moments and our worst moments in a day", she said. I read a sutta where the Buddha spoke to the monks about women and compared a woman to a snake. I did not like that. Acharn Sujin answered that this sutta can remind us of our accumulated defilements. If right understanding is not developed, accumulated defilements can cause the arising of many kinds of aksuala, and then we are like a snake. In other words, we should profit from the message contained in a sutta, learning how dangerous akusala is. Moreover, by this sutta the Buddha warned the monks of the danger of getting involved with women.

Acharn Sujin helped me to see how accumulations in past lives can lead to harm. We never know how these accumulations can condition cittas at the present moment. We may do things we did not believe ourselves capable of.

When I listened to her lectures in the temple I became sometimes depressed when I realized how difficult the development of right understanding is. Would I ever be able to reach the goal? But I had no inclinations to look for another way that could hasten the development of right understanding. Acharn Sujin explained that clinging to progress will not help us at all. When we realize more that it takes aeons to develop right understanding we shall be less inclined to think in terms of progress. Before this life there were aeons of ignorance, and in this life we are fortunate to be able to listen to the teachings and begin to understand the way of development of the eightfold Path. But it has to be a long way before we reach the goal. We can learn to accept that this will take more than one life.

Time and again Acharn Sujin repeated what the Buddha said in the "Exhortation to the Pāṭimokkha": "Patience is the greatest ascetism."

8

Practising the 'process'

Suzaki wrote:

"So, practising the 'process' (may I also say, sīla-samādhi-paññā?) will lead to elimination of suffering."

Nina: Acharn Sujin taught me what is kusala and what is akusala by her example. Observing the precepts is not a matter of rules one has to follow. She explained that there is no self who can direct the arising of kusala, that it is sati which conditions refraining from akusala and performing kusala. Since I was in the diplomatic service I went to cocktail parties and took drinks. Acharn Sujin would never say, "Don't drink". She would explain that it is sati that makes one refrain from akusala. Gradually I had less inclinations to drinking. I did not know that killing snakes or insects was akusala. When I was in Acharn Sujin's house, we were having sweets, and when flies were eating some crumbs on the floor, Acharn Sujin said, "We let them enjoy these too". I had never considered before to give flies something they would enjoy, it was a new idea to me. I learnt more in detail what was kusala, what akusala. I began to refrain from killing insects and snakes. She also taught me that

it is kusala sīla to pay respect to monks, because the monks observe so
many rules. She taught me to kneel down and pay respect in the proper
way. She taught me the importance of the Vinaya, and she explained
that we laypeople should help the monks by our conduct to observe
the Vinaya. We should not give money to them, but hand it to the
layperson in charge. When we are in conversation with the monks we
should not chat on matters not related to Dhamma. Together with her
elderly father we visited temples and offered food. We often had lunch
with her father in his favoured restaurant where they served finely sliced
pork (mu han in Thai). We did not talk about Dhamma very much at
such occasions, but I noticed Acharn Sujin's feeling of urgency, never
being forgetful of the Dhamma, whatever she was doing. I was clinging
very much to Dhamma talks, but throughout the years I learnt that we
do not need to talk about Dhamma all the time, but that we should
reflect on Dhamma and apply Dhamma in our life. Acharn Sujin is
always such an inspiring example of the application of Dhamma.

When we read the "Visuddhimagga" we see the three divisions of
sīla (wholesome conduct or virtue), concentration and paññā. We may
think of a specific order. However, Acharn Sujin explained that this
is the order of teaching, that there is not a specific order according to
which we should practise. When we carefully read about sīla, we see
that all degrees of sīla are dealt with, from the lower degrees up to the
highest degrees: the eradication of all defilements.

Having kindness for flies and abstaining from killing is sīla. Being respectful to monks is sīla. Being patient in all situations is sīla.
Satipaṭṭhāna is sīla. We read in the Gradual Sayings (Book of the
Threes, Ch II, § 16, The Sure Course) that a monk who possesses three
qualities is "proficient in the practice leading to the Sure Course" and
"has strong grounds for the destruction of the āsavas". These three
qualities are moderation in eating, the guarding of the six doors and
vigilance. We read concerning the guarding of the six doors:

> And how does he keep watch over the door of his sense fac-
> ulties?
>
> Herein, a monk, seeing an object with the eye, does not grasp
> at the general features or at the details thereof. Since covet-
> ing and dejection, evil, unprofitable states might overwhelm

one who dwells with the faculty of the eye uncontrolled, he applies himself to such control, sets a guard over the faculty of the eye, attains control thereof. . .

The same is said about the other doorways. The six doorways should be guarded. How does one, when seeing an object with the eye, not "grasp at the general features or at the details thereof"? In being mindful of the reality which appears. It is satipaṭṭhāna which is the condition for abstaining from akusala.

As to concentration or calm, there are many degrees of concentration. Each kusala citta is accompanied by calm. Calm is not a feeling of calm, it means the absence of akusala. When we cling to silence and to being calm, there is lobha, not calm. Paññā has to be very keen to know exactly which moment is akusala and which moment of kusala, otherwise we shall not know the characteristic of calm. When there is awareness of nāma or rūpa there is also calm at that moment. As paññā grows, calm grows as well. The eradication of defilements is the highest degree of calm. Acharn Sujin often stressed: when there is right awareness of a nāma or rūpa there is at that moment higher sīla, higher concentration and higher paññā.

Acharn Sujin helped me to see what is akusala and what is kusala in the different circumstances of daily life. She often said, the teachings are "not in the book", they are directed to the practice of everyday life. Also the Abhidhamma is not technical, it helps us to have a more refined and detailed knowledge of different cittas as they occur at this moment. When I said that I had enjoyed reading a beautiful sutta, she answered, "It is so sad when we only think of what is in the book, when we do not apply it." I realized that we may cling to what we read instead of seeing it as a reminder to develop understanding.

Acharn Sujin introduced me to her friends at her house, where they consulted books of the Tipiṭaka and discussed points of the Dhamma. She explained to me, "All we study and discuss is not just for ourselves, it is to be shared with others." This impressed me very much because I knew very little about sharing kusala with others. It had not occurred to me that even studying the teachings is not just for oneself. She would always help me to have more kusala cittas. When we were in a temple and we had things to offer to the monks she would hand the gifts and books to me, asking me to present them. I was glad to have the opportunity to pay respect to the Triple Gem and show my reverence to the monks. In fact she was helping others all the time to have kusala cittas. We visited Khun Kesinee who wanted to print my book "Buddhism in Daily Life". Khun Kesinee said, "Khun Sujin has given me life". This was so true, because she taught us all a new outlook on life, she taught us how right understanding can be developed in our ordinary daily life. She taught us to develop understanding of all phenomena of life in a natural way. Her daughter Khun Amara wrote "The Lives and Psalms of the Buddha's Disciples", inspired by the Thera-therigatha". These are the stories of men and women in the Buddha's time who proved in their daily lives that the Path can be developed and enlightenment be attained. Acharn Sujin and I were very busy to correct the printing proofs of my book, sometimes at night. When we had not heard anything from the printer and I wondered about this, she just answered, "No news." This was a good lesson to leave things to conditions and not to expect anything. Later on I thought many times of these words. It is clinging when we expect things to be the way we like them to be.

I was glad to meet many of her friends and take part in their life of giving and sharing. We went to temples together with Acharn Sujin, presenting dāna, or attending cremation ceremonies. On Sunday, I drove Acharn Sujin to the temple where she gave lectures on satipaṭṭhāna and afterwards we sat outside the temple where people asked her more questions about awareness in daily life. Her lectures were put on tape for a radio program. In the course of years the radio stations which sent out her program expanded all over Thailand and to neighbouring countries.

I accompanied Acharn Sujin to different places where people had invited her for a lecture. People were wondering whether there can be awareness of nāma and rūpa while driving a car. The answer was that it is just the same as being at home, it is normal life. Seeing, thinking or hardness appear time and again. When walking on the street we discussed seeing and thinking of concepts. There were holes in the pavement and if one would only be aware of colour and seeing but not think, one would fall into the holes. We learn that in the ultimate sense there are only nāma and rūpa, that there are no people, no things. This does not mean that we should not think of people and things. Also thinking of concepts is part of our daily life, we could not function without thinking of concepts. Thinking is a conditioned reality, it is nāma, not self. We can think with different types of citta, some are kusala and many are akusala. In the development of satipaṭṭhāna, we come to know our daily life just as it is.

9

'Formal' meditation

Suzaki wrote:

"From just skimming to read 'Buddhism in Daily Life', it appears that you do not put high importance to 'formal' meditation. Was this the case in your beginning of the Path? Did you start to do 'formal' meditation later? If so, how and how effective was it? Or, are you suggesting that it depends on people?"

Nina: I left Thailand after almost five years, but there were opportunities to return many times and take part in pilgrimages to India and Sri Lanka together with Acharn Sujin. She taught at the Thai language school to foreigners and several of them took an interest in the teachings. Among them were the late Bhikkhu Dhammadharo and Jonothan Abbot. Later on I also met Sarah who visited me from England. I found discussions on the Dhamma very useful since these helped me to clear up misunderstandings about nāma and rūpa. I had correspondance with people all over the world and this also helped me to clarify for myself the meaning of satipaṭṭhāna in daily life.

People are always wondering how to act in order to have more understanding. Acharn Sujin would stress that we should not think of ourselves, and that we become less selfish by paying more attention to the needs of others. This is a simple advice, but it is very basic. We cling to ourselves all the time, but the aim is detachment from the idea of self. If we are always selfish, how can we become detached? On all the India trips she would speak about the perfections which should be developed together with satipaṭṭhāna. Generosity, loving-kindness (mettā) and patience are essential qualities that should be developed, they are conditions for thinking less of ourselves. I learnt a great deal from my Thai friends on these trips. I noticed how alert they were to help others, even with small gestures. When we are sitting with others at the table for a meal, we can notice whether we take hold of dishes or reach for food only with the idea of wanting things for ourselves, or whether we are also attentive to the needs of others. I began to understand that there are countless moments of thinking of ourselves. I learnt in the situation of daily life that when kusala citta arises, there is a short moment of detachment. However, very shortly after kusala citta we are likely to cling to an idea of "my kusala". Generosity is only a perfection if we do not expect anything for ourselves, if it leads to less clinging. The aim of the development of perfections is detachment, eradication of defilements.

Acharn Sujin would often remind us of the need to apply the Dhamma in our daily life, reminding us how circumstances change from moment to moment. Each moment is actually a new situation. Each moment is conditioned. Whatever we experience through the senses, be it pleasant or unpleasant is conditioned by kamma. Once during a pilgrimage we stayed in a Thai Temple where different rooms were assigned to our group. I received the worst room, without bathroom and full of moquitos. I could hardly sleep and the next day I complained about this. I was used to having Vip treatment in the diplomatic service but Acharn Sujin helped me to see that unpleasant experiences are conditioned. Nāma is nāma and rūpa is rūpa, and it is not important what status of life people have. She asked me whether I was not glad afterwards to have those experiences. I agreed because now I found such experiences a good lesson. She helped us to understand kamma and vipāka in different situations of our life.

Some of her listeners thought that they should look for other circumstances, different from the present one, in order to have more conditions for sati. To them Acharn Sujin explained that seeing here is the same as seeing in another place, hearing here is the same as hearing in another place. Seeing is always seeing and hearing is always hearing, they are ultimate realities with their unalterable characteristics. We learnt that the Abhidhamma is not theory, that it can be directly applied, and this is satipaṭṭhāna. She would often remind us, "And how about this moment now?" Whatever questions people asked, she would always guide them to the present moment.

Bhikkhu Dhammadharo said that he was sometimes lost for a long time, without sati. Acharn Sujin asnwered that this shows that one has to develop right understanding in daily life, that one has to understand one's natural life. Then one can see the conditions for different nāmas and rūpas, conditions one has accumulated. One can check for oneself whether there is clinging to nāma and rūpa.

We need the Vinaya, the Suttanta and the Abhidhamma to support the development of right understanding. We should listen, study and consider the Dhamma. Paññā cannot suddenly arise. When we have intellectual understanding we can compare this with a plant that has to grow. We see at first buds, and we do not know yet when it will bloom. This will happen when the conditions are right.

10

Understanding of mind-matter

Suzaki wrote:

" The aim is understanding of mind-matter relationship, by dissecting or rather becoming aware of specific happenings that we experience in our daily life (that we were unaware of before). Such insight will enable us to become aware of what is going on in terms of cause and effect relationship, to see the cause of suffering, etc."

Nina: During a pilgrimage in India with Acharn Sujin, Bhikkhu Dhammadharo, Jonothan and other friends we discussed Dhamma all night in the train to Bodhgaya. During that night we discussed the difference between thinking of nāma and rūpa and direct awareness of them. We may notice that realities appear through different doorways, that sound is experienced through ears and hardness is experienced through the bodysense. However, we may take noticing realities for direct awareness of them. Acharn Sujin said, "You may believe, 'I have developed a great deal of understanding, I sees that there is nothing else but nāma and rūpa.' " She then explained that in reality this is only thinking, not direct understanding of one nāma or rūpa at a time.

Hearing is nāma, it experiences sound. Sound is rūpa, it does not experience anything. When hearing arises we think almost immediately of the meaning of the sound, its origin, of words which were spoken and the meaning of those words. Thinking is another type of nāma, different from hearing. Her remarks were an eye-opener to me. This shows again how important discussions on the Dhamma are. Without them our misunderstandings of the Dhamma would not appear. That night in the train passed very quickly, and before we realized it we were in Bodhgaya. One of our friends offered breakfast to Bhikkhu Dhammadharo and to the Samanera (novice) who was also present. We also stayed in Varānasī, in Hotel de Paris. When we were walking in the garden of that hotel, we heard a band with drums, and immediately we had an image of people marching and playing. Acharn Sujin explained that we build up stories on account of what we experience through the senses. Sound, hearing and thinking are ultimate realities, the stories we think of are concepts or ideas, different from ultimate realities. It is difficult to distinguish between different realities; it is direct understanding, paññā, that is able to do so. If we try to separate nāma from rūpa or if we try to think of both nāma and rūpa, there is only thinking, no awareness of either of them. Paññā cannot suddenly arise, it is gradually developed by studying, considering what we learn, discussing, asking questions.

We may be thinking of ourselves and others, walking in the garden of Hotel de Paris, but if we die now, the story comes to an end. Actually, each citta that falls away is a moment of dying. With the citta that falls away, the story comes to an end. Many years later Lodewijk and I walked to Hotel de Paris again, and then we saw that it had become neglected and that nothing of it's old glory was left.

One may believe that knowing what is going on is right awareness. Someone may know that he sees or that he hears, but that is not satipatthāna. When right awareness arises, it is mindful of the characteristics of nāma and rūpa as they appear one at a time. Right mindfulness and right understanding arise when there are conditions for their arising. Throughout all these years with Acharn Sujin we discussed again and again what seeing is: the experience of what appears through eyesense. We discussed what hearing is: the experience of what appears through the earsense. We are always forgetful of seeing and hearing, because we are more interested in concepts such as people, things and events. We can never be reminded enough of nāma and rūpa, because these are ultimate realities paññā has to understand. Right understanding of nāma and rūpa leads to detachment from the idea of self.

We were reminded that awareness is not self, it cannot be induced. Acharn Sujin asked us: "Who is aware?" When we answered, "Awareness is aware", she said, "That is in the book, but in your mind?" Such remarks made us realize how much we are still clinging to the idea of "my awareness".

11

Elimination of suffering

Suzaki wrote:

"Such insight will enable us to become aware of what is going on in terms of cause and effect relationship to see the cause of suffering, etc. Such cause and effect relationship lead to the experiential understanding of the four noble truths. So, practising the 'process' (may I also say, sila-samadhi-panna?) will lead to elimination of suffering.

Nina: My husband and I took part of many excursions with Acharn Sujin and other friends whenever we visited Thailand again. We went to nature reserves in the north of Thailand, to Nakom Phanom and other places in the provinces. For our Dhamma discussions Acharn Sujin always tries to arrange for pleasant surroundings and a relaxed atmosphere. With the help of her sister Khun Jid and our friend Khun Duangduen she sees to it that we have delicious and well-balanced meals. There is no end to their hospitality. The right climate and suitable food can be favourable conditions for the citta that develops right understanding. During our visits to Thailand and during our pilgrimages to India we discussed Dhamma and whenever we talked about personal problems in daily life, she would give us the most practical advice. This helped us to see our problems in the light of the Dhamma. When we discussed deep subjects of the Dhamma such as the Dependent origination and the four noble Truths, she would always relate these to our daily life.

We read in the Tipiṭaka about the four noble Truths: dukkha, the cause of dukkha which is craving, the cessation of dukkha which is nibbāna and the way leading to the cessation of dukkha, which is the eightfold Path.

Acharn Sujin stressed that we should not have merely theoretical understanding of the four noble Truths. Dukkha and the cause of dukkha pertain to our life at this moment. The way leading to the cessation is the development of right understanding of the realities appearing at this moment. When insight has been developed stage by stage nibbāna can be attained.

We read in the "Kindred Sayings"(V, 420, Dhamma-Cakkappavattana vagga, §1), that the Buddha said, "in short, the five khandhas are dukkha". The five khandhas are actually all conditioned realities, nāma and rūpa of our daily life. When the arising and falling away of nāma and rūpa, thus their impermanence, is realized, dukkha can be understood. What falls away immediately is not worth clinging to, it is dukkha.

We have to develop insight stage by stage. We have to develop understanding of hardness when it appears through the bodysense during all our activities in daily life. We do not have to think, this is hard, and we do not have to think of the place where it touches; its characteristic can be known when it appears. Gradually we can learn that the characteristic of nāma is different from the characteristic of rūpa. When we take nāma and rūpa as a whole, the arising and falling away of nāma and rūpa as they appear one at a time cannot be realized. They can not be realized as dukkha and we shall continue to take them for a person or a thing that exists.

Craving, the cause of dukkha, arises time and again and it causes us to continue in the cycle of birth and death. Acharn Sujin reminded us to be aware of clinging at this moment. We should know when there is clinging to awarseness, to having a great deal of understanding. If we do not realize such moments we do not follow the right Path. Intellectual understanding of the fact that each reality arises because of its own conditions can help us to follow the right Path, and then we shall not be inclined to try to select particular realities as objects of mindfulness and try to make mindfulness arise. It arises because of its own conditions. She said, "Awareness is like an atom in a day", meaning that there are not many moments. How could this be otherwise; we have accumulated such a great deal of ignorance.

We are in the cycle of birth and death, and during this cycle, cittas arise and fall away, succeeding one another. Each citta that falls away conditions the arising of the following citta, and in this way all wholesome and unwholesome qualities of the past have been accumulated from moment to moment. Even so all wholesome and unwholesome qualities that arise at the present time are accumulated and they will condition our life in the future. When ignorance arises today, it does so because it is conditioned by past moments of ignorance, even during aeons. When understanding arises today, it does so because it is conditioned by past moments of understanding. Even if there is a short moment of right understanding now, it is not lost, it is accumulated and thus there are conditions for its arising later on. Acharn Sujin said that this is like saving a penny a day, which can become a big fortune.

During all our journeys and visits to Thailand she stressed that the four noble Truths are realized in different phases. First there should be firm understanding of what the object of right understanding is and how right understanding should be developed. This is the first phase (sacca ñāṇa, understanding of the truth). When understanding of the truth, the first phase, is firmly established, one will not deviate from the right Path, that is, right awareness and precise understanding of the characteristic of the reality that appears. The first phase is the foundation of the practice, which is the second phase (kicca ñāṇa, understanding of the task). This again is the foundation of the realization of the truth (kata ñāṇa, understanding of what has been done).

I remember that we were walking in India with one of the Thai monks and that Acharn Sujin was repeatedly stressing these three phases. Hearing the Dhamma again and again helps us to remember what was explained and to reflect on it. When we read about the four noble Truths we may not realize that they can only be understood and applied in different phases and that we can begin right now. Acharn Sujin would always remind us that there is seeing at this moment. We do

not have to be in a quiet place to understand seeing; there is seeing no
matter where we are. Seeing can gradually be known as a reality that
experiences only what appears through the eyes, visible object. This is
the beginning of the first phase of understanding the four noble truths.

The Buddha taught the development of understanding of our life at
this very moment. The Abhidhamma is not technical, not theoretical,
it teaches about citta, cetasika and rūpa, realities arising all the time.
I am most grateful to Acharn Sujin for pointing out to us time and
again that we should understand our life at this very moment. What
she explained is completely in conformity with the Buddha's teachings.
Nina.

Part III

What is Most Precious?

12

Preface

Acharn Sujin and friends were invited again for Dhamma discussions in Vietnam by Tam Bach and other Vietnamese friends at the end of August and the beginning of September 2017. Before this journey Dhamma discussions were arranged in Thailand, in Kaeng Krachan and Nakorn Nayok. I only attended the discussions in Nakorn Nayok. Here I received a great lesson, namely, that one never knows what will happen the next moment. It all depends on conditions and it is beyond control. I suddenly lost my balance and fell down. Since there was no fracture I could get up and continue to attend the sessions. Thanks to Hang, a Vietnamese friend who had helped me during former trips in many ways, I could continue my journey to Vietnam in a wheelchair. Hang had special connections so that she could arrange a wheelchair for me.

I am most grateful to her for all her kindness, consideration and patience in constantly helping me in the wheelchair and out of it, to go up and down on steep staircases, to overcome all the troubles and hardship. She kept on being optimistic and seeing things from the sunny side. Without her I could not have continued this journey and I would have missed all the opportunities for hearing and considering the Dhamma. Hang said all the time: "no worry", reminding me that we keep on being preoccupied with ourselves when we worry about the future and how to face difficulties. When I was annoyed about my laundry she said: "It is past, it is all gone." It is very helpful to be reminded that whatever happens are all conditioned dhammas that cannot be controlled. This was a topic that was raised again and again during our journey. We kept on reminding ourselves: "All gone, all gone".

During the discussions Acharn Sujin was assisted by Sarah and Jonothan and they helped me and others not to be forgetful of the truth of life, to realize what is most precious: understanding the reality of the present moment. We are absorbed in our thinking of stories and worries which are not real. Seeing, hearing or thinking are real, they are realities that do not last and that are not self.

13

The best time to understand Truth

Most precious in life is understanding whatever reality appears now. Most of the time we are thinking of concepts and ideas about people and things that seem to stay. Through the Buddha's teachings we learn that realities such as seeing, feeling or hardness only arise for an extremely short moment and then fall away. There is no self who can cause their arising or control them.

Because of ignorance we are misled about the truth of realities that are impermanent, unsatisfactory (dukkha) and non-self, anattā.

Without the Buddha's teachings no one knows that life is seeing, hearing, smelling, tasting, experiencing tangible object through the bodysense and thinking. Each moment of consciousness or citta experiences only one object at a time and then it falls away, never to return.

When we are convinced that hearing true Dhamma and right understanding are the most valuable in our life we appreciate the opportunity for listening we still have in this human plane of existence.

Most of the time we are forgetful of what life really is: moments of seeing, hearing or thinking which arise and fall away immediately. We keep on thinking of different situations which seem to last, of people, of concepts that are not realities.

Throughout our sessions there were dialogues with children and adults about the realities of life. These were most useful for all of us. In this way we were reminded about what is really true.

When we were staying in Nakorn Nayok, Sarah had a lively conversation about realities with Vincent's twelve year old daughter Nana who lives in Taiwan. They talked about the different feelings that arise. When we hear kind words there is mostly happy feeling, whereas when we hear unkind words unhappy feeling is bound to arise.

Nana was asked what kind of feeling arises when seeing or hearing. There is not happy feeling nor unhappy feeling but indifferent feeling. She was asked what feeling arises when one is doing good deeds. Is it not usually happy feeling? Feelings are different at each moment. Sarah asked Nana whether it is "you" who feels pleasant or unpleasant; actually, what is the reality that feels it?

Nana answered: "Only feeling."

There are two types of reality: one type of reality experiences something, it is nāma, and one type does not experience anything, it is rūpa. Conciousness, citta, and its accompanying mental factors, cetasikas, experience different objects. Sound or hardness are rūpa, they do not experience anything.

Sarah asked Nana why feeling is nāma. Nana answered that it is nāma because it experiences things.

We are forgetful of the fact that feeling feels, that not a self feels. We are led by feelings. We find it very important how we feel in a day. We are distressed when others do not treat us well. We think that others are to be blamed instead of understanding that the real cause of our distress is within us. Whatever occurs is conditioned by many different factors, and nobody can be master of whatever happens in our life.

When seeing right now we always have the idea of "I see". Seeing is a citta that is accompanied by mental factors, cetasikas, which condition it. Citta is the leader, the principal, in experiencing an object and the accompanying cetasikas experience the same object but they each perform their own function. Citta and cetasika condition each other by conascence-condition. They arise at the same physical base, and fall away together at the same time. Some cetasikas accompany every citta, such as contact, feeling, remembrance or concentration. Contact (phassa) contacts the object of citta so that citta can experience it. Remembrance or recognition, saññā, marks or recognizes the object citta experiences. Concentration, ekaggatā cetasika, focusses on the object and it is the condition that each citta experiences only one object at a time. When seeing arises it experiences only visible object, when hearing arises it experiences only sound. Some cetasikas are beautiful and some are akusala and they accompany different cittas. Actually, citta itself is not kusala or akusala, its function is just to experience an object. The accompanying akusala cetasikas or kusala cetasikas cause citta to be akusala or kusala.

Sarah asked Nana: "What is the best time to understand the truth?" Nana gave the right answer, saying: "Now".

We are inclined to think of the past but this has already gone, never to return. When we are thinking of the future, of what we are going to do, we are quite absorbed in concepts and we are forgetful of the thinking itself that is a reality which is conditioned, non-self. We forget that the only time reality appears is now. This is the time to understand its true nature.

Seeing appears now. We can learn that there are conditions for its arising. It is conditioned by eyesense and visible object. Seeing is a citta that is result, vipāka. It is the result of kusala kamma or akusala kamma. When it is the result of kusala kamma it experiences a pleasant object and when it is the result of akusala kamma it experiences an unpleasant object. Nobody can select the object that is experienced. Having more understanding of the conditions for the realities that arise and learning more details helps us to realize that there is no self who can direct realities or cause their arising. Seeing is often dealt with as an example, but when we have understanding of the conditioned nature of seeing we shall also have more understanding of the other realities that arise.

Each conditioned reality arises for an extremely brief moment and then it falls away. When we think of the situations of life and of people it seems that people and things stay on. We are often lost in stories instead of knowing what is real at this moment. Without the Buddha's teaching we do not know what life really is. Life is seeing, hearing, thinking, and they all fall away immediately. Life is only one moment of experiencing one object at a time.This does not mean that we should not think of concepts of people. We should not try to change our way of thinking, but there can be more understanding of what life truly is.

Nana had prepared some of her own questions. She asked what "nimitta" (sign) is. While we are seeing now there are numerous cittas arising and falling away in succession, very rapidly. Countless visible objects are experienced by moments of seeing-consciousness and what is known is only the sign of visible object. There is a sign or mark of visible object that has fallen away. It is impossible to experience just one visible object since citta that is seeing-consciousness arises and falls away etremely fast, but a sign of the characteristic of visible object can be experienced. The sign of visible object that remains is like a shadow of visible object. As was explained before, the experience of the nimitta can be compared to a burning torch that one swings around so that a circle of fire appears. There seems to be a circle that remains but in reality there is no circle.

The sign or nimitta of what arises and falls away very fast appears as if it is still there. On account of the nimitta of realities we think of concepts or ideas. At this moment a dhamma such as visible object appears for an extremely short moment and then it falls away. But since dhammas arise in succession there seems to be a continuity which is steady, so that we take what is experienced for 'some thing'. Evenso is there the nimitta of citta, viññāṇa-nimitta, that experiences different objects. There is a nimitta of each of the five khandhas.

Nana asked what kamma is. It is cetanā cetasika, translated as intention or volition. It accompanies every citta. It sees to it that the other accompanying cetasikas each perform their own task. Cetanā that accompanies vipākacitta, citta that is result, is different from cetanā that accompanies kusala citta or akusala citta. When it accompanies kusala citta or akusala citta and it is of sufficient strength, it is able to produce the appropriate result. Kindness to others is wholesome kamma. Nana agreed that knowing the truth is the best kamma.

The Buddha taught that all realities are non-self. However, because of ignorance and clinging it is hard to accept the truth.

We read in the "Kindred Sayings"(IV, Saḷāyatana vagga, Kindred Sayings on Sense, Fourth Fifty, Ch III, § 193, Udāyin):

Once the venerable Ānanda and the venerable Udāyin were staying at Kosambī in Ghosita Park. Then the venerable Udāyin, rising at eventide from his solitude, went to visit the Venerable Ānanda, and on coming to him ... after the exchange of courtesies, sat down at one side. So seated the venerable Udāyin said to the venerable Ānanda:

"Is it possible, friend Ānanda, just as this body has in divers ways been defined, explained, set forth by the Exalted One, as being without the self ... is it possible in the same way to describe the consciousness, to show it, make it plain, set it forth, make it clear, analyze and expound it as being also without the self?"

"Just as this body has in divers ways been defined, explained, set forth by the Exalted One, as being without the self, friend Udāyin, so also is it possible to describe this consciousness, to show it, make it plain, set it forth, make it clear, analyze and expound it as being also without the self.

Owing to the eye and visible object arises seeing-consciousness, does it not, friend?"

"Yes, friend."

"Well, friend, it is by this method that the Exalted One has explained, opened up, and shown that this consciousness also is without the self."

(The same is said with regard to the other doorways.)

"Owing to the eye and visible object arises seeing-consciousness", the Buddha explained. His words are very direct and impressive. Is there seeing now? Acharn often asked this question during the discussions. It brings us back to the present moment. There is seeing time and again but without the Buddha's words we would never know the truth of seeing. It does not arise because a self wants to see. Nobody can cause its arising. It arises just for a moment and then it is gone, never to return. Acharn emphasized again and again that we should carefully consider each word spoken by the Buddha: "Owing to the eye and visible object arises seeing-consciousness."

Before we went to Vietnam we were invited by Khun Duangduen to her home in Bangsai. She received us with great hospitality and offered us a luncheon in a restaurant located in the same area as her house. Here we enjoyed an incredible variety of health foods. Before and after the luncheon we had a Dhamma discussion in a small group while seated by the waterside. Acharn explained about right awareness that should be very natural. It does not matter whether or not it arises. Attachment to it is bound to come in very quickly. At the moment of right awareness there is no thinking about realities. Acharn said: "Very natural means: whatever appears by conditions can be object of right awareness. Unexpectedly. It takes aeons and aeons for sati and paññā to develop, from moment to moment."

We discussed about seeing the danger of being in the cycle of birth and death, saṃsāra. We may well read about the danger or discuss it but there is not enough understanding of the danger of saṃsāra. I had a dialogue with Jonothan about this subject:

Jonothan: "Why are you interested in developing understanding?"

Nina: "We want to know the truth."

Jonothan: "What is the truth we are going to know?"

Nina: "The truth the Buddha taught about no self, the truth of all realities. That is what we want to know."

Jonothan: "Is that dukkha (unsatisfactory)?"

Nina: "All conditioned realities are dukkha. But we do not quite understand dukkha, the impermanence of realities."

Jonothan: "All realities are dukkha, there is no future."

Nina: "Because they fall away. There is so much thinking about it."

Jonothan: "We come to understand this intellectually at first. The cessation of dukkha takes place only at arahatship, parinibbāna, the end of saṃsāra."[1]

Nina: "There is hearing, thinking, but not understanding. It is so much theory for me."

Jonothan: "It is theory for all of us, when understanding is of the intellectual level. You asked about the connection with seeing the danger of saṃsāra."

---

[1]The arahat has eradicated all defilements and, therefore, he does not have to be reborn. He has reached the end of dukkha, the arising and falling away of realities.

Acharn Sujin: "We should not try to see the danger, but it is by understanding on and on and on... Ignorance cannot be eradicated all at once."

Acharn explained that that the actual moment of seeing the danger of life must be vipassanā ñāna[2]. One can see the danger of akusala dhammas in daily life. Realizing the danger of life has to be from now on. There is nothing that does not arise and fall away from this morning up to now. There is no one there.

I said that realizing this from now on is very hard. Acharn answered that it is not a matter of self, but of citta and cetasikas. When I said that we just listen and consider, she answered: "Citta and cetasikas. They develop."

It is beneficial to be reminded that citta and cetasikas perform their tasks, not a self who can do anything.

Sarah reminded me that wise consideration is paññā that develops naturally and easily. She said: "It is not 'how can I understand', or trying to work it out. This is natural, but self, clinging to the self gets in the way all the time and hinders the natural considering or understanding."

Acharn emphasized again: "Paññā begins to listen carefully, consider carefully, and in that way it develops."

---

[2]This is paññā of the level of direct understanding of realities.

14

The Functions of Citta

Seeing at this moment is life. It is conditioned, no one can make it arise. Each moment that arises and falls away is life. As Acharn said, "Without understanding reality right now, there is no understanding of life." Life is not permanent; each reality that is conditioned to arise, falls away in splitseconds. Nobody can stop the succession of realities that arise and fall away. As Acharn said, "It has gone completely. So rapid, it seems like it is permanent". The citta that has fallen away is succeeded immediately by the next citta and, thus, it seems that citta can stay.

When citta arises, it performs a function. Seeing is a function of citta. Seeing is vipākacitta, result of kamma. When it experiences a pleasant object it is the result of kusala kamma, and when it experiences an unpleasant object it is the result of akusala kamma. We should not try to find out whether seeing is kusala vipākacitta or akusala vipākacitta, it is just one short moment that falls away immediately.

Different cittas perform different functions. The term "function" (in Pali: kicca), helps us to understand that there is no self who acts, but that it is citta that performs a function. Seeing arises in a process of cittas which each perform their own function. Before seeing arises, there has to be adverting-consciousness (āvajjana-citta) which does not see but just adverts to visible object that impinges on the eye-sense. Then seeing arises and after it has fallen away it is succeeded by two more vipākacittas which receive the object and which investigate it. Then determining-consciousness (votthapana-citta), which is kiriya-citta[1], arises. This is only one moment of citta that will be followed by kusala cittas or akusala cittas that perform the function of "javana" or "going through" the object. It depends on accumulated conditions whether kusala citta or akusala citta arises. There is no one who could determine this.

Birth is a function of citta and dying is another function of citta. Birth-consciousness (paṭisandhi-citta) and dying-consciousness (cuti-citta) are results of kamma. No one can condition birth-consciousness to arise in a specific place or country. No one can know when death will come. It depends on kamma when a lifespan will be ended. It may seem unusual to see dying as a function of citta. But this is reality. There is no person, only citta, cetasika and rūpa arising and falling away. Dying-consciousness is the last moment of a life-span which is followed immediately by the rebirth-consciousness of the following life. This is just like now: seeing arises and is immediately followed by the next citta in the process which is receiving-consciousness: it does not see but still experiences visible object while receiving that object. There is life and death at each moment, when a citta arises and falls away.

Cittas can be kusala, akusala, vipāka or kiriya. These are the four "natures", "jātis", of citta. This was also a topic discussed during the sessions. In a process of cittas there are not only kusala cittas, akusala cittas and vipākacittas, cittas that are result, but also kiriyacittas. Kiriyacitta is not kusala, akusala or vipāka. Before seeing arises in a process of cittas, there is a kiriyacitta, the eye-door adverting-consciousness that adverts to visible object. Another kiriyacitta in the process of cittas is the determining-consciousness, votthapana-citta, arising after seeing and the two vipākacittas that follow upon seeing. The determining-consciousness that is only one moment, is succeeded

---

[1]Kiriyacitta is neither kusala citta nor akusala citta, nor vipākacitta.

by kusala cittas or akusala cittas.

It depends on the appropriate conditions of what jāti a particular citta is. Acharn said: "There are four jātis every day. One can begin to understand that there is no one, no self."

Citta and its accompanying cetasikas are of the same jāti. They condition one another by conascence-condition, meaning, they arise and fall away together. Thus, when the citta is kusala, all accompanying cetasikas are also kusala, and it is the same in the case of akusala citta, vipākacitta and kiriyacitta. When we are helping someone else with kusala citta the accompanying feeling which may be pleasant feeling or indifferent feeling is also kusala. When the kusala citta falls away there may be akusala citta with clinging to the person we are helping or to an idea of "my pleasant feeling". In that case the accompanying feeling which may be pleasant or indifferent, is also akusala. We may be ignorant of realities believing that the feeling that is kusala stays on, whereas, in reality, it is akusala. It is not self but just feeling that feels and it only lasts for an extremely brief moment. When we consider realities wisely it will be clearer that feeling is only a conditioned dhamma.

Cittas arising in processes experience an object through one of the six doorways, the doorway of the eye, the ear, the nose, the tongue, the bodysense or the mind. Only one object through one doorway at a time can be experienced. Life is the experience of one object and then it is gone, never to return. Each citta that falls away conditions the arising of the next citta. This is proximity-condition, anantara-paccaya. Cittas arise in succession, and also in a specific order. When the adverting-consciousness has fallen away it is succeeded by seeing or one of the other sense-cognitions. This order cannot be changed.

Seeing sees only visible object, but very soon after seeing we think of people and things. Cittas succeed one another so rapidly that it seems that we can see and think all at the same time. However, we could not think of persons and things if there had not been seeing. We may understand this intellectually, but it still seems that we see and recognize people and things at the same time.

We usually think of people and events with akusala citta, with attachment or aversion. One may wonder whether one should change one's way of thinking. We should not try to change our way of thinking,

that would be unnatural. When we try to change our thinking there is
clinging to an idea of self who can do so. Thinking is also a conditioned
reality. We can learn that it is different from seeing or hearing. When
we learn about different realities, there will be more confidence in the
Buddha's teaching of non-self.

There are not only cittas arising in processes, in between the processes of cittas there are cittas that are life-continuum, bhavanga. They
keep the continuity in the life of an individual. The bhavanga-citta does
not experience an object through a doorway. It experiences the same
object as the rebirth-consciousness, throughout life. Kamma produces
the first citta in life, the rebirth-consciousness which is vipākacitta and
it experiences the same object as that experienced shortly before dying.
The rebirth-consciousess is succeeded by bhavanga-citta. When we are
fast asleep and not dreaming bhavanga-cittas arise. We do not know
any object through the sense-doors or the mind-door, we do not know
where we are and who we are, who our parents are. Acharn asked us:
"Is there anyone at the moment of being fast asleep? Where are you,
your property, family and friends?"

When we wake up cittas arise again that experience objects through
one of the six doorways.

The cycle of birth and death goes on endlessly, consisting of cittas
arising in processes and cittas that do not arise in processes, bhavanga-
cittas. Dying-consciousness, cuti-citta, is the last citta of this life-span.
It is of the same type as the bhavanga-citta and it experiences the same
object.

Acharn asked whether there is seeing in a dream. We think of many
stories, when dreaming. She explained:

"At this moment there is seeing and memory of people and things.
Just like in a dream. What is the difference between moments of dreaming and of being awake? There is no seeing in a dream. Memory makes
it seem so real. When one wakes up where are those that appeared in a
dream?"

Nothing can arise without conditions. But it is very difficult to
understand conditions. One is occupied with oneself and this causes
many problems. I worry about what will happen to me, tomorrow, or
after tomorrow when I have to travel. I remarked that it is so good to be
reminded that one is occupied with oneself, to learn about conditioned

realities that cannot be controlled. They are all conditioned dhammas. This is a great support when we face problems. Also akusala citta is a reality of life and it should be understood as conditioned, non-self.

We read in the "Kindred Sayings" (III) "Kindred Sayings on Elements", The First Fifty, § 8, "Grasping and Worry"(2), that the Buddha, while he stayed at Sāvatthī, said:

"I will show you, brethren, grasping and worry, likewise not grasping and worrying. Do you listen ...

And how, brethren, is there grasping and worry?

Herein, brethren, the untaught many-folk have this view: 'This body is mine: I am this: this is myself.'[2] Of such an one the body alters and becomes otherwise. Owing to the altering and otherwiseness of body, sorrow and grief, woe, lamentation and despair arise in him ..."

The same is said about the other four khandhas, the khandha of feeling, of perception (remembrance or saññā), of saṅkhāra-khandha (the other fifty cetasikas, apart from feeling and remembrance) and of consciousness (viññāṇa).

The Buddha said:

"And how, brethren, is there no grasping and worry?

Herein, brethren, the well-taught Ariyan disciple has this view: 'This body is not mine: I am not this: this is not myself.' But inspite of the altering and otherwiseness of body, sorrow and grief, woe, lamentation and despair do not arise in him. . ."

The same is said of the other four khandhas.

Only the arahat, the perfected one has eradicated all kinds of clinging and, thus, he has no grasping and worry.

Sarah had a dialogue with Trung, the brother of Tran Thai's wife Tiny Tam. Sarah asked him what is seen now and he answered that it was people and things.

---

[2]These three ways of clinging denote: clinging without wrong view, conceit and clinging with wrong view.

Sarah: "Just visible object that is seen. Afterwards we think of people and flowers. What sees visible object?"

Trung: "The 'I',".

Sarah: "Is the 'I' that can hear the same as the 'I' that can see?"

Trung: "Yes."

Sarah: "Is that 'I' real or just imagination?"

Trung: "An idea."

Sarah: "Just an imaginary 'I', no 'I' to be found. Does that make sense?"

Trung: "Yes."

Later on Sarah had another dialogue with Trung and it appeared that he had considered realities more.

Sarah: "Eyesense cannot experience anything, only citta can experience something. So visible object contacts the eyesense and seeing sees visible object. Without these two seeing cannot see.

What is heard now?"

Trung: "Sound."

Sarah: "What hears that sound?"

Trung: "Hearing-consciousness."

Sarah: "What is seen now?"

Trung: "Light or visible object."

Sarah: "Light or visible object, just that which is seen.

When there is the idea of people and flowers there are just ideas that are thought about. In dreams thinking is real, but are people, flowers, strange events real or imagined?"

Trung: "Imagined."

Sarah: "Seeing is real, light or visible object is real, thinking is real. Flowers and people are ideas. Is this interesting or useful?"

Sarah said that she appreciated his interest. Trung came to the sessions also the following days and he listened attentively to the discussions.

This was a dialogue about all the different realities that appear in a day and we have heard about this many times. However, it is always useful to be reminded again and again about what is real since our ignorance and attachment are deeply rooted. It will take aeons of listening and carefully considering realities before there will be clear understanding of realities as impermanent and non-self. It seems, when we think of our house, that our house is still existing and belongs to us. Acharn frequently reminded us of the truth. She said:

"You think of your house. Where is your house? You are just dreaming about your house. Can one say that life is just like a dream, no matter at night or at day time. There is nothing in a dream. What is the use of clinging to what appears very shortly." We should not try to stop dreaming, or wish for life to be different. Life should be understood. Thinking is real, but the stories one thinks of are not real.

During the sessions the listeners had many questions and several of these pertained to calm as a method to have more kusala. People believed that if one goes to a quiet place in order to have more loving kindness, mettā, it would arise more frequently. However, from the beginning it should be understood what calm is and what mettā is. Mettā can arise naturally in daily life. At the moments of kindness there is calm already. Calm (passaddhi) is a cetasika arising with each kusala citta.

One point that was raised was that the thought of foulness of the body will eliminate lust or attachment. There will not be true calm if one tries to cause citta to be in a certain way, motivated by an idea of self. One should know that whatever citta arises is conditioned, and that nobody can control citta. Many akusala cittas arise in our life and they can be understood as non-self. They are all dhammas. Recollection on the foulness of the body is one of the subjects of samatha, the development of calm. If one understands the right conditions for calm there can be temporary release from attachment. But if one just focusses on foulness without right understanding of what true calm is, it will not be beneficial.

People raised questions as to paying respect to one's ancestors. This is a duty stemming from the Vietnamese tradition. It is not helpful to speculate about one's ancestors who could notice one's good deeds done in order to honour them. When the dying-consciousness has fallen away and it is succeeded by the rebirth-consciousness, there is no longer the same individual. However, one can be grateful for what they have done in the past and think of them with kusala cittas. People also wonder how to pay respect to the Buddha although he has passed finally away. The best respect to the Buddha is to study his words and develop understanding of what is real. Now is the way to show respect to him.

Someone mentioned a Mahāyāna belief that there is a joint or collective kamma. A group of people receives the same kind of result due to kamma that they have collectively performed. This is not possible because each person will receive the result of a deed he has performed himself. He is heir to his own kamma, as the Budha said. Seeing arises now and it is the result of past kamma, a deed one has performed oneself.

Each of the questions raised can be brought back to the present moment.

We are thinking about concepts and situations time and again and then we are forgetful of what is true in the ultimate sense.

When we hear the words "being alone" we tend to think about this in conventional sense. Acharn reminded us of the real meaning of being alone, of the fact that there is no one there. She said:

"There is always thinking about situations. Each moment is alone. Seeing is alone. Just live alone. There is thinking about people, but thinking is alone. Just alone each moment. This will lead to less attachment. There is no one with us, citta just arises and falls away. Where are those people we are thinking about. We are happy being with friends, but this arises alone."

Citta is always alone, there is nobody there when seeing arises. Besides citta, cetasika and rūpa there is no person.

When intellectual understanding, pariyatti, develops it will become quite firm and there will be more confidence in the truth. Then it can condition right awareness and direct understanding of realities, paṭipatti. Without confidence there are no conditions for direct understanding or satipaṭṭhāna. We may be attached to the idea of pariyatti that has to become firm and condition paṭipatti. Each person has to find this out by himself, but it is only paññā that knows. Pariyatti has become really firm when there is no self involved. Instead of thinking too much about pariyatti and paṭipatti, it would be better to attend to what is appearing now. This is what is really important. There is no need to think about terms like pariyatti and paṭipatti, or all the other terms one finds in the texts. What appears now, just now? Is it seeing, hearing, hardness or thinking? This is the only way leading to the development of paññā. Paññā is only an element, devoid of self.

From the beginning there should be more and more understanding that no self studies, considers and develops intellectual understanding.

This is already difficult, because the idea of self comes in unnoticed. This is so because of ignorance and attachment that has been accumulated for aeons.

Some people believe that they have reached already the stage of paṭipatti, direct understanding. They believe that they can be aware of seeing, hearing or thinking. Someone mentioned that there is a fine borderline between thinking and direct awareness. However, only paññā can know about the difference between the moments of right awareness and the moments that there is merely thinking of awareness. It is of no use to try to find out whether awareness has arisen. Right awareness and right understanding of the level of satipaṭṭhāna arise together and they do so because of their own conditions. Nobody can select the object they take. Whatever reality appears, be it kusala or akusala, pleasant or unpleasant, can be the object of sati and paññā.

15

What is Death?

Nothing lasts, there is death at each moment in life. When a citta arises and falls away there is birth and death in the ultimate sense.

Two boys, Duc, sixteen years old, and Tri, twelve years old, were very sad because their grandmother had just passed away. Sarah had a dialogue with them:

"When seeing or hearing now there is no sadness. At the moments of helping or giving, there is no sadness. Your grandma started a new journey. What she would wish is that you study, help your parents and study Dhamma.

The world before hearing the teachings is the whole world. But after hearing the teachings it is that which arises. Each world is different: seeing is not hearing. After it has arisen it is old and then it passes away, never to return. We can think about the world in the sense of whatever appears now.

Understanding what the Buddha taught brings about respect to anything he taught. He is the person who enlightened the truth of everything."

Sarah asked them whether they understood this a little bit and it appeared that they did. In the case of death and mourning it is important to consider realities. Instead of thinking again and again about the dear person one lost and one's sadness it is good to be reminded of what is really important in life. Mostly we are involved in stories and concepts instead of considering realities wisely.

Sarah said:

"Is there seeing now? Does it last for a little time or for a long time? It seems to last for a long time but everything passes very quickly. What about unhappy feeling? A little while ago you told me you had unhappy feeling and now you are smiling. So, does unhappy feeling last? Everything seems to last. We learn a little bit more and then we understand a little bit more. We learn that it passes very quickly. What seems so important now will be forgotten very quickly."

Sarah explained that there is just this moment now and the boys agreed. They understood that it is useful to find out what life is at this moment. When we help people to consider the present moment they will be less inclined to think with sadness about their loss. It is natural to be sad about a loss, but one can learn that even sadness is a conditioned reality that does not last. We are attached to pleasant feeling and when we lack the company of a dear person we cry. We only think of ourselves.

Sarah explained that when holding the microphone it is not the microphone that is touched but just tangible object such as hardness or temperature. The world the Buddha taught is just what is seen now, heard now, touched now. One may think of one's deceased grandmother but what is real is just thinking now and then gone.

Duc said that he had regrets about his wasting of opportunities for kindness towards his grandmother and he was wondering whether he could come into contact with her in order to correct his former attitude. Jonothan explained that this is not possible and that it is not useful to have regrets about the past. One cannot always express how one feels about someone who is close to us.

I said to them that their interest and the way they asked questions was helpful to all of us. It was an opportunity to exchange thoughts about realities, about what is real now. Their dialogue with Sarah helped all of us to consider more ourselves what is real in life. We should consider more seeing and hearing. What is touched is not a thing like a microphone, but a reality such as solidity. We should have more understanding of what is real and what is only a thought or idea, which is not real.

I said that if their grandmother could know about their interest in the Dhamma she would really be happy. Understanding about the truth can develop very, very slowly. It is normal that it grows so slowly. It may take many lives, not just one life. It is good that understanding can begin just now.

The boys were shedding tears but in the course of the conversation about realities they dried their tears. The next day the cremation took place and a friend who attended the ceremony said that the boys were smiling.

When we reflect wisely about death, knowing that it can come any time, we can realize what is precious in life: just understanding this moment. We should remember that there is birth and death at each moment when a citta arises and then falls away. It is very natural to be involved in stories while thinking of grief caused by the loss of a dear person. However, it is beneficial to know the difference between thinking of situations and understanding the realities of citta, cetasika and rūpa. We do not try to change thinking of situations, but understanding can be developed of realities. In the ultimate sense there is no dear person who passed away nor people who are grieving. As we heard so many times these days: there is no one there. Our life is only citta, cetasika and rūpa. Through the Dhamma we learn to see our life in a different way.

Sarah reminded us that we are not crying for the beloved one but for ourselves. We are so attached to the pleasant feeling we derived from his or her company. One by one our dear ones will pass away. She said: "Wise people who are courageous will understand life as it is: however life goes, facing difficulties, there are still just dhammas: citta, cetasika and rūpa arising and falling away."

We were reminded time and again that no matter life is happy or unhappy now, the only thing that matters is understanding of the realities appearing at the present moment. It is useless to wish for more calm and more kusala.

Kusala citta with calm can only arise when there are the right conditions.

Just now so many things seem to appear at the same time. All this, we call the world, appears because citta experiences different objects. Through the Buddha's teachings we learn that there is one citta at a time, an extremely short moment. It arises and falls away never to return. We are misled by the outer appearance of things. We seem to see continuously, hear continuously. But we learn that, time and again, there is a different citta that experiences an object through one of the six doorways, of the senses and of the mind-door.

Whatever subject we consider, we have to distinguish the world of concepts, of people, I, you, different things that seem to last, and the real world of ultimate realities. Otherwise we shall not know the truth.

When we think of death we usually think of death in conventional sense, as the end of a lifespan. But when we consider the arising and falling away of citta, there is actually birth and death of citta.

Acharn said that in childhood she was very afraid of death. But when she understood that there is momentary death of citta all the time, all fear disappeared. She said:

"But now there is each moment. Nothing to be afraid of. Are you afraid of tomorrow, are you afraid of death? So, understand the death of reality which arises and falls away, never to return, and that is the real meaning of death. So, is there time to be afraid of death anymore? Because it is just right now. When there is more understanding there will be less sorrow or unpleasant moments... Great sorrow will come from the dear one's death. One can understand what conditions sorrow, the unknown attachment that arises most in one's life."

Attachment is mostly not known. When it is strong such as greed for a delicious meal, we may notice it. But often there are countless more subtle moments such as attachment to seeing, to what is visible, to the eye.

We were reminded all the time that the difference between seeing and visible object, between nāma and rūpa, has to be clearly understood so that realities can, one at a time, be directly known. But we should not mind if this is not yet the case. At the moment of right understanding there is also patience.

Acharn said: "What is there now. Is there seeing or what? Seeing is conditioned, it cannot arise by itself. It is conditioned just to arise and see, that is all. No matter what you call it."

Those are simple words, but did we really consider them enough? No matter what we call seeing, this reality appears and can be understood. We can call it by any name, in any language, but its characteristic does not change. It experiences visible object. It is an ultimate reality, different from conventional notions.

Acharn said: "It is gone completely, never to return in saṃsāra or anywhere in the world. No matter what you call it, is it true?"

A precious moment is understanding what has not been understood before. If one has not listened to the Buddha's teachings there will always be ignorance covering up the truth. We were reminded time and again that when there is ignorance, seeing is not understood as a moment of seeing, just a conditioned dhamma. We tend to think of seeing as if it is lasting. It seems that we see and perceive people and things at the same time. When intellectual understanding has conditioned direct understanding of the level of insight knowledge, vipassanā ñāṇa, the arising and falling away of realities, one at a time, can be clearly understood. Direct awareness, sati of the level of satipaṭṭhāna, and direct understanding arise together at those moments.

The reality of mindfulness or awareness, sati, was often discussed. Some people believe that mindfulness is knowing what one is doing. However, it has a reality as object, not a situation or a conventional idea one may think of, such as an idea of doing the washing, of eating or of walking. Or one may think: "I am aware". Awareness cannot arise with an idea of self. People may have misunderstandings when they read about applying knowledge during awareness. It entirely depends on conditions what the object of awareness and understanding will be. We learn from the teachings that no self can apply anything, but there may still be an idea of myself applying, even if we do not expressively think this in words. From the beginning there should be more and more understanding that no self studies or considers realities. This is already difficult, because the idea of self comes in unnoticed. This happens because of ignorance and attachment that has been accumulated for ages.

People confuse mindfulness with an idea of concentration. Mindfulness or concentration are terms one thinks of in conventional sense, as if they are lasting. The Buddha taught very precisely about them as spe-

cific cetasikas, dhammas arising because of the appropriate conditions
that do not last.

Concentration or one-pointedness (ekaggatā cetasika) accompanies
each citta and it is the condition that citta experiences only one object
at a time. Seeing only experiences visible object, it cannot know any
other object. It can be kusala, akusala or neither kusala nor akusala.
Sati is a sobhana (beautiful) cetasika that can accompany only sobhana
cittas[1]. Sati is non-forgetful of what is wholesome. There are many
levels of sati: sati of the level of dāna, of sīla, of samatha, of tranquil
meditation or of vipassanā.

Acharn emphasized that paññā can know the difference between moments of sati and moments without sati. Only paññā that has been
developed more can know the difference. She said: "Sati and paññā are
not you. If there is only intellectual understanding the characteristics
of sati and paññā cannot be known."

Acharn explained that when there is understanding of the level of
pariyatti the object does not appear well, but when sati and paññā
of the level of satipaṭṭhāna arise the object of understanding "appears
well". The object cannot appear well in the beginning, when paññā has
not been developed enough. When understanding has been developed
more, the object of understanding begins to appear well. Then paññā
will know the difference between the moment of sati and the moment
without it. She said that it is a very short moment but that it is there.
The characteristic of the object is truly understood as not self, as an
element. This is paññā of a higher level, different from intellectual
understanding of an object. But it has intellectual understanding of the
present reality as a condition for its arising.

When understanding has been developed further to the degree that
levels of insight knowledge (vipassanā ñāṇa) arise the object appears
clearer and clearer.

Sati and paññā of the level of vipassanā can directly know the arising
and falling away of realities. Then the real meaning of momentary death
of citta will be understood.

---

[1]Sobhana cittas include not only kusala cittas but also kusala vipākacittas accompanied by sobhana cetasikas and kiriyacittas of the arahat accompanied by sobhana
cetasikas.

16

Every moment is present moment

Understanding what has not been understood before is most valuable. Without the Buddha's teachings we would always have an idea of "I see, I hear", from life to life. He taught us that there is no self who is there, no one who experiences, not a person or thing that is experienced. Ignorance will always cover up the truth. During the discussions we often heard the words "seeing is not self" and we considered those words. But when seeing arises there is still the idea of "I see". There will be this idea so long as the characteristic of seeing does not appear to paññā that has been developed more. Even when we do not expressively think "it is me" there is still the idea of self. We only know this through the Buddha's teaching. The view of self is only eradicated by the sotāpanna, the person who has attained the first stage of enlightenment.

Seeing arises for one extremely short moment and then shortly afterwards we think of people and things we believe that we see. The difference between seeing and thinking should be known.

Acharn asked someone a few questions about seeing.

Acharn: "When it is not 'I', what is it?"

Answer: "Seeing."

Acharn: "What is seeing?"

Answer: "Citta."

Acharn then explained: "If you do not use words like citta or nature of citta, there is a reality which sees. A reality which just arises to see. The more there is the understanding of the reality which arises to see, the more understanding develops. There is no one there and it falls away instantly. When there is the idea of people and things there is no seeing at that moment."

Acharn often asks the listeners questions in order to help them to consider the truth for themselves. The Buddha taught the Dhamma in such way that people would develop their own understanding. Then they will have more confidence in the teachings.

Acharn asks people why they want to study the Dhamma. It is just for the sake of understanding the truth. The aim is not becoming a better person, not trying to have more understanding; then one still thinks of self. Understanding is not "I".

Life just exists in a moment. The moment of seeing is so short, and also what is seen, visible object, does not last. She asked why one clings to mountains, trees and people. What is the use of clinging to what is gone immediately. Clinging accumulates and at such moments there is no understanding of the truth. Through the development of understanding of realities there can eventually be a little less attachment to what is not worth clinging to.

Our whole life is the succession of realities that arise and fall away. We were often reminded of citta that sees alone, hears alone or thinks alone. We think of situations and stories about people, but the thinking itself is alone. Citta arises and experiences an object and then falls away immediately. Only one citta arises at a time; when seeing arises there is no other experience at the same time. "Even right now you are alone. Citta just arises and falls away", Acharn said. When we are happy with friends, happy feeling arises alone. Citta is always alone, each moment.

Someone may wonder whether helping or giving is meaningful if there is no person. Here we have again two different worlds, the world of the situations and persons, and the world of what is real in the ultimate sense, citta, cetasika and rūpa.

We should consider citta. The citta that arises with generosity is wholesome. It can think in a wholesome way. There is no need to think of a person, it is the behaviour of citta, just for a moment, that matters. Understanding of realities leads to more wholesomeness. It is purer. For example, when we want to help others they may react with irritation. That does not matter, we need not think of situations, like reactions of others; there is the wholesome citta that arises and nobody can change it.

We lead our ordinary life in different situations, with different people, but in between thinking of situations, citta with right understanding of what life really is can arise. Thinking is a reality and the stories one thinks of are not real. By knowing the difference between stories and realities understanding can grow and develop. Life is really seeing visible object, thinking about it, hearing sound, thinking about it, all different realities that do not last.

This cannot be clearly understood in the beginning. When paññā is more developed to the stage of direct understanding of realities, it can penetrate the arising and falling away of whatever appears now. Then it becomes clearer that all we find so important only stays for a splitsecond. It will be clearer that what appears now, just one moment of seeing visible object, is real, and all concepts we think about are just speculations, thoughts or ideas which are not real. There will eventually be less ignorance and clinging to self.

After being in Hanoi for a few days we went to Mai Chau for a pleasant stay in the country with Dhamma discussions. We visited a picturesque village in Mai Chau Valley by an electric car where we had luncheon. We passed a traditional "homestay", where guests stay together with the family on the same floor. Those are simple houses of wood and bamboo, usually without electricity. Women who look after their cattle just continue with their needle work while walking on the street.

The dining room of the resort in Mai Chau was a roofed verandah, an ideal place with fresh air for Dhamma discussions. Here Acharn had a conversation with Tadao, our Japanese friend, about seeing and what is seen. She explained the Dhamma in the way of asking questions and would not stop until she had an answer to her questions. People may answer what they have learnt from the texts without really investigating the truth themselves. She would ask what is there when seeing. Everyone should really find out by himself what reality is there.

She explained that in the beginning there should be understanding of what is real and what is not real. What is seen, visible object, is real, seeing is real. She asked: "Can seeing which arises and falls away be anyone? Is seeing real, can it be you?"

When we say that seeing is not "I" there is only an idea about reality, it is not the actual moment when seeing arises. At that moment we are usually forgetful and we do not investigate the truth for ourselves. It has to be one's own understanding of whatever appears now. She said that understanding of what appears now is the test of one's own development of understanding.

She asked Tadao "What is there now when seeing?" She repeated this question several times. Tadao said: "Things". Acharn then asked what the thing is that can be seen. She said: "That which can be seen is a reality. It is real. Can anyone make it arise? No one can do anything at all, right? What is seen now? What is that thing that is seen? You did not answer my question. The question was about the thing, what is it?"

This way of question and answer helps to understand realities. One should not just think about words and follow what one learnt from the teachings. One has to investigate the reality appearing now.

People think that they see a table with four legs. Acharn said: "You talk about shape and form but it has to be seen. What is really seen brings about the idea of four legs." She reminded us of the truth by repeating that what has to be understood should be now, now. If there would not be seeing of visible object there could not be thinking of a table.

After hearing the teachings one begins to realize what is really seen. The idea of people or table comes later on, after seeing. She said:

"There must be seeing, like a flash. Thinking comes later. We do not talk about thinking, we talk about seeing before there can be the understanding that there is nothing besides seeing and what can be seen. So, no one there at all. This is the beginning of understanding that there is no one. We learn to understand the absolute truth of each moment as it is. At this moment of seeing there is no one. There are only different realities."

She said that there is the idea of self all the time but that one should learn to understand what appears, little by little, in order to eradicate the idea of self in that which is seen. She talked about seeing again and again because it is the object of ignorance from aeons ago.

She asked what nāma is. A reality that arises to experience something. "Can anyone see nāma ?", she asked, and the answer was no. She then asked the same about hearing and the other sense-cognitions. When we answer that seeing is nāma, not self, it does not mean that we have really understood what nāma is. We have ideas about reality but there is no direct awareness at the moment when seeing arises.

By her questions Acharn helps us to understand the difference between intellectual understanding and direct awareness and direct understanding of seeing or any other reality that appears now. Paññā that is developed from moment to moment can clearly know realities that appear now. But as soon as we are wishing for this knowledge, there is no understanding of the fact that all realities of our life arise because of their own conditions and are not self. When sati and direct understanding arise it will be known precisely when there is wrong view.

The development of paññā to the stage of insight knowledge, vipassanā ñāṇa, takes aeons. When it arises it knows directly the arising and falling away of realities. Without direct awareness of seeing it cannot be known that it arises and falls away. That is why Acharn often said that paññā is not enough yet. However, understanding can begin to know different characteristics of realities. If it does not begin now how can awareness and direct understanding ever arise?

Jonothan reminded us repeatedly that the development of right understanding does not mean that there will be less akusala, a change of personality for the better and more calm. There is no point in wishing for these things. No matter life is pleasant now or unpleasant now, the only thing that is worth while is understanding realities that appear at the present moment.

Jonothan said: "Every moment is present moment". There are no methods to be followed for causing the arising of awareness of realities.

Acharn said: "Why do you think of practising. There is no need to think about it. Forget it." She reminded us that the aim of listening to the Dhamma is just for the sake of understanding, nothing else.

There were several questions about the way to develop calm. One of the listeners mentioned that a good location and confortable wheather would be favourable conditions for the understanding of the Dhamma. Acharn remarked: "Why wait." One may have the idea that a quiet place is necessary in order to develop understanding, but that is attachment and this is not a helpful condition for understanding of whatever appears now.

One may be attached to comfortable surroundings and wants to have only pleasant feeling. One may have the illusion that one can control one's life. We always dream of another place, thinking there will be more awareness. We are forgetting realities at this moment.

Sarah remarked:

"Whatever arises does so by conditions, not by anyone's will. Can anyone control what hearing hears, what is experienced through the bodysense? It arises so quickly by conditions, long before anyone can even think about it. When we try so hard to avoid unpleasantness, the realities are attachment and the wrong idea of 'I can control' ".

Someone said that one should meditate before listening to the Dhamma. By concentration on breath he would become calm and this would help to solve the problems of life such as stress. One dislikes stress that arises when there is aversion (dosa), accompanied by unpleasant feeling. However, one may not know when there is attachment to pleasant feeling. The real cause of problems in life are ignorance and attachment. No matter aversion, attachment, ignorance, whatever dhamma arises, they are all conditioned realities. It is an illusion that one can control one's life just by concentration on a subject like breath without any understanding of what true calm is. Calm, the cetasika passaddhi, arises with each sobhana citta (beautiful citta). True calm as it is developed in samatha accompanies right understanding of the way how to develop it with a suitable meditation subject.

Jonothan explained that the beginning of samatha, the development of calm, is knowing the difference between kusala and akusala. Without knowing the difference there cannot be the development of kusala. Some people believe that they should concentrate on a meditation subject such as in-and-outbreathing but they may not have any understanding of what breath is nor of kusala citta and akusala citta.

Kusala citta is always accompanied by the wholesome roots[1] of non-attachment and non-aversion and it may be accompanied by understanding as well. Akusala citta is always accompanied by the root of ignorance, moha, and it may at times by accompanied by attachment (lobha) as well or by aversion (dosa) as well. There are many degrees of these roots and one may not know them when they are more subtle. For instance, attachment is not only desire for a beautiful painting one wants to have, it is also attachment to seeing right now or to bodily wellbeing, moments that are not known. Aversion is not only anger or sadness, but it can also arise when there is a slight feeling of uneasiness. Ignorance follows very often seeing, hearing and the other sense-cognitions. It is ignorance of what realities are.

Jonothan explained that non-attachment or detachment arises naturally, by the development of understanding, after a long time. By thinking about detachment and by trying to have it, there will not be any detachment. He said:

"Samatha begins to develop when kusala citta arises naturally in one's daily life. That is when the characteristic of calm that is kusala can be known. If one thinks to just take an appropriate meditation subject, such as in-and-out- breathing or a kasina[2] it is wrong. Taking a particular meditation subject cannot make the citta kusala. That is why Acharn says that right understanding is necessary for both samatha and vipassanā."

The development of samatha has to be right from the beginning. The development of samatha is not necessary for the attainment of enlightenment. Many people became enlightened without any attainment of jhāna.[3]

There can be moments of calm in daily life and then the citta is for that moment free from akusala, there is detachment. This is different from trying to be detached. Sarah mentioned that there were conditions to reflect naturally on death, because a friend's mother had passed away. Such reflection may condition calm. She said that one can reflect that

---

[1] Some cetasikas are roots, hetus, which are the foundation of the beautiful citta or the akusala citta.

[2] A coloured disc, or a disc made of earth.

[3] See the Susima Sutta (S II, 199-23) and the Visuddhimagga (666-67) which deals with dry insight, sukkhavipassanā.

life is short: "Death can come at each moment. There can be calmness. What is precious in life is understanding at this moment."

17

The right Path and the wrong Path

Just now, at this moment, many things seem to appear at the same time. All this which we call the world, could not appear if there were no citta. Citta experiences an object. Through the Buddha's teachings we learn that there is one citta at a time, an extremely short moment. It arises and falls away never to return. We seem to see continuously, hear continuously. But we learn that at each moment there is a different citta that experiences an object through one of the six doorways, of the senses and of the mind-door.

Whatever subject we consider, we have to distinguish the world of concepts, of people, I, you, different things that seem to last, and the real world of ultimate realities. Otherwise we do not know the truth.

The difference between realities and concepts cannot be grasped at once. That is why there was so much repetition in all the explanations during the sessions. We have accumulated ignorance and wrong view for aeons.

Realities can be directly experienced, but first more intellectual understanding, pariyatti, is needed. We have to listen to the Buddha's teaching who speaks about seeing, hearing and all realities. Are they permanent or impermanent he asked. Impermanence is not just thinking about the fact that things do not last. The falling away of seeing or hearing can be experienced but not immediately. It needs countless times of considering what seeing is, as different from thinking about people. What hearing is, as different from thinking about the rain or thunder one perceives. Very gradually there can be a little more understanding of seeing and other realities that appear without trying to know them. That is why it is useful to discuss about seeing and other realities.

Thus, considering realities is most important. We should not have any expectation that realities can clearly appear one at a time immediately. Patience is important.

We are reminded all the time that the difference between nāma and rūpa, such as seeing and visible object, has to be clearly understood so that realities can, one by one, be directly known. When we take realities as a "whole", as a collection of phenomena, there is no precise knowledge of their different characteristics and we take them for self. But we should not try to distinguish nāma from rūpa, that is done with an idea of self. Understanding cannot be made to arise by an idea of self.

Acharn said: "What is there now. Is there seeing or what? Seeing is conditioned, it cannot arise by itself. It is conditioned just to arise and see, that is all. No matter what you call it."

Those are simple words, but did we really consider them enough? No matter how seeing is called, this reality appears and can be understood. We can call it by any name in any language, but its characteristic does not change. It experiences visible object. It is an ultimate reality, different from conventional notions.

Acharn said: "It is gone completely, never to return in saṃsāra (the cycle of birth and death) or anywhere in the world. No matter what you call it, is it true?"

If one has not listened to the Buddha's teachings there will always be ignorance covering up the truth.

Acharn said: "What is most precious in life. Does one understand the truth of seeing right now? Life goes on from moment to moment. There is seeing now and it is gone completely. Everything arises and falls away in splitseconds. Without the Buddha's teaching who knows that seeing arises and falls away. The truth of life is not easy to understand. What is precious is understanding what was not understood before. Everything is gone. Can anything belong to you? Realities arise and fall away each moment. When there is no understanding there will be the idea of 'I see, I hear', from life to life."

There are many misunderstandings about practice. In the texts the word practice is used and it is actually the translation of the Pali term paṭipatti. There is nobody who practises, practice arises only because of the right conditions. It is the development of direct understanding and it is conditioned by intellectual understanding, pariyatti. Intellectual understanding is not just study of texts and deep reflection on what one has learnt. It is more than that, it pertains to reality now, although we know that the understanding of the present reality is not precise yet. It refers to the reality of this moment, such as seeing that appears now. It can be understood as a conditioned reality, not self. It is the beginning of understanding that there is no one there.

As Acharn often explains: "One begins to understand: it is this moment only which is real. And then it is completely gone, there is nothing. Seeing is gone, where is the 'I' who sees? No one."

When someone asked how understanding develops by reflection, she replied:

"By understanding better and better, no other way."

Pariyatti is not the direct understanding of realities, paṭipatti, but it is the condition for it. Paṭipatti conditions paṭivedha, the direct realization of the truth by the stages of insight knowledge[1] and enlightenment.

Some people think that they have to follow a meditation practice in order to realize the truth, a special method such as focussing on a subject like breathing. However, when on clings to an idea of self that can cause the growth of paññā it will only lead to more clinging with wrong view.

Some people think that there are specific times for practice, such as sitting quietly. There is an idea of "I am practising" and they do not

---

[1] There are different stages of insight, vipassanā. The first one is knowing the difference between nāma, the reality that experiences an object, and rūpa, the reality that does not experience anything. In the course of the different stages of insight there is more and more detachment from realities.

realize that awareness and right understanding can only arise because of their own conditions, not when there is an idea of self that can follow a method to cause their arising. No one can cause the arising of any reality, such as seeing or hearing, they arise naturally. Instead of clinging to an idea of practice one should consider what the Buddha taught about the realities that appear all the time, like seeing, visible object, hearing, sound or thinking. When we carefully consider the Buddha's words, for example that seeing arises because of conditions, it can lead to the development of right understanding. But there should not be any expectations that understanding can grow quickly.

Retreats are organized in Vietnam and all over the world. People believe that it is easier to develop understanding of one's citta when there is silence. One can quietly follow different moments of thinking. Again, one should find out whether one is motivated by attachment to the idea of self who wishes to be wise and calm.

It is said that people's behaviour improves in a meditation center. However, one cannot tell from someone's outward behaviour whether or not there are kusala cittas. Kusala citta arises for an etremely short moment and then falls away, and it is bound to be followed by akusala cittas which are unknown. One may think of oneself as a good person, and that is conceit. It is necessary to often hear about realities that arise and fall away, otherwise there is the idea that one has to do something special to have more calm and wisdom.

The right Path and the wrong Path was a subject discussed several times during the sessions. There are misunderstandings as to the development of the eightfold Path. The factors of the eightfold Path are sobhana cetasikas which all develop together[2]. Some people think that the factors of the eightfold Path have to be developed one after the other, but they develop together. The object which the citta and the accompanying path-factors experience has to be a reality that presents itself at the present moment, such as seeing, hardness, attachment, kindness. It is an ultimate reality; conventional notions, such as person or tree, are not the object of the path-factors. There must be the factor of right

---

[2]They are: right understanding (sammā-diṭṭhi), right thinking (sammā-sankappa), right speech (sammā-vācā), right bodily action (sammā-kammanta), right livelihood (sammā-ājīva), right effort (sammā-vāyāma), right mindfulness (sammā-sati) and right concentration (sammā-samādhi).

understanding of the eightfold Path accompanying the other cetasikas. Realities such as right effort and right mindfulness without right understanding are not factors of the eightfold Path. Right understanding knows the object that appears as non-self. When someone thinks of self trying to develop the eightfold Path he is on the wrong Path.

We usually think of situations, stories which are not realities, we are dreaming, living in a phantasy world. Acharn always helps people to return to the present moment. She said:

"Is there seeing right now? Is it truth? Who can make it arise or change it into thinking? It is not me. Who can stop seeing right now? One cannot do anything, it is completely gone. The seeing is not you, it is a reality. There is no one at all, only different realities."

Some people think that they should first have less akusala cittas before they can develop understanding. They try to abandon attachment to people and situations. If one tries to have less attachment one should ask oneself what type of citta arises at such moments. One wishes to be a good person with good qualities, and at such moments there is clinging to an idea of self. It is very meaningful that there are four stages of enlightenment when defilements are successively eradicated. First wrong view must be eradicated and this occurs at the first stage of enlightenment, the stage of the "streamwinner" (sotāpanna). Later on, at the third stage of enlightenment, the stage of the "non-returner" (anāgāmī), attachment to sense objects is eradicated. Thus, so long as realities are taken for self it is impossible to eradicate attachment to them. The development of understanding takes aeons.

We read in the "Kindred Sayings" (III), "Kindred Sayings on Elements", "Directly Knowing" (I § 24)[3], that the Budha said, while he was at Sāvatthī:

"Bhikkhus, without directly knowing and fully understanding form[4], without becoming dispassionate towards it and abandoning it, one is incapable of destroying suffering..."

The same is said about the four nāma-khandhas: feeling, perception (saññā), formations (saṅkhāra-khandha, the other fifty cetasikas) and consciousness (viññāṇa-khandha). The Buddha said:

---

[3] I am using the translation by Ven. Bodhi.
[4] Rūpa, physical phenomena.

"Bhikkhus, by directly knowing and fully understanding form, by becoming dispassionate towards it and abandoning it, one is capable of destroying suffering..."

The same is said about the other khandhas. First there should be intellectual understanding of the reality appearing now, such as seeing, hearing, hardness, or whatever appears. They do not belong to a self but they are mere passing dhammas. There are many moments of akusala we are ignorant of. One may not know when feeling at ease, laughing, or looking at the table, that there are bound to be many moments of attachments and ignorance. Ignorance usually follows seeing or hearing.

Sometimes people are told to be aware now, but this is impossible, as Acharn explained. Right awareness of the eightfold Path and also the other path-factors arise because of the appropriate conditions, they are not self. It is not a matter of trying to have awareness and understanding. Trying to think of Dhamma or to walk slowly in order to have awareness are methods that do not lead to right understanding of realities, and, thus, they are the wrong Path.

Acharn said: "When intellectual understanding is not enough to condition right awareness, it cannot arise. All dhammas are anattā, so, awareness and right understanding are anattā. Can anyone know the next moment: seeing, hearing or thinking? Right awareness arises only when there are conditions."

It is not known what the next moment will be, it may be seeing, hearing, clinging, awareness and understanding or dying-consciousness. It depends entirely on conditions that are beyond our power. Nobody can condition the arising of seeing, and evenso, nobody can condition the arising of awareness. It can arise unexpectedly, if one does not cling to it.

People are often wondering when there are sati and paññā. That is why Acharn explained about these realities time and again.

Acharn asked: "When listening to Sarah and Jonothan, is there any understanding? That is sati and paññā, not you. At the moment of hearing there is no understanding. Understanding comes afterwards, it cannot be hearing."

Hearing is a vipākacitta that just hears sound, it does not know the meaning of what is heard. Acharn said: "Whenever there is understanding it is only a reality; there are sati, paññā and other wholesome cetasikas arising together, but they are unknown. We can understand that the moments of seeing and hearing are not the moment of understanding. This is the beginning to understand at which moment there are sati and paññā and at which moment there are no sati and paññā."

Acharn explained that in the beginning there is only intellectual understanding of realities. There is not yet direct understanding of the arising and falling away of realities, which is a higher level of paññā. There can be thinking about sati and paññā but their characteristics do not appear as they are, just one at a time.

Someone may take thinking of realities for right awareness. Acharn explained: "Usually in a day hardness arises but it is not known. It appears to ignorance and attachment, not to right awareness and right understanding."

Only right understanding can know the difference between such moments. Someone touches a table and he believes that he clearly knows hardness at such a moment. He should find out whether there is an idea of self touching, even if he does not expressively thinks in that way. He may think of hardness but without right understanding that knows it as just a conditioned reality that does not last for an instant.

Acharn explained that one misleads oneself while believing that he has awareness at the moment he is told to be aware. Each word of the Buddha points to the development of right understanding. Only the right intellectual understanding of whatever appears now can lead to direct understanding, to paṭipatti, sati and paññā of the level of satipaṭṭhāna.

The development of intellectual understanding, pariyatti, may take more than one life until it is so firm that it can condition direct understanding. Only direct understanding knows the characteristic of sati and of paññā. We should not try to find out whether pariyatti is already firm, as we were reminded so often. We should just persevere to learn a little more about seeing now, hearing now, hardness now. They arise because of their own conditions and nobody can manipulate them. It is as Acharn often said: understanding is not enough yet.

Some people have an idea of practice of vipassanā, insight, by focussing on an object with concentration, in order to make satipaṭṭhāna, mindfulness of realities, arise. They try to focus on breathing or try to have mettā, kindness. Instead of mettā one has attachment. Sarah explained that this is not the same as mettā arising naturally in daily life. All such methods are wrong concentration of the wrong Path.

Concentration, ekaggatā cetasika or samādhi, may be right concentration or wrong concentration. When there is awareness and right understanding of the reality appearing at this moment without any expectation of a result, there is at that moment also right concentration. There is no need to think of concentration, it arises already because of conditions.

Acharn explained that we should remember that all are dhammas, arising by conditions. There should be no selection of the reality that appears, its arising depends on conditions.

The words "no selection" that she often used are very helpful. It reminds us that all are just passing dhammas arising each by their own conditions. "We cannot do anything, there is nobody there", as Acharn said, time and again. Following the right Path with detachment is the way to have more confidence that all dhammas are anattā. The Path leading to enlightenment is the Path of understanding of anattā, Acharn said. At the end of the session on that day someone of the listeners expressed her great appreciation of these explanations on the right Path.

18

One cannot do anything

The Dependent Origination, Paṭiccasamuppāda was briefly referred to during the sessions. It is the Buddha's teaching about the conditions leading to the cycle of birth and death. The first link is Ignorance, leading to kamma, and kamma leads to rebirth and vipākacittas (result) throughout life. The first javana-cittas of every living being are cittas rooted in attachment, lobha, thus, there is immediately craving, there is clinging to life.

Someone remarked that one should just cut off craving, tanhā, which is one of the links of the Dependent Origination, and that this would lead to the end of the cycle. This is impossible since there is no self who could change conditioned realities. It is with the eradication of ignorance of realities through fully developed paññā that the chain of conditions is broken. It will take aeons to develop paññā stage by stage. Only when right understanding to the degree of arahatship has been developed there will not be rebirth. Then there will be the end of the cycle.

Often during the discussions there was reference to the "three Rounds" (vaṭṭas) of the cycle of birth and death. When seeing or hearing arises it is the round of vipāka, the result of kamma. We cling to vipāka and then there is the round of defilement, kilesa. Defilements lead to the committing of kamma. So long as defilements have not been eradicated there will be conditions for kusala kamma and akusala kamma that condition rebirth. Kamma will produce again vipāka and in this way the round goes on and on. Attachment and aversion are not always of the degree of kamma, an evil deed, but they are defilements (kilesa) that accumulate and when they have become strong they can lead to evil speech and deeds that harm others, to akusala kamma that is able to produce result.

The Visuddhimagga[1] deals with the three rounds in the chapter on the Dependent Origination (XVII, 299). We read:

> "With triple round it spins forever: here formations and becoming [2] are the round of kamma. Ignorance, craving and clinging are the round of defilements. Consciousness, mentality-materiality sixfold base [3], contact and feeling are the round of result. So this Wheel of becoming, having a triple round with these three rounds, should be understood to spin, revolving again and again, for ever; for the conditions are not cut off as long as the round of defilement is not cut off."

Sarah explained:
"After seeing attachment arises, it arises beyond anyone's control and falls away instantly."

Someone may think that since it does not stay why we should worry about it, dwell on it, or reason about the causes of attachment.

Sarah: "If one thinks that one can stop attachment and ignorance arising after seeing, it is the wrong idea of self that can control or stop or change reality.

---

[1] This is an Encyclopedia composed by the commentator Buddhaghosa who lived in the fifth century A.D.

[2] Formations, abhisaṅkhāra, refers to kusala kamma and akusala kamma. Becoming, bhava, to kamma process becoming, kamma in this life.

[3] Consciousness, viññāṇa, refers to the vipākacitta that is rebirth-consciousness and to vipākacitta throughout life. Mentality-materiality, nāma-rūpa, to the cetasikas that are vipāka and rūpa produced by kamma.

Just as seeing arises naturally by conditions, attachment arises. When hearing more about realities, sati can arise naturally, but not by anyone's doing anything.

Listening and considering carefully does not mean how many hours one can come to these discussions. It means that even a few words, like 'seeing arising by conditions now', or 'what is the meaning of dhamma', has to be very carefully considered. The careful considering leads to awareness and understanding without any expectation."

Acharn explained that life is anattā even from the beginning, from the moment of birth-consciousness. Kamma conditioned the citta and accompanying cetasikas at that moment; they are vipāka, result of kamma. Kamma also produced three groups of rūpa, kalapas, at that moment: one group with bodysense, one group with the heartbase and one group with sex, femininity or masculinity. Even the moment of birth is anattā. Hearing the teachings now is kusala kamma and this can condition the next birth-consciousness.

We still have the opportunity to hear the teachings and develop understanding. She said: "Understanding means understanding of seeing and hearing in daily life." Pariyatti is not theoretical understanding, it is understanding of what appears now, time and again, like seeing and hearing.

If there is only thinking of the fact that all dhammas are anattā, there will not be any understanding right now of dhamma as anattā. Seeing lasts only for one moment but people think: 'I see'. Life exists only in one moment. Acharn repeated this very often and this is most beneficial. We always forget this when we are taken in by the events of life. Ignorance is a kind of sickness and the Buddha is the true physician who can cure it.

Acharn explained that just knowing that there is ignorance is not enough. One should understand more and more that it is conditioned, by the accumulation of aeons ago. No one can stop conditions for the arising of anything.

Hearing a few words is not enough. When we were in a restaurant Acharn said: "We have to continue developing understanding amongst akusala." Delicious food was waiting for us and it is natural to have attachment to flavour. Even after seeing, shortly after it has fallen away, we are bound to be attached to seeing or to visible object. This is completely unknown. Cittas arise and fall away succeeding one another so fast. When we consider the countless moments of akusala, Acharn's words that understanding is developed in the midst of akusala become more meaningful. Akusala cittas arise almost all the time, but, in between, understanding of whatever appears can be developed, just for an extremely short moment.

"One cannot do anything", this was often repeated. It was said to remind us that there are only conditioned realities arising and falling away. When seeing has arisen can one prevent it from arising? Can one cause the seeing that has fallen away to return and see again?

Seeing was taken as an example of a conditioned reality, but when we have more understanding of its conditioned nature we shall also understand that other realities that arise are conditioned and cannot be altered or manipulated. One cannot do anything. This can also be said of different kinds of defilements that arise, that are not welcome. However, thanks to the Buddha's teachings understanding of whatever appears can be developed, in the midst of akusala.

Acharn said: "What we take for the world, people and things are only different realities. It is the absolute truth, nobody can change this characteristic. When you touch something hard is it you who makes it hard? Actually, there is no you, only different dhammas."

Someone asked whether good deeds, like giving, releasing animals[4] or chanting texts would be a way of sharing merit with the dead. When someone is reborn in another plane of existence, such as one of the heavenly planes, where he can know about someone else's good deed he may appreciate the wholesome deeds of someone else and have kusala citta on account of it. This can be called the sharing of merit. However, we cannot know in which plane someone else is reborn, a plane where he could know about someone else's kusala. It is of no use to speculate about this.

It is difficult to know whether the citta of someone else is kusala or akusala. When one sees other people doing good deeds or abstaining from deeds that can harm others it cannot be known from the outward appearance of a deed whether or not the citta is kusala. Every citta that arises does so for an extremely short moment and it falls away instantly.

---

[4]This is a custom done near a temple or pagoda: releasing birds that have been caught, in order to make merit.

Kusala citta can be followed closely by akusala citta, but since cittas succeed one another so rapidly one may take akusala citta for kusala citta.

Someone thought that he could constantly be aware of postures. There cannot be awareness and understanding all the time. When one thinks in that way there is no understanding. Posture is an impression of a whole, a situation, such as walking. It is not a nāma or rūpa that can be directly experienced. We can just think of it.

Some people want to change their lifestyle or give up their job in order to have more time for the Dhamma. However, such a wish is motivated by clinging to the idea of self . This hinders the development of understanding. One should lead one's life naturally.

What is morality, sīla? This was one of the topics of discussion that came up. It is not following rules. There may be the conventional way of thinking about good morality when considering kusala sīla. However, we should know what kusala sīla is in the ultimate sense. It is the behaviour of citta, only for a very short moment. Kusala citta does not last, it falls away within splitseconds. From the outward appearance of deeds by others we can never know what the citta is like.

When performing a good deed such as helping others, one may have an idea that such moments last. Or when one abstains from akusala one may think of a story of not retorting unkind words to someone who spoke in an unpleasant way. All the time during which one does not retort unkind words one may keep silent with aversion. Then one misses the real meaning of abstaining from akusala which is just a short moment of kusala citta. Or there may be moments of conceit, while thinking, "I am better than the person who spoke unkindly, or see how good I am". When we have more understanding of citta it will be clearer that kusala sīla is the behaviour of kusala citta which arises and then falls away immediately.

If one knows the difference between understanding the ultimate realities of citta and cetasika and the conventional way of thinking, there will be more understanding of what sīla is, the behaviour of citta now. We are used to thinking in a conventional way but if we do not know the difference between the conventional way of thinking and the understanding of ultimate realities, there will be a great deal of confusion in life.

In the ultimate sense, there is no person, only citta (consciousness), cetasika (mental factors accompanying citta) and rūpa (physical phenomena) which arise and fall away instantly. What arises and falls away immediately cannot be taken for a person or self.

We have to lead our daily life naturally, and so, we think of our fellowmen, to treat them with respect and concern for their wellfare. At the same time there can be more understanding of ultimate realities. What is the citta like that thinks of others, is it kusala or akusala? It is not my kusala or akusala, just dhammas arising because of their own conditions. When there is right understanding, kusala will be purer, there will be less thinking of self.

One may think in a conventional way of monkhood, thinking of the person who wears a yellow robe. However, we have to consider the true meaning of monkhood by way of ultimate realities. It is not the wearing a yellow robe that makes someone a monk. It is the behaviour of citta of someone who leads the monk's life, different from the laylife. The monk should lead the life of an arahat, a perfected one, who truly sees the danger of being in the cycle of birth and death.

Acharn, her sister and I had a wheelchair at the airport in Bangkok. We had a conversation with the young men who pushed those wheelchairs and it appeared that several of them had been ordained as a monk for three months, just to please their parents. They said that they did not have much understanding of the Vinaya. One should have understanding of the teachings first, before being ordained.

In Vietnam Acharn spoke about the true meaning of monkhood. She stressed the importance of first studying the teachings. One should not think of being ordained in order to study the teachings later on. Even the first five disciples of the Buddha were not ordained yet before they had understanding of the teachings. One should have true understanding of the teachings in order to know whether one has accumulations for leading the life as a monk or for leading the laylife.

In the Buddha's time laypeople who developed understanding and attained enlightenment, could even attain the third stage, the stage of the "non-returner"(anāgāmī), and this meant they had eradicated clinging to all sense objects. But those who attained the fourth stage, the stage of the arahat, had eradicated all kinds of clinging and all defilements and they could not lead the laylife anymore. The monk's life is the life of the arahat. It is a life of fewness of wishes. They should never ask for anything, they are dependent on the requisites of robes, food, lodging and medicines given to them by laypeople. It is their duty to "review" these requisites every time they use them.

Acharn explained that it is disrespect to the Buddha to just wish to become a monk and be his son or heir without developing understanding of his teachings. Only those who have accumulations to lead the monk's life, study the teachings and develop understanding could ask to be ordained as a monk.

Acharn said: "The monk's life is quite different from the laylife. When the monk wakes up he remembers, 'I am not a layman anymore.' Before having his meal he must think about it that this is given. So he would make use of this gift in the best way. The best thing in life, especially in the monk's life, is studying the teachings carefully and follow the Vinaya, the rules of Discipline. Each word of the Vinaya comes from the Buddha himself. Who else is better than him to lay down the Vinaya, the rules of the monk's life." Acharn said that if the monk does not live in this way it is so dangerous to be a monk. He is like a thief who steals what is given to the virtues ones.

We read in the "Visuddhimagga" (I, 125) about four kinds of use and one kind is "use as a theft". The commentary to the "Visuddhimagga", the "Paramattha-mañjūsā" (61) states:

> " 'Use as theft': use by one who is unworthy. And the requisites are allowed by the Blessed One to one in his own dispensation who is virtuous, not unvirtuous; and the generosity of the givers is towards one who is virtuous, not towards one who is not, since they expect great fruit from their actions".

Acharn said: "That is why in the Buddha's time someone would understand the teachings before becoming a monk and he would realize that his accumulations are so great that he could renounce the laylife."

Acharn explained that the Buddha's Path, no matter for laypeople or for monks, is the way to have less and less attachment. Clinging to the idea of self should be eradicated first, before clinging to sense objects can be eradicated. Each word of the Buddha pertains to understanding of reality right now.

At the end of the last session one of the monks spoke with great appreciation and confidence about Acharn's explanations on the development of understanding. He said that this was the right Path. He was hoping that at rebirth in a future life he would be able to listen to Acharn again.

There were long photo sessions and many of the listeners found that these days they had learnt a great deal from the discussions. They expressed their gratefulness and appreciation to Acharn, Sarah, Jonothan and friends. It was very inspiring to see the confidence and enthusiasm of those who had listened during these sessions.

The Buddha's words about the truth of life should be understood, not just followed. The best thing he shared with everyone is understanding and this is what is most precious in one's life.

Part IV

Considering the Truth

19

Preface

Acharn Sujin and friends were invited again for Dhamma discussions in Vietnam by Tam Bach and other Vietnamese friends in February 2017. Friends from Thailand, Australia, Taiwan and myself joined this journey. Sarah and Jonothan were assisting Acharn and they gave us all many helpful reminders and explanations about the reality appearing at the present moment. In Vietnam Tran Thai made the travel and accommodation arrangements for us.

Before the sessions in Vietnam, there were a few days of Dhamma discussions in Thailand, in Nakorn Nayok, a place outside Bangkok. Here we could meet old friends from Thailand, U.S.A. and Italy. Vincent from Taiwan joined us with his wife Jane and their eleven-year-old daughter Nana. We discussed details of cetasikas, mental factors that accompany citta, such as contact, feeling and concentration. Knowing more details helps us to see that citta and cetasikas that arise together condition one another. Nobody can cause the arising of particular realities, they are all dhammas devoid of self. We also discussed the factors leading to enlightenment. Without the proper conditions, enlightenment cannot be attained.

In Vietnam the sessions took place first in Saigon where we met many friends who attended sessions at former occasions. The listeners had numerous questions which were profitable for all of us. After Saigon, the sessions were held at a very special place in Hoi An, namely at the newly constructed resort An Villa of Tran Thai and Tiny Tam. It is a "home-stay" and it has the friendly atmosphere as we find it in a family home, a Dhamma home, and here we spent delightful hours of discussions.

Acharn reminded us many times that only listening and reading is not enough. We should deeply consider the truth of Dhamma. In this way understanding can grow. The development of understanding should be very natural. We should not imagine that we have to go to a special tranquil place or engage in special actions in order to have more understanding. Understanding can be developed in the midst of akusala. It does not matter what types of realities arise, they are all just conditioned dhammas.

20

The reality of this moment

In our daily life we are quite occupied with all the chores we have to do, with our work, with our social life. We meet people and talk to them and we are absorbed in the stories they tell us. We find our thoughts, speech and actions very important and we take them for self. But the Buddha taught that there is no person, no "I" or "you", only ever-changing realities. If we truly understand this, we shall know the meaning of "living alone", without the idea of a person or self.

Before we heard the Buddha's teaching of non-self or anattā, we found it quite normal to believe: "I see, I hear, I think". Seeing, hearing and thinking arise, but there is no person who sees, hears or thinks. They are realities arising because of their appropriate conditions. They are present for an extremely brief moment and then they fall away, never to return. How could they be a self or how could they belong to a self?

We read in the Visuddhimagga[1] (XV, 15 in the section on the āyatanas, sense-fields) about conditioned realities:

---

[1] This is an Encyclopedia composed by the commentator Buddhaghosa who lived in the fifth century A.D.

"...they do not come from anywhere previous to their arising, nor do they go anywhere after their falling away. On the contrary, before their arising they had no individual essence, and after their falling away their individual essences are completely dissolved. And they occur without power (being exercisable over them) since they exist in dependence on conditions...

Likewise they should be regarded as incurious and uninterested. For it does not occur to the eye and visible object, etc., 'Ah, that consciousness might arise from our concurrence'. And as door, physical basis, and object, they have no curiosity about, or interest in, arousing consciousness.

On the contrary, it is the absolute rule that eye-consciousness, etc., come into being with the union of eye with visible object, and so on. So they should be regarded as incurious and uninterested..."

As Acharn often reminded us: "Before seeing there is nothing, and after seeing there is nothing". Seeing does not come from anywhere, it arises for an extremely brief moment when there are the right conditions and then it falls away, never to return.

When we stayed in Nakorn Nayok, before going to Vietnam, we had a valuable experience, listening to the discussion of Vincent and Jane's daughter Nana with Acharn, Sarah and others. We can really learn from an eleven-year-old child. Nana was very happy to have bicycle rides with Sarah and Jonothan in the early morning. Nana began to take an interest in the Dhamma and when questions were posed to her, she deeply considered these before she answered.

Nana asked Acharn: "What is most important in life?"

Acharn answered: "Right understanding of whatever appears. Do you understand what is there now? Seeing, hearing? You are without understanding, but you think that you understand. Seeing sees, is it you that sees? Can you see your father?"

Nana answered that this is just thinking. Nana said that she did not like it when her dad was angry with her. She came to understand that her daddy was not real and that there was just thinking about him being angry. Sarah asked her what the problem was: her dad being angry or thinking and feeling unhappy. Nana answered: "Thinking and feeling unhappy".

Sarah asked: "Is it good or not good when you are angry?"

Nana said: "Not good."

Sarah asked her whether she could prevent being angry and Nana understood that this is not possible.

These are all basic questions about the real cause of problems we have in life and in our dealings with other people. We tend to forget that in reality our own defilements are the cause of all trouble and not other people or the outward circumstances. We may have intellectual understanding of the truth but when we face contrariwise situations or when we have disagreements with people, we tend to forget the truth of realities.

Nana had truly accumulated an interest in the Dhamma and she considered the truth. Sarah explained that some realities are good and some are not good. Nana understood that anger is not good and kindness and helping others is good.

Hearing about basic principles of the Buddha's teachings such as in the discussions with Nana is valuable to all of us. We are forgetful of the truth that a person does not exist. We are taken away by the stories about people and then there are ignorance and attachment time and again. We cannot be reminded enough of the truth. Acharn said: "We have to begin again and again."

When someone said that it is so difficult to realize that there is no one, nothing, Acharn answered:

"There is not direct understanding yet. That is why we talk about seeing, so there will be a moment of direct understanding. Even touching now is real, but there is no understanding; no matter how many times there is touching. But when there is understanding, it is intellectual understanding until the moment there is touching with right understanding. We talk a lot about realities but there is not yet a moment of understanding of what is real as not self."

I said to Acharn: "It is so helpful that you explain all the time about this moment. This moment of touching or this moment of thinking. The present moment. Until there is direct understanding of that by conditions."

This understanding does not arise by anyone's will. Otherwise it is wrong, because there is the idea of "I". The idea of "I am doing something, I am concentrating on an object, I am being aware." If this is not clearly understood there is no way that the idea of self can be eradicated. We forget that it is not "I" who studies Dhamma, who is listening to the Dhamma, who learns about realities.

Sarah asked Nana: "Why is there the idea of my mommy?"

Nana: "Thinking."

Sarah: "Why is there the idea of my mommy, not my daddy?"

Nana: "Thinking."

Sarah: "Thinking and memory."

Remembrance (saññā) is a mental factor (cetasika) arising with every citta. There could not be thinking of a person or a thing without remembrance assisting the citta that thinks.

We have to listen more to the right friends who explain the teachings and we have to carefully consider what we hear again and again, so that there will be intellectual understanding (pariyatti) of what appears at the present moment. Intellectual understanding can condition direct understanding of the truth (paṭipatti). There should be no expectations as to when direct understanding will arise, it depends on conditions, nobody can cause its arising.

When people visited the Buddha he would ask them whether seeing is permanent or impermanent. We read in the "Kindred Sayings on Sense" (IV, Ch III, § 82, the World) that a monk said to the Buddha:

> " 'The world! The world!' is the saying, lord. How far, lord, does this saying go?"

> The Buddha answered:

> "It crumbles away, monks. Therefore it is called 'the world'. What crumbles away? The eye... objects... eye-consciousness..."

It seems that seeing can stay, but it arises because of eyesense and visible object, just for a moment and then it falls away. It is the same with hearing and the other sense-cognitions. We tend to cling to an idea of the whole body that exists, that is sitting, standing, walking or lying down. When we take the body as a whole it seems to last and we believe that we can manipulate it. There are only elements

arising because of their own conditions, there isn't anybody who can
cause their arising. They appear one at a time through one doorway at
a time. When we look at the body, only visible object appears, when we
touch it only tangible object appears such as hardness or softness, heat
or cold. These are realities, not concepts of a whole. There is no body
that is sitting. Realities can be directly experienced when they appear
one at a time, without having to think about them, whereas concepts
cannot be directly experienced, they are just objects of thinking. When
understanding of realities is being developed, the whole world crumbles
away, including the body, and the person. There is nothing left.

Some cittas are result, some are cause. Rebirth-consciousness (paṭisandhi-citta) is the first citta arising in life and it is the result of a good
or a bad deed (kusala kamma or akusala kamma) committed in the past.
Birth as a human is the result of kusala kamma. Birth as an animal
or birth in a hell plane is the result of akusala kamma. Seeing, hearing and the other sense-cognitions arising in the course of life are also
cittas that are result (vipākacittas), they experience pleasant objects
or unpleasant objects. On account of what is experienced, akusala cittas or kusala cittas arise that experience the object in an unwholesome
way or in wholesome way. These are cittas that are cause, they can
motivate unwholesome or wholesome deeds that will bring their results
accordingly.

Only one citta arises at a time and every citta is accompanied by
several mental factors, cetasikas, that each perform their own function
while they experience the same object as the citta. Some cetasikas are
beautiful (sobhana), some are akusala and some are neither.

Attachment (lobha), aversion (dosa) and ignorance (moha) are akusala
cetasikas that have been accumulated during countless lives and, thus,
they can condition the arising again of attachment, aversion and ignorance. Each kusala citta is accompanied by the beautiful cetasikas of
non-attachment (alobha) and non-aversion (adosa), and it may be accompanied by understanding, paññā, as well. Cetasikas are a condition
for citta and citta conditions cetasikas. The understanding of conditions
is essential for understanding the nature of anattā. Nobody can cause
the arising of any reality, its arising depends entirely on conditions.

Citta and cetasika are realities that are mental, in Pali: nāma. They
experience an object. They are different from physical realities, in Pali:

rūpa. There are twenty-eight kinds of rūpa, but only seven kinds appear all the time in daily life. They are: visible object, sound, odour, flavour, and the three tangible objects of solidity, appearing as hardness or softness, temperature, appearing as heat or cold, and motion, appearing as motion or pressure. These rūpas condition citta and cetasikas just by being the object they experience. The rūpas that are the sense-bases are essential conditions for the sense-cognitions. Seeing-consciousness could not arise if there were no eyesense, hearing could not arise if there were no earsense, all sense-cognitions need their own physical base. The sense-bases themselves are classified along with the seven sense objects as gross rūpas[2], even though they are not experienced directly by those who begin to develop the Path. They can only be experienced through the mind-door.

We are so used to thinking of self and what appears to the self. The Buddha taught what is real at this moment, like seeing, hearing and thinking. They arise and are present for such a short time, we cannot imagine how short.

When there is some understanding of the reality at this moment, such as seeing that appears now, we can begin to understand what reality is. Seeing is a mental reality, nāma, that experiences what is visible. It seems that we immediately see people. This shows us that cittas arise and fall away extremely rapidly, succeeding one another. Seeing that sees visible object is one moment and thinking of people is another moment, different from seeing. Seeing is vipākacitta, the result of kamma, and thinking is kusala citta or akusala citta. One may think wisely of unwisely, depending on accumulated conditions.

One may think about someone else with kindness, and this is a cetasika, mettā cetasika, arising with kusala citta. The citta with kindness falls away immediately but since each citta is succeeded by a next one, without a break, kindness is not lost; it is accumulated from one moment of citta to the next moment so that there are conditions for the arising again of kindness. It is the same with the accumulation of unwholesome qualities. One may think with attachment, aversion and ignorance. These akusala cetasikas fall away with the akusala citta,

---

[2]Twelve rūpas are gross because of impinging: the seven sense objects and the five sense-bases. The other sixteen kinds of rūpas are subtle.

but they are accumulated from moment to moment so that there are conditions for their arising again.

The Buddha taught about realities and their conditions to help people to realize that whatever arises is uncontrollable, non-self. He spoke time and again about seeing, visible object, hearing, sound and thinking, because these arise all the time. We cannot select what kind of object we shall experience, desirable or undesirable, this depends entirely on conditions which are beyond control. It is not easy to understand different realities appearing one at a time. That is why we have to listen and to consider the realities that appear now, again and again.

During the discussions in Vietnam, someone said that the more she listens, the more confused she becomes. This is not surprising because there were countless lives in the past with ignorance. We should be happy to have an opportunity now to listen to the Dhamma. Ignorance cannot be eradicated by a few moments or even many years of listening. During the discussions we hear again the same things such as explanations of the nature of seeing, hearing or thinking that arise now. However, this is not boring, because it can remind us to consider the present reality at those moments. Did we really consider seeing as being different from thinking of what is seen? We cannot expect to understand the truth of realities immediately. Seeing does not know what is seen, it does not know whether there are people and things present in the room. It just sees. The idea of self, of "I see, I hear" is deeply rooted.

Acharn repeated many times: "Be patient and truthful to seeing now. Otherwise it is not possible to understand directly its arising and falling away." We have intellectual understanding of the arising and falling away of realities, but when paññā is more developed, it can realize directly their arising and falling away. Then it will become clearer that it is impossible to control realities.

It is in the beginning not easy to know the difference between realities, namely, citta, cetasika and rūpa, and concepts of persons and things we can think of but which are not real.

During the discussions, someone spoke of her child with concern about his opinions as to the eating of meat. She thought that one should not eat meat since animals have to be slaughtered in order to obtain it. Acharn spoke about clinging to an idea of "my child". Someone may cling to his child and strongly believe that the child exists. Because of ignorance and attachment, there is an idea of "my child". The Buddha taught that there is no person, no self. In that sense we can say that we are living alone. We forget that there is no one there, only different cittas, cetasikas and rūpas, conditioned elements. No matter whether there are people around or not, there are just seeing, thinking, thinking of stories, situations.

Sarah said: "No courage to live alone, to understand reality at this moment, no matter the circumstances. No courage to understand what appears now, seeing now, visible object now, kusala, akusala, not anyone who does anything."

Nina: "I see people, not visible object."

Acharn: "The 'I' comes in very quickly."

Sarah: "Not enough understanding, not enough courage to live alone, even at that moment of thinking and clinging to 'I'. There is lobha (attachment) at that moment. It is real, but it is not my clinging, or my thinking, my wrong understanding. Just thinking, citta, cetasika and rūpa."

Acharn: "Are you alone now? In order to understand realities one does not need so many stories. Consider that which experiences and that which now appears. Dhamma means that which now appears."

We are all alone. Seeing arises for a moment and then falls away, it is no one. Thinking arises and falls away, it is no one. There can be only one citta at a time, arising and falling away. Where is the person? But, at first there is only intellectual understanding which cannot eradicate the belief in a person. When this has become firmer, there can be more confidence in the truth and it can condition direct awareness of realities appearing now, one at a time. Then it will be understood more clearly that a person does not exist.

We read in the "Kindred Sayings" (Second Fifty, Ch 2, § 63, By Migajāla) that Migajāla addressed the Buddha:

" 'Dwelling alone! Dwelling alone!' lord, is the saying. Pray, lord, to what extent is one a dweller alone, and to what extent is one a dweller with a mate?"

"There are, Migajāla, objects cognizable by the eye, objects desirable, pleasant, delightful and dear, passion-fraught, inciting to lust. If a brother be enamored of them, if he welcome them, if he persist in clinging to them, so enamored, so persisting in clinging to them, there comes a lure upon him. Where there is a lure there is infatuation. Where there is infatuation there is bondage. Bound in the bondage of the lure, Migajāla, a brother is called 'dweller with a mate.',"

The Buddha said the same about the other objects experienced through the other sense-doors and the mind-door. Even if that person would live in solitary places, he is still called "dweller with a mate", because craving is the mate he has not left behind.

The Buddha explained that when there is no clinging to those objects, the lure fades away:

"When there is no lure, there is no infatuation. Where there is no infatuation, there is no bondage. Freed from the bondage of the lure, Migajāla, a brother is called 'dweller alone.'

So also with regard to savours cognizable by the tongue, and mind-states cognizable by the mind...

Thus dwelling, Migajāla, a brother, though he dwell amid a village crowded with brethren and sisters, with lay-brethren and lay-sisters, with rājahs and royal ministers, with sectarians and their followers,- yet is he called 'dweller alone'. Why so? Craving is the mate he has left behind. Therefore is he called 'dweller alone'."

21

Against the stream of common thought

A friend asked: "What is understanding?" This is a basic question and I tried to answer this: "It is the opposite of ignorance. Now there is ignorance of many things. We think of cups, of food with attachment. We know that there are many moments of attachment and these are always accompanied by ignorance. We learn that seeing does not see people or things, that that is already thinking. This shows how fast cittas arise and pass away. We are misleading ourselves all the time."

Our friend thought that there was a choice to be made and because of this either understanding would arise or attachment and aversion. I answered: "There is no choice, there is no one who can choose or select anything. It just happens by conditions. They are all realities, it does not matter what arises. We should not try to change realities; some we would rather not have. They are all dhammas and understanding can understand them little by little."

Acharn explained that one should be truthful to the truth, and understand the present moment. One should not think: "What can I do to cling less to the self."

All that appears naturally can be object of right understanding. When clinging to the self appears, it can be known as just a dhamma, arisen because of conditions. It is difficult to really see the difference between the world of concepts and ideas and the world of realities such as seeing, visible object, hearing, like, dislike and thinking. Life lasts as long as one moment of citta that experiences one object at a time.

We read in the "Kindred Sayings" (I, VI, The Brahmā Suttas, Ch I, § 1, The Entreaty) that the Buddha, after his enlightenment, contemplated the Dhamma that is subtle and deep, difficult to understand. He thought:

> "This that through many toils I have won,
> Enough! Why should I make it known?
> By folk with lust and hate consumed
> Not this a Dhamma that can be grasped.
> Against the stream of common thought.
> Deep, subtle, fine, and hard to see,
> Unseen it will be by passion's slaves,
> Cloaked in the murk of ignorance."

We read in the commentary to this sutta[1] :

> "Living at ease (appossukkatā, lit. "little zeal") means lack of desire to teach. But why did his mind so incline after he had made the aspiration to Buddhahood, fulfilled the perfections, and attained omniscience? Because as he reflected, the density of the defilements of beings and the profundity of the Dhamma became manifest to him. Also, he knew that if he inclined to living at ease, Brahmā would request him to teach, and since beings esteem Brahmā, this would instil in them a desire to hear the Dhamma."

We read that then Brahmā Sahampati entreated the Buddha to preach the Dhamma. The Buddha surveyed the world with the eye of a Buddha and saw beings who were easy to teach and who were difficult to teach. He answered Brahmā Sahampati, making known his inclination to teach.

---

[1] As given in the translation by Ven. Bodhi in the "Connected Discourses of the Buddha".

The Dhamma is subtle and deep, difficult to understand. It goes "against the stream of common thought". The idea of self is deeply ingrained. We believe that a self sees, hears or thinks, is attached or has aversion. That is why the Buddha taught for forty-five years so that people would understand that what is taken for a person or self is only citta, cetasika and rūpa that arise because of their proper conditions.

During the sessions we discussed birth and death. We believe: "I was born and I will die", but what was born? Not the "I", only citta, cetasika and rūpa. The first moment of life cannot be by anyone's will, it has conditions to arise. Life goes on by conditions, from moment to moment. When we see life in a conventional way, we think of a whole lifespan that is ended by death. But in order to understand the truth, we have to consider life from moment to moment. For example, when seeing arises, life is seeing, and this arises and falls away immediately. After seeing there may be thinking with attachment or aversion and these are always accompanied by ignorance. Sometimes understanding may arise. All these are different moments that are gone immediately. So are birth and death, there is birth and death of citta at each moment. This is the only way to really understand the truth of life.

Some people are afraid of death but the dying-consciousness (cuti-citta), the last moment of this life, falls away and is succeeded immediately by the following citta that is the rebirth-consciousness (paṭisandhi-citta) of the next life. There is nothing to fear, cittas arise and fall away, succeeding one another extremely rapidly. The change from one life to another life occurs without there being time to think about it. Even now, the next moment can arise in another plane of existence.

Sarah reminded us: "Hearing, considering, understanding and sharing that understanding of dhammas as anattā is by far the most useful way to spend this life which may come to an end at any time."

The arahat has no more conditions for rebirth since all defilements have been eradicated. Summarizing the three kinds of death: death in conventional sense which is the end of a lifespan, momentary death (khanika maraṇa) which is the falling away of every citta that has arisen, and final death (samuccheda maraṇa) of the arahat.

Considering life at this moment, the momentary birth and death of citta, helps us to see what is really true, different from conventional ideas one may think of but which are not real. The Buddha taught

realities by way of many different aspects so that we would understand
that there is no person, no self, only citta, cetasika and rūpa.

In Hoi An, in the resort An Villa where we stayed, the Dhamma
discussions were held on a veranda under a roof, close to a swimming
pool. During the discussions, I saw people catching a snake by the side
of the pool. I was so absorbed in the "story" about the snake that I was
forgetful of realities. It is helpful to remember that many visible objects
appear one after the other, all different because of different conditions.
This leads to thinking of shape and form and the concept of a snake.
The snake is not a reality, but the thinking is. It is essential to know
the difference between concepts and realities.

Rūpa is different from nāma. Seeing is nāma and visible object
is rūpa. Rūpa does not think, remember, feel, like or dislike. It is
important to learn the different characteristics of nāma and rūpa. If they
are not distinguished from each other, we are bound to take whatever
appears for self.

Citta and cetasika are different types of nāma. Every citta experiences an object, it is the "leader" in experiencing an object. Only one
citta arises at a time and it is accompanied by several cetasikas, mental
factors, which assist citta in cognizing the object.

Cittas can be classified in many ways and one of these is the classification by way of "jāti" (literally birth or nature). Cittas can be of
the following four jātis: akusala, kusala, vipāka (result of kusala kamma
or of akusala kamma) or kiriya (inoperative, neither cause nor result).
Each citta is accompanied by several cetasikas. Some cetasikas accompany every citta, some accompany cittas of the four jātis but not every
citta, some accompany only akusala citta and some accompany only
kusala citta.

Citta and its accompanying cetasikas are closely associated and they
condition one another. The cetasikas which accompany the citta arise
together at the same physical base, experience the same object as the
citta, and they fall away together with the citta. The cetasikas which
accompany citta are of the same jāti as the citta they accompany. When
the citta is kusala, all accompanying cetasikas are also kusala, even those
kinds of cetasikas which can arise with each type of citta. When the
citta is akusala, all the accompanying cetasikas are akusala. Feeling,
for example, is a cetasika which accompanies each citta. When there is

pleasant feeling, it can accompany kusala citta or akusala citta rooted in attachment, but its quality is different in each case.

When generosity arises, there is no person who is generous, generosity is a cetasika performing its function while it assists the kusala citta. When attachment arises, there is no person who is attached, attachment is a cetasika performing its function. Citta is the principal, the leader in experiencing an object and the cetasikas that experience the same object as the citta perform each their own function while they assist the citta.

Seven cetasikas arise with every citta, no matter whether it is kusala, akusala, vipāka, or kiriya (inoperative, neither kusala, akusala, or vipāka). We have read about these cetasikas, the "universals" (sabbacittasādhāraṇa), in the text books and we have studied them, but while we were in Nakorn Nayok we had an opportunity to discuss about them in more detail. We were reminded that they are realities appearing in daily life, conditioned dhammas that are not self. It is beneficial to consider their true nature again and again.

Contact, phassa is mentioned first among the seven "universals". It is not physical contact, but it is mental. It accompanies the citta and contacts the object so that citta and cetasikas can experience the object for an extremely brief moment. Contact is mentioned first because without contact there would not be the experience of any object. When seeing arises it is accompanied by contact that contacts visible object. When hearing arises it is accompanied by contact that contacts sound. At first we may believe that there can be seeing and hearing at the same time. But they arise at different bases and experience different objects, thus, from different conditions. They are different realities.

One may like to experience a specific object, but it is impossible to cause phassa (contact) to contact such or such object. This reminds us that there is no self who can select an object.

Feeling is another cetasika that accompanies every citta. Sometimes feeling is pleasant, sometimes unpleasant, and sometimes indifferent. When contact contacts an unpleasant object such as a disagreeable odour, there is likely to be unpleasant feeling arising with the akusala cittas after smelling-consciousness has fallen away. Smelling-consciousness is accompanied by indifferent feeling. When contact contacts a pleasant object such as a beautiful sound, there is likely to be pleasant feeling arising after hearing has fallen away. Seeing, hearing, smelling and tasting are always accompanied by indifferent feeling, but the vipākacitta that is body-consciousness is either accompanied by unpleasant bodily feeling or by pleasant bodily feeling. These feelings are mental, but they are called bodily feeling because they accompany body-consciousness. They are also vipāka, conditioned by kamma.

It is difficult to distinguish between feeling that is vipāka and feeling that is akusala. When painful bodily feeling arises, unpleasant feeling that accompanies akusala citta rooted in aversion may arise immediately. We find feeling very important but mostly we are ignorant of realities. People wish to have pleasant feeling all the time but it falls away immediately. Sometimes it accompanies kusala citta such as citta with generosity, but mostly it accompanies citta rooted in attachment.

The following sutta reminds us of the diversity and complexity of feelings. We read in the "Kindred Sayings" (IV, Kindred Sayings about Feeling, 2. The Chapter on Solitude, § 12, The Sky), that the Buddha said:

> "Just as, brethren, divers winds blow in the sky – some winds blow from the east, some from the west, some from the north, some from the south, winds dusty, winds dustless, cool winds and hot winds, winds soft and boisterous – even so in this body arise diverse feelings – feelings pleasant, feelings painful, also neutral feelings."

The Buddha then speaks about a monk who has understanding and awareness of all kinds of feelings and is without defilements.

When feeling appears it can be understood as a conditioned dhamma devoid of self. Nobody can choose what kind of feeling arises, it is beyond control.

Another cetasika that accompanies every citta is concentration or one-pointedness (samādhi or ekaggatā cetasika). It focusses on the object that citta experiences and it performs this function for an extremely brief moment. It is the condition that citta knows only one object. There are actually six worlds: the world of experiencing visible object, of experiencing sound, of experiencing odour, of experiencing flavour, of experiencing tangible object and of thinking. The conditions for citta experiencing an object through one of the six doorways are different and this makes it clear that there is no self who coordinates all that is experienced.

Concentration or samādhi is of many degrees and it is developed in samatha in order to suppress the "hindrances"[2]; it is one of the jhāna factors leading to the attainment of jhāna (absorption). It is also one of the eight Path factors leading to enlightenment. It focusses on the nāma or rūpa that appears at the present moment, so that paññā can know it as it really is, as impermanent, dukkha and anattā.

Remembrance, saññā, is another cetasika accompanying every citta. It remembers and marks the object that is experienced at that moment so that it can be recognized later on. The translation of saññā as memory or remembrance should not mislead us, saññā is not remembrance as we understand it in a conventional way. It is a cetasika that arises for an extremely short moment together with the citta and the other cetasikas it accompanies. It performs its function of recognition or marking the object experienced by the citta it accompanies. Without saññā there could not be any thinking about pleasant and unpleasant objects.

One may be attached to a pleasant object with happy feeling. Attachment and happy feeling fall away immediately but saññā remembers this happy feeling. This leads to more and more clinging to happy feeling. Saññā conditions attachment. Since saññā accompanies every citta while it performs its function, it has the same object as the citta and, thus, its object can be a reality, a nāma or rūpa, or a concept.

The recognition of a person or a thing, which are concepts, is the result of many different processes of citta and each moment of citta is accompanied by saññā. Because of many moments of saññā, we can follow the trend of thought of a speaker or we ourselves can reason about something, connect parts of an argument and draw conclusions. All this is not due to "our memory" but to saññā, which is not self but only a kind of nāma. What we take for "our memory" or "our recognition" is not one moment which stays, but many different moments of saññā which arise and fall away.

There are several aspects to akusala saññā and kusala saññā. Akusala saññā leads to taking realities for permanent (nicca-saññā) and for self

---

[2]The hindrances (nīvaraṇa) are: sensuous desire (kāmacchanda), ill-will (vyāpāda), sloth and torpor (thīna-middha), restlessness and worry (uddhacca-kukkucca) and doubt (vicikicchā).

(attā-saññā).

Jonothan said: "Attā-saññā accumulates, it influences the way the world is seen now."

We think of people and things, of the world in conventional sense, and we forget that in reality there are only citta, cetasika and rūpa that are gone immediately after they have arisen.

When saññā accompanies kusala citta, it is kusala. Firm saññā that is kusala is mentioned in the "Atthasālinī" (I, Part IV, Chapter I, 121) as a condition for the arising of sati of the level of satipaṭṭhāna. It states that the proximate cause of mindfulness is firm remembrance (saññā) or the four applications of mindfulness (satipaṭṭhāna). There can be mindfulness of the nāma or rūpa which appears because of firm remembrance of all we learnt from the teachings about realities of daily life. We can learn by reading and by discussing. When we are reading, we should not forget that the Buddha's words pertain all the time to whatever appears right now. Listening is mentioned in the scriptures as one of the most important conditions for the attainment of enlightenment, because when we listen time and again, there can be firm remembrance of the Dhamma.

Mindfulness is different from remembrance, saññā. Saññā accompanies every citta; it recognizes the object and marks it, so that it can be recognized again. Mindfulness, sati, is not forgetful of what is wholesome. It arises with sobhana cittas. But when there is sati which is non-forgetful of dāna, sīla, of the object of calm or, in the case of vipassanā, of the nāma and rūpa appearing at the present moment, there is also kusala saññā which remembers the object in the right way, in the wholesome way. Saññā accompanying insight which remembers in the right way the reality that appears, as non-self, is anattā-saññā.

Apart from contact (phassa), feeling (vedanā), concentration (samādhi or ekaggatā cetasika) and remembrance (saññā), there are three more cetasikas among the "universals" accompanying every citta: volition (cetanā), attention (manasikāra) and life faculty (jīvitindriya). They condition every citta and also the other cetasikas that they accompany. When conditions are understood more it will become clearer that all realities are anattā.

Apart from the seven "universals", there are other cetasikas that accompany cittas of the four jātis of kusala, akusala, vipāka and kiriya, though not every citta. These are the six "particulars" (pakiṇṇakā) and among them are "thinking" (vitakka) which touches the object so that citta can experience it, effort or energy (viriya) and decision (adhimokkha). Seeing does not need thinking and effort for the experience of visible object, but the cittas that succeed it in the same process and still experience visible object, although they do not see, need these "particulars"[3] .

Akusala cetasikas such as attachment (lobha), aversion (dosa) and ignorance (moha) only accompany akusala cittas. Sobhana (beautiful) cetasikas, such as non-attachment (alobha), non-aversion (adosa) and understanding (paññā) accompany sobhana cittas.

All cetasikas are realities occurring in daily life, they are not merely textbook terms. They condition citta and they condition each other and when we truly consider their functions it becomes clearer that there is no self who can control realities. All the classifications of realities given by the Buddha have as their aim helping beings to understand that each reality that appears is non-self.

---

[3]The other particulars are: sustained thinking (vicara), enthusiasm (pīti) and wish-to-do (chanda).

22

Inner and the outer sense-fields

I was talking with Alberto, a friend from Italy, about accumulated tendencies. Accumulations have such a strong impact and we are overwhelmed by them at times. I am worried, for example, about many things I have to do in daily life and I am thinking about how to act. Alberto reminded me that we always take accumulated tendencies for self.

Acharn said: "We always forget that all are dhammas. We are concerned about 'myself'. Thinking, 'how can I do this, what about me tomorrow morning'. Develop understanding, it does not matter what is arising. It is gone completely."

We were discussing conceit (māna), what conceit is and when it arises. Acharn made it clear that if we name it and keep on thinking about it, it is already completely gone. The present reality is not conceit at such a moment. We are just speculating about what happened in the past instead of knowing the characteristic of the present reality. She brought us back to the present moment by saying that there is seeing right now. Seeing sees visible object which is there, accompanied by the

137

four great Elements of solidity, cohesion, temperature and motion.

When we consider rūpas, physical phenomena, we may see them by way of science, in a conventional way, but in reality they arise and fall away each moment. We think of the body as a whole, but what we take for our body are in reality many groups or units, consisting each of different kinds of rūpa, and the rūpas in such a group arise together and fall away together. Rūpas do not arise singly, they arise in units or groups.

There are four conditioning factors that produce rūpas of the body: kamma, citta, temperature and nutrition. Kamma is actually the cetasika volition or intention (cetanā) that arises with every citta. When it is kusala or akusala it can motivate a good deed or a bad deed that produces result. Kamma is a mental activity which is accumulated. Since cittas that arise and fall away succeed one another in an unbroken series, the force of kamma is carried on from one moment of citta to the next moment of citta, from one life to the next life. In this way kamma is capable to produce its result later on. A good deed, kusala kamma, can produce a pleasant result, and an evil deed can produce an unpleasant result. Rebirth-consciousness is the mental result of kamma, vipākacitta, but at that moment kamma also produces rūpas and kamma keeps on producing rūpas throughout life; when it stops producing rūpas our lifespan has to end. Kamma produces particular kinds of rūpas such as the senses.

Citta also produces rūpas. Our different moods become evident by our facial expressions and then it is clear that citta produces rūpas.

Temperature, which is actually the element of heat, also produces rūpas. Throughout life, the element of heat produces rūpas.

Nutrition is another factor that produces rūpas. When food has been taken by a living being, it is assimilated into the body and then nutrition can produce rūpas. Thus, some of the groups of rūpas of our body are produced by kamma, some by citta, some by temperature and some by nutrition. If we see the intricate way in which different factors condition the rūpas of our body we shall be less inclined to think that the body belongs to a self.

There are not only rūpas of the body, there are also rūpas which are the material phenomena outside the body. If we do not study rūpas, we may not notice their characteristics that appear all the time in daily life.

We shall continue to be deluded by the outward appearance of things instead of knowing realities as they are.

Seeing sees visible object. Visible object is a rūpa that arises in a group of rūpas. These are the four Great Elements of solidity, cohesion, temperature, motion, and in addition odour, flavour and nutritive essence. Although these rūpas arise together, only one kind of rūpa at a time can be the object that is experienced. When there are conditions for seeing, only visible object is seen. Visible object is conditioned by the other rūpas that arise in the same group. For example, solidity may be hard or soft at different moments and this conditions visible object to be different too at different moments. Different visible objects that appear lead to thinking of shape and form and this again is a condition to think of concepts of persons and things. On account of what is seen, heard or experienced through the other senses, we think of concepts. Gradually we can learn to see the difference between realities and concepts.

When there are conditions for the arising of sati of the level of direct awareness, understanding can know what appears as just a conditioned reality. Acharn also explained that no matter we talk about realities as stated in the teachings, we have to come back to seeing right now, hearing right now.

People have many problems in daily life, they have worries and anxieties, but one should remember Acharn's reminder of "Is there seeing now?" There is seeing time and again and its characteristic can be known when it appears without having to think about it. After seeing has fallen away we often think with attachment, aversion and ignorance about what was seen. These three unwholesome roots (akusala hetus) are the real problems in life. One thinks that the cause of unhappiness is one's partner, a colleague at work, or the way one was treated by others. But the real cause is the accumulated attachment, aversion and ignorance.

Intellectual understanding (pariyatti) can condition direct understanding of realities (paṭipatti) and in this connection Acharn mentioned that the understanding of the āyatanas (bases or sources) can be a supporting condition for direct understanding.

All realities can be classified as twelve āyatanas, translated sometimes as "sense-fields" (Visuddhimagga, Ch. XV, 1-17)[1]. There are six inward āyatanas and six outward āyatanas. The six inward āyatanas are: eyesense, earsense, smelling-sense, tasting-sense, bodysense and mind-base, including all cittas.

The six outward āyatanas are: visible object, sound, odour, flavour, tangible object and mind-object (dhammāyatana), including cetasikas, subtle rūpas and nibbāna.

Āyatana implies association of realities, and this shows that the teaching of āyatanas is not abstract. Association of dhammas takes place at this very moment, but usually we are ignorant of this. There could not be hearing now if there were no association of sound, earsense and hearing. Different characteristics appear one at a time, and there can be understanding of them. That is the real study of āyatanas.

When we see, hear or think, we believe that a self experiences objects, but in reality there is the association of the inward āyatanas and the outward āyatanas, the realities "outside". When seeing sees visible object there is the association of eye-sense, visible object, seeing-consciousness and the seven cetasikas that accompany every citta, the "universals".

Understanding what āyatanas are will help us to know the difference between reality and concept. When touching the body, there is a meeting between tangible object and the rūpa that is bodysense, so that there are conditions for body-consciousness that experiences tangible object. Only for a very short moment, only at the moment these āyatanas associate, namely, mindbase (manayatana which is citta), accompanied by cetasikas (dhammāyatana), tangible object (photabbāya-tana) and bodysense (kāyāyatana). They meet for an extremely short time and then they are gone. This reminds us how fragile and insignificant what we take for body is. There is no whole body, it does not exist. It is only an idea we may think of.

Sarah explained that the āyatanas associate for a short moment and that it could not be any other way.

She said: "It all shows that there is no self at all involved, no one who can control anything for an instant. Understanding more about these realities and their conditioned nature and 'coming together' is the way that understanding develops with detachment and awareness

---

[1]See also Book of Analysis, Vibhaṅga, II, Analysis of Bases.

which leads to the abandoning of the idea of self and other defilements. It's the only way. Right understanding leads to the development of direct awareness of what appears now very naturally. If there is any expectation of awareness or expectation of understanding arising now, it shows the deep clinging to the idea of self again, not the detachment which right understanding brings at this moment. It really is the 'fine point' or 'balancing on a pinhead' of dhammas arising by conditions very naturally and without any expectation of what will arise next. This is the only way that satipaṭṭhāna and the Path can develop. The detail about the āyatanas shows the real subtlety and depth of the Buddha's Teachings."

Acharn said that there should be no expectation for the arising of awareness, but when one has understanding of the āyatanas, there will be a condition for that moment unexpectedly. One will understand more and more that all dhammas are anattā. It is most helpful that Acharn emphasized the importance of understanding the āyatanas. We have read about their classification many times but the truth of these realities should be considered over and over again. "Are there āyatanas now?" Acharn asked us.

The dhammas of our life arise and fall away, they are dukkha, unsatisfactory or suffering. Someone of the listeners asked what suffering is. He tried to walk slowly and stop thinking in order to have less worry. We are so involved in stories, thinking, "What happens to me, what shall I do." We forget the real meaning of dukkha the Buddha taught: the arising and falling away of realities right now. Since they fall away immediately, they are unsatisfactory, not worth clinging to. So long as we are involved in stories, thinking of concepts instead of understanding whatever reality appears now, there is no way of solving any problem in life. When we think of suffering and of what we have to undergo in our life we forget that each reality that appears now falls away immediately, even thinking or worry. We need patience to consider all the different realities of our life.

The Buddha, in his previous lives when he was still a Bodhisatta, considered all realities over and over again with endless patience. This was the only way to develop the wisdom leading to enlightenment and becoming the Omniscient Buddha. Acharn asked me several times to speak about the three kinds of Bodhisattas, beings destined for enlightenment: someone who will become a Sammāsambuddha, Omniscient Buddha, someone who will become a Paccheka Buddha, Silent Buddha, and someone who is a Savaka Bodhisatta, who is a "Learner"[2] . In the beginning, I did not quite understand the meaning of Savaka Bodhisatta, but by repeatedly discussing this term I better understood what a Savaka Bodhisatta is and how we can become a Savaka Bodhisatta by developing understanding of realities, even for countless lives.

The Sammāsambuddha has attained perfect understanding of the truth of realities, all by himself, without the help of a teacher. Through his enlightenment, he reached omniscience. The Buddha could attain enlightenment because he developed for innumerable lives direct understanding of seeing which appears at the present moment, of visible object which appears at the present moment, of all realities which appear at the present moment. Direct understanding of realities can only be developed now.

The Silent Buddha, Paccheka Buddha, has also attained enlightenment all by himself, but he has not accumulated wisdom to the same extent as the Sammā-sambuddha. He cannot proclaim to the world the truth he has realized.

The Savaka Bodhisatta develops understanding during innumerable lives until the moment of enlightenment. He knows the value of understanding of realities appearing at the present moment.

A moment of understanding is not lost, it is accumulated from moment to moment. Conditions for attaining the first stage of enlightenment, the stage of the "stream-enterer" (sotāpanna) are[3] : association with good people (sappurisa-saṃsevo), hearing the true Dhamma (saddhammassavanaṃ), thorough attention (yoniso manasikāro), practice of the Dhamma in accordance with the Dhamma (dhammā-nudhammap-paṭipatti).

As to "wise attention", the commentary explains that this is attention to impermanence, dukkha and anattā.

As to the practice of the dhamma in conformity with the dhamma, the commentary states that practice in conformity with the dhamma relates to lokuttara dhamma, and that previous practice is necessary,

---

[2]Cariyāpiṭaka-aṭṭhakathā, nidānakathā.
[3]See "Dialogues of the Buddha", DN 33.1.11(13)

which is, according to the subcommentary, vipassanā, the development of insight.

The word "practice" is a translation of the term paṭipatti, meaning the development of direct understanding.

This phrase is also explained in the commentary to the Mahāparinib-bānasutta: "Those who practise a dhamma consistent with the dhamma (dhammānu-dhamma-paṭipannā). Those who practise the teaching of insight (vipassanā) which is consistent with the teachings of the noble (ariyadhammassa)."

The teaching of the noble is of the path (magga), or else also the ninefold supramundane dhamma[4] .

These are the essential conditions leading to the penetration of the four noble Truths. Gradually the true nature of the realities that appear can be penetrated. As we read, there has to be wise attention to the characteristics of impermanence, dukkha and anattā. However, first of all there have to be right awareness and direct understanding of the realities appearing through the six doors. Nāma has to be known as nāma and rūpa as rūpa. We read, consider and discuss Dhamma just in order to understand the reality of this moment. When a moment of understanding arises, understanding is accumulated little by little. This is the way that paññā can grow to the degree of lokuttara paññā. We need confidence and courage so that we do not become disheartened about the long way we have to travel.

We learn from the statements about the three kinds of Bodhisattas that whatever occurs in life has been conditioned. We can become "learners", savaka Bodhisattas, by continuing to develop understanding of what appears now with confidence and without expecting anything. We are beginners and what can be understood depends on conditions. Some people seek peacefulness but everything that arises now, also when it is not peaceful, should be known as not self.

We heard a great deal about citta, cetasika and rūpa, which are conditioned realities arising for a short moment and then falling away. They can be considered in our daily life. However, we are inclined to cling to situations, to cling to thinking of other people and "self". That

---

[4]This refers to the eight lokuttara cittas and nibbāna. For each of the four stages of enlightenment there is the magga-citta and the phala-citta, the result of the magga-citta.

is not the world of realities. We forget that all that is real now in our life are citta, cetasika and rūpa. Intellectual understanding of what is real can eventually lead to direct understanding, to satipaṭṭhāna.

Satipaṭṭhāna is developed in being mindful of whatever appears so that direct understanding can grow. Mindfulness, sati, is a cetasika that arises only with certain types of citta and lasts for an extremely short moment. Remembering this helps us not to try to control or manipulate this type of cetasika. All that can be done is listening and considering the truth of this moment and understanding it a little more, so that we can become a "savaka", a learner, who will once attain enlightenment and full understanding. This is possible, the Buddha taught the way. But when we are hoping or expecting results, there is clinging and this hinders the development of understanding. We shall listen again and again to the truth of seeing, visible object, hearing, sound, and all that is reality. This is the way to have more confidence in the Buddha's teaching of anattā.

Some people wonder why we discuss seeing and hearing all the time. They are realities of daily life that arise and fall away extremely rapidly, but they are unknown. There is seeing now but no one pays attention to it, it falls away in split seconds. What is seen is only what impinges on the eyebase but we think immediately of shape and form and take it for something that stays. Understanding of seeing, visible object and all other dhammas appearing at this moment develops very gradually and hearing about them and discussing them is never enough.

Seeing is an element that experiences an object and visible object is an element that is seen, it does not experience anything. So long as the different characteristics of mental realities, nāma, and physical realities, rūpa, are not distinguished, it is impossible to understand them as anattā. It is not sufficient to merely think that nāma is different from rūpa. Understanding can come to realize the different characteristics of seeing and visible object, hearing and sound, of all mental realities and physical realities, when they appear at this moment.

Sarah explained: "Without even an intellectual understanding of them, there cannot be any understanding of kusala and akusala (wholesome and unwholesome states) and there can't be even a beginning of following the right Path."

People want to know the difference between kusala dhammas and akusala dhammas when they appear in daily life, but first the difference between the elements that experience an object and the elements that do not experience anything should be directly known. Intellectual understanding (pariyatti), when it is firm enough, can condition direct understanding (paṭipatti), as was often emphasized during our discussions.

23

Factors leading to enlightenment

In Nakorn Nayok we discussed the thirty-seven factors leading to enlightenment (bodhipakkhiya-dhammas). They are not theoretical terms, they are realities that can be developed in daily life. We should first consider what the meaning is of enlightenment. Acharn said people are usually dreaming about enlightenment as some desirable state, without understanding its meaning. It is actually perfect understanding of the truth. This has to begin by understanding the truth of this moment. She said:

"Most important is understanding this moment, otherwise it is gone without understanding, thus, with ignorance. Each moment in life is gone, by conditions. Without conditions nothing can arise, such as seeing, it cannot arise without eyesense. Just learn in the beginning to understand the reality and to understand that it is conditioned. Know by how many conditions in order to understand that it can never be yours. It is only a reality that is conditioned to arise and nobody can stop its arising. Like now, nobody can stop the arising of seeing. So, there is no you. You think, at the moment of seeing, that you see, but actually seeing is not you. Learn to understand each moment as not me."

Someone asked: "What conditions knowing that seeing is not: 'we see' or 'I see'?"

Acharn answered: "One just wants to keep the 'I', not to abandon the 'I'. One should not just listen and read, but consider deeply the truth. It takes time. Do not forget that all dhammas are anattā, no exception."

She explained that people think of "my problem", but that this is not the understanding of dhammas as anattā.

The factors of enlightenment, bodhipakkhiya-dhammas, are wholesome qualities that, when fully developed, can lead to enlightenment. However, the attainment of enlightenment is entirely dependent on conditions. We can take our refuge in the Buddha, the Dhamma and the Sangha. The Dhamma as our refuge includes these factors leading to enlightenment. They are the following factors:

- the four applications of mindfulness,

- the four right efforts,

- the four roads to power (iddhi-pāda),

- the five faculties (indriyas),

- the five powers (balas),

- the seven factors of enlightenment (bojjhanga),

- the eightfold Path.

As to the four Applications of Mindfulness, these are all nāmas and rūpas that appear now, no matter under what application they have been classified. Thus, at one moment there can be mindfulness of rūpa, the next moment of feeling, of citta or of dhamma. The application of mindfulness of dhamma includes rūpa and nāma under different aspects. It all depends on sati and paññā what object they take. Sati and paññā are mere dhammas, not self, and they cannot be directed to specific objects. The classification as four applications is given so that people can be reminded that all realities in all situations can be object of mindfulness and understanding. When pariyatti, intellectual under-standing of the present reality, is quite firm, it can condition the arising of direct understanding. Direct understanding is developed through satipaṭṭhāna.

As to the four right efforts, we read in the "Dialogues of the Buddha" (Dīgha Nikaya, XXXIII, Sangīti Sutta, D. III, 1, 221):

"Four great efforts (sammappadhānā): Here a monk rouses his will (chanda), makes an effort, stirs up energy, exerts his mind and strives to prevent the arising of unarisen evil un-wholesome mental states. He rouses his will... and strives to overcome evil unwholesome mental states that have arisen. He rouses his will... and strives to produce unarisen whole-some mental states. He rouses his will... and strives to maintain wholesome mental states that have arisen, not to let them fade away, to bring them to greater growth, to the full perfection of development."

The word "will" used here is a translation of chanda. Chanda is also translated as zeal or wish-to-do. There are several kinds of chanda: zeal of craving, of wrong view, of energy, of dhamma. Dhamma-chanda, zeal for the dhamma, is intended here.

Right effort or energy accompanies right understanding of the eight-fold Path. It is not self, but a cetasika performing its function. When there are conditions for sati to be mindful of whatever dhamma appears through one of the six doorways, understanding can develop so that the reality that is the object can be seen as a mere dhamma, not self. The accompanying energy performs its function already and there is no need to think of applying effort.

When there is mindfulness of visible object which appears now, see-ing which appears now, sound which appears now, hearing which ap-pears now, or any other reality which appears now, right understanding of the present reality is being developed. This is the most effective way to avoid akusala, to overcome it, to make kusala arise and to maintain kusala and bring it to perfection. At that moment right effort performs its task of strengthening the kusala citta with right understanding so that there is perseverance with the development of understanding of realities.

Effort or energy has nothing to do with effort in conventional sense. Even at the level of pariyatti there has to be wholesome energy, kusala viriya, and right understanding of realities will lead to the four right efforts. At this moment effort, viriya, can maintain the kusala that has arisen. This means it is a support for the arising again of kusala citta.

There are four "Roads to Power", iddhipāda. They are classified among the factors leading to enlightenment. Iddhipāda is also translated as basis of success. They are: chanda (wish-to-do), citta (firmness of kusala citta or concentration), viriya or energy, and vīmaṃsā or investigation, another word for paññā.

The "roads to power" are actually four predominant factors. Whenever we wish to accomplish a task, one of these four factors can be the predominance-condition for the realities they arise together with. Chanda, viriya and citta can be predominant in the accomplishment of an enterprise or task both in a wholesome way and in an unwholesome way, whereas vimaṃsa, investigation of Dhamma, which is paññā, a sobhana cetasika, can only be predominant in a wholesome way. In the context of the "bases of success", only the factors which are sobhana are dealt with.

Citta can be a predominance-condition for the accompanying cetasikas, but not all cittas can be predominance-condition. Predominance-condition can operate only in the case of javana-cittas accompanied by at least two roots. All mahā-kusala cittas (kusala cittas of the sense-sphere) and all mahā-kiriyacittas (of the arahat), have the two roots of alobha, non-attachment, and adosa, non-aversion, and, in addition, they can have the root which is paññā, thus, they have two or three roots and, therefore, they can be predominance-condition for the accompanying dhammas. When we accomplish a task with cittas which are resolute, firmly established in kusala, the citta can be the predominance-condition for the accompanying dhammas.

With regard to investigation of the Dhamma, vīmaṃsā, this is paññā cetasika. When we listen to the Dhamma, consider it and are mindful of realities, vīmaṃsā can condition the accompanying citta and cetasikas by way of predominance-condition.

Without the conditioning force of one of the four predominance factors, it would not be possible to attain jhāna.

We read in the "Visuddhimagga" (III,24):

"...If a bhikkhu obtains concentration, obtains unification of mind, by making zeal (chanda) predominant, this is called concentration due to zeal. If... by making energy predominant, this is called concentration due to energy. If... by making (natural purity of) citta predominant, this is called concentration due to citta. If... by making inquiry (vimaṃsā) predominant, this is called concentration due to inquiry (Vibhanga 216-219)..."

The Bases of Success can also lead to supernatural powers like walking on water, knowing one's former lives (Visuddhimagga, Ch XII, 50-53).

In the development of vipassanā, right understanding of nāma and rūpa, one also needs the "four bases of success" for the realization of the stages of insight wisdom and for the attainment of enlightenment. The arising of awareness and understanding of realities is beyond control, it is due to conditions. We need patience and courage to persevere studying and considering nāma and rūpa, and, if there are the right conditions, to be aware of them in daily life.

Among the factors pertaining to enlightenment are five faculties, indriyas, sometimes referred to as "spiritual faculties". These are sobhana cetasikas (beautiful mental factors) included in the "factors of enlightenment" (bodhipakkiya dhammas) that should be developed for the attainment of enlightenment. They are: faith or confidence (saddhā), energy (viriya), mindfulness (sati), concentration (samādhi) and understanding (paññā).

Indriya means principal, or leader. There are several indriyas, but each indriya is a leader, a leader in its own field. Mindfulness is an indriya, a "controlling faculty", a "leader" of the citta and accompanying cetasikas in its function of heedfulness, of non-forgetfulness of what is wholesome. The five wholesome controlling faculties, the "spiritual faculties", must be developed in samatha in order to attain jhāna and in vipassanā in order to attain enlightenment. It is our nature to be forgetful of the reality which appears now, but gradually mindfulness can be accumulated. It can even become a "power" (bala). As understanding develops, the accompanying spiritual faculties also develop.

We are so often taken in by thinking of people and situations, and this is with attachment and ignorance time and again. We would wish not to be absorbed, but that is not the development of understanding. Whatever arises, even being absorbed, is a reality that can be object of right understanding. Acharn often tells us to begin again and again with the development of right understanding.

She said: "There is not yet direct understanding and that is why we talk about seeing so that it will be object of right understanding. Even touching now is real, but there is no understanding, no matter how often we touch. But when understanding arises, it is intellectual understanding, until there will be a moment of touching with direct understanding."

Among the factors of enlightenment, there are five powers, balas. We read in the "Dialogues of the Buddha" (Dīgha Nikāya, Saṅgītisutta, IV, sutta 26) about four powers, since in this section confidence is omitted. The five powers are: confidence (saddhā), energy (viriya), mindfulness (sati), concentration (samādhi) and understanding (paññā).

They are unshakable by their opposites. Lack of confidence is the opposite of confidence, indolence is the opposite of energy, forgetfulness is the opposite of mindfulness, restlessness the opposite of samādhi and ignorance the opposite of paññā. The commentary states that all of them refer to samatha, vipassanā and magga (lokuttara magga), and that they can be mundane or supramundane. In the case of magga, lokuttara magga-citta, they accompany lokuttara citta and they are also lokuttara. They experience nibbāna.

Confidence (saddhā) is also one of the powers. We should have more confidence in the power of kusala dhammas and this confidence is a condition for their development.

Among the factors pertaining to enlightenment, there are seven factors of enlightenment, bojjhaṅgas. We read in the "Dialogues of the Buddha" (Dīgha Nikaya, XXXIII, Saṅgīti Sutta, D. III, 2, 252):

"Seven factors of enlightenment (sambhojjhaṅgā): mindfulness, investigation of phenomena (dhammavicaya), energy, delight (pīti), tranquillity, concentration, equanimity."

Dhammavicaya, investigation of realities, is another term for paññā. The enlightenment factors develop together with paññā that understands more and more the true nature of nāma and rūpa that appear at the present moment. All factors develop together and are leading to enlightenment and in that case they are still mundane. When enlightenment has been attained, they are lokuttara and nibbāna is the object experienced at that moment. When insight is developed, there is also calm. One is not disturbed by unwholesome thoughts about persons and situations when right understanding of dhammas is developed. One begins to see thinking about them as an impersonal element devoid of self.

Right concentration, sammā-samādhi, focusses on the object of vipassanā in the right way. When there is mindfulness of one object at a time as it appears through one of the sense-doors or the mind-door, right concentration focusses on that object, and at that moment right understanding can investigate it so that it will be seen as it really is. When right understanding arises, there is right concentration, which is conascent with it.

There are many types of concentration and many levels of it. It is actually the cetasika that is one-pointedness, ekaggatā cetasika. It accompanies each citta and it is the condition that each citta experiences only one object. All accompanying cetasikas share that same object. When seeing arises, one-pointedness focusses on visible object, and only that object is experienced. When hearing arises, it focusses on sound. Hearing is a moment that is quite different from seeing, they experience different objects. There is no self who can choose what object will be experienced, this is dependent on several conditions. Although there is concentration with each citta, usually it does not appear. When jhāna is being developed with right understanding of the object which can be a condition to be removed from sense objects, samādhi grows until it is access-concentration, upacāra samādhi, and attainment concentration, appanā samadhi, which is absorption-concentration or jhāna.

We can be easily deluded and take for right concentration, sammā-samādhi, what is wrong concentration, micchā-samādhi. When it is conascent with lobha, it is wrong concentration. We are inclined to take samādhi for 'my concentration', and, therefore, it is important to remember that it is only a dhamma conditioned by many different factors. It is conditioned by the citta it accompanies and by the conascent cetasikas.

The factors of the eightfold Path are among the factors pertaining to enlightenment: right view (sammā-diṭṭhi), right thought (sammā-sankappa), right speech (sammā-vācā), right action (sammā-kammanta), right livelihood (sammā-ājīva), right effort (sammā-vāyāma), right mindfulness (sammā-sati), right concentration (sammā-samādhi).

These are sobhana cetasikas each performing their own function. One should not just remember their names but they are dhammas each with their own characteristic and these can gradually be known when they appear. The factors of the eightfold Path all develop together with right view, paññā. It is not "I" who practices, but the factors of the eightfold Path that will come to fulfilment at the moment of enlightenment. The object of the Path factors is a reality such as seeing or visible object that appears at the present moment. Sammā-sankappa, right thinking, is vitakka cetasika which is sobhana. When right thinking is a factor of the noble eightfold Path it has to accompany right understanding, paññā. Right thinking "touches" the nāma or rūpa which appears so that paññā can understand it as it is.

There are three cetasikas which are sīla, namely: right speech (sammā-vācā), right action (sammā-kammanta) and right livelihood (sammā-ājīva). They are actually the three abstinences or virati cetasikas which are: abstinence from wrong speech (vacīduccarita virati), abstinence from wrong action (kāyaduccarita virati), abstinence from wrong livelihood (ājīvaduccarita virati).

Paññā can realize that the cetasika which abstains from akusala is non-self, that it arises because of its appropriate conditions. The three abstinences which accompany cittas of the sense-sphere, kāmāvacara cittas, arise only one at a time. However, when lokuttara citta arises, all three abstinences accompany the lokuttara citta and then nibbāna is the object. They fulfil their function of path-factors by eradicating the conditions for wrong speech, wrong action and wrong livelihood.

Sammā-vāyāma or right effort is another factor of the eightfold path. It is viriya cetasika (energy or effort), which strengthens and supports the accompanying dhammas. When it accompanies right understanding of the eightfold Path, it is energy and courage to persevere being aware of nāma and rūpa which appear one at a time through the six doorways. At the moment of mindfulness of nāma and rūpa, right effort has arisen already because of conditions and it performs its function; we do not need to think of making an effort. When we think, "I can exert effort,

I can strive", akusala citta has arisen with clinging to the idea of self
reaching the goal. Wrong effort may arise without our noticing it. Right
effort, when it accompanies right understanding, supports the other
factors of the eight-fold Path, but we should remember that it arises
because of its own conditions, that it is non-self.

Sati of the level of satipaṭṭhāna is right mindfulness of the nāma
or rūpa which appears so that understanding of that reality as non-self
can be developed. Mindfulness does not last, it arises just for a moment, but it can be accumulated. Mindfulness and right understanding
cannot arise without the appropriate conditions: listening to the teachings as explained by the right friend in Dhamma, considering what one
has heard and applying it in daily life. Moreover, all wholesome qualities developed together with satipaṭṭhāna are supportive conditions for
paññā. When we learn to be less selfish and develop kindness, thoughtfulness and patience, these qualities support paññā to become detached
from the idea of self. Sati that accompanies right understanding of the
eightfold Path is a factor of the noble eightfold Path.

One may wonder how, in the development of insight, the faculty of
mindfulness, the power of mindfulness, the path-factor right mindfulness
and the enlightenment factor of mindfulness can be developed. The
answer is: through mindfulness and understanding of the nāma and
rūpa which appears right now. There is no other way. Sights, sounds,
scents, savours and tangible objects are most of the time objects of
attachment, aversion and ignorance. If mindfulness arises and right
understanding of the object is being developed, one is at that moment
not enslaved to the object nor disturbed by it.

Sammā-samādhi, right concentration, is another path-factor accompanying sobhana citta. Kusala citta which is intent on dāna, sīla or
bhāvanā is accompanied by right concentration which conditions the
citta and accompanying cetasikas to focus on an object in the wholesome way. Right concentration, which is a factor of the noble eightfold
Path, has to accompany right understanding of the eightfold Path.

All these enlightenment factors are not theory. They are realities
to be developed. Several factors are the same types of cetasikas but
they are shown under different aspects. For example the faculties (indriyas) when developed more can become powers, balas. Then they
have become unshakable. When sati has become a power, it can arise

any time and at any place, no matter the circumstances. We see that many conditions are necessary for the attainment of enlightenment.

24

Everything is dhamma

After our discussions in Thailand, we flew to Vietnam where we first had four days of discussions in Saigon. Among the listeners were many old friends who had been to Dhamma sessions before. They took a great interest in the discussions and posed many questions. It was the time of New Year's celebration, "Tet" in Vietnamese, and it is the custom to give money with one's good wishes for the New Year. People gave money to be spend on charity such as the printing fund for Acharn's books and a few of my books that were translated into Vietnamese. These books were out of print. Friends had also composed a book with collections of Dhamma discussions with Acharn translated into Vietnamese, that were held in Vietnam at several occasions. There were sessions in the morning and the afternoon, and one of the nuns who always listened with great attention remarked that time went by too quickly while attending the sessions.

One of the listeners found it difficult to study Dhamma. She found that she knew just seeing, but she was not mindful of thinking. How could she be mindful?

Acharn asked: "What about understanding? Each word of the Buddha should be carefully studied, like seeing. Without the Buddha's word, it is not possible to understand seeing as not self. Seeing now is taken for 'I see'. Consider whether this is a reality which is not self. Right understanding has to develop right now."

She explained that seeing is not that which is seen. We should be truthful and patient in order to understand seeing now. Truthfulness and patience are perfections that should be developed together with paññā, they are indispensable. Otherwise there are no conditions to know directly the arising and falling away of each reality that appears. She often referred to the perfections[1] that should be developed together, because without these there can never be the eradication of ignorance, attachment and other defilements. We should learn more about realities so that we shall have more confidence in the Buddha's teachings. Without the accumulation of the perfections, it is impossible to understand what appears now. One follows ignorance and attachment all the time. The perfections support paññā. We need courage and energy so that we shall not be discouraged when the development of understanding is so slow. Mettā, lovingkindness, is a condition to be concerned for others and to think less of ourselves. The perfection of determination is indispensable so that the development of paññā can continue.

Acharn said that just considering the words: "Life is so short" can be a perfection, because one understands that the best moment in life is hearing, understanding whatever appears now. The perfection of truthfulness means being truthful to reality now as non-self. Acharn said: "One has to consider one's blindness and the great understanding of the Enlightened One. Consider, consider, consider so that there would be understanding gradually. There is ignorance after seeing, but it is unknown all the time."

Acharn said that the moment of listening to the Buddha's teachings is paying respect to him. Each of his words is most valuable, just one word like 'dhamma'. There is nothing except dhamma. Each word is very deep and subtle. Whatever is real and appears at the present

---

[1]The perfections are liberality (dāna), good morality (sīla), renunciation (nekkhamma), wisdom (paññā), energy (viriya), patience (khanti), truthfulness (sacca), determination (adiṭṭhāna), loving kindness (mettā) and equanimity (upekkhā).

moment through one of the six doors, the sense-doors or the mind-door, is dhamma. She explained:

"Right now there is just thinking about seeing. Who knows what seeing is. It has already arisen and fallen away. Without conditions, nothing can arise, like seeing. Without the eye base, seeing cannot arise. One has read before that all dhammas are anattā, which means no self."

We have heard many times those words said by Acharn, but actually one should not forget that they are not Acharn's teaching, but the teaching of the Buddha. He explained all the conditions for the dhammas that arise. We have read about these in the textbooks, but we have not deeply considered them when they occur in daily life now. That is why we appreciate reminders of realities. It is true that when there is no understanding at the moment of seeing, there is always an idea of "I see". We may not expressively think that it is self that is seeing, but the idea of self is still there. Ignorance cannot know it, but when a moment of understanding arises, it knows when there is an idea of self that is thinking or acting. It is not eradicated until one has reached the first stage of enlightenment, the stage of the sotāpanna (streamwinner). That is why Acharn reminded us that we should listen and consider the Buddha's words "on and on and on, until one becomes enlightened."

Enlightenment seems far away, it is actually perfect understanding. However, there can be a beginning of understanding of the reality that appears at this moment, be it sound, visible object or whatever appears now. Paññā has not been sufficiently developed so as to distinguish the reality that experiences and the reality that does not experience. Seeing is nāma, it experiences visible object, and visible object is rūpa, it does not experience anything but it can appear. Seeing could not arise if there were no visible object and no eyesense which is another rūpa. Nāma and rūpa have different characteristics and as long as these are not distinguished from each other we take all that occurs for self. When paññā is more developed it can realize the difference between nāma and rūpa. This is not a matter of remembering that this is nāma (a mental reality) and that is rūpa (a physical reality), but we should consider the characteristic of the reality that appears now. When hardness appears its characteristic can be gradually understood as a reality that does not know anything, without having to think about it. When seeing appears it can be understood as a reality that experiences visible object.

After our sessions in Saigon, we went to Hoi An where we stayed in An Villa, a resort with eight rooms adjacent to a swimming pool. It is very suitable for Dhamma discussions. There is space for many people who come to Dhamma sessions. They can be seated under a roof as a protection against rain and sunshine. We were the first guests staying here and we attended the inauguration ceremony. Photos were shown picturing how the idea originated for a Dhamma home. A committee was formed by Tran Thai, Tiny Tam, family members and friends to execute their plans. After the ceremony, there was a party at the poolside and delicious springrolls and other snacks were served. The service given by the attendants who cleaned the place and took care of our rooms was with so much kindness and thoughtfulness. Every day the breakfast menu was different and prepared with the utmost care. Hang helped me every day with difficult steps, and besides this she had early morning ocean swims and she baked black bread for breakfast. Staying in An Villa was an unforgettable experience to us since it really is like a family home. One always wants to return there.

Every day we went out for luncheon to a different restaurant and all these places had lush tropical gardens full of flowers, or they were situated at the riverside. Vincent helped me with great patience as we were walking along to these places, waiting to let the quick walkers pass.

During the discussions, both in Saigon and in Hoi An, the Vietnamese listeners were very keen to learn more and they posed many questions. Someone asked: "How can we figure out what is citta and how can we have more kusala cittas? Which citta is kusala and which akusala? What is the right Dhamma?"

People think of making merit by releasing animals at the Pagoda. It is very difficult to know when the citta is kusala citta and when akusala citta. Cittas arise and fall away very rapidly and kusala cittas alternate with akusala cittas. Acharn would say: "Only paññā can know". It cannot be known by paññā that is still weak. Usually we think of what is seen, heard or experienced by the other sense-doors but the kusala citta or akusala citta that follows is not known. They do not appear until there are conditions to understand this moment directly. Without listening to the Dhamma, it is not known that often our deeds and speech are motivated by clinging to the idea of self. Acharn said:

"Even moving one's hands is motivated by akusala citta. How can this be known without direct understanding? No one can force oneself to have understanding of citta right now. When the moment of experiencing is not known as not self, how can one know the exact moment of kusala citta and of akusala citta? Do not work out: this is kusala, this is akusala. One should rather know the reality which experiences and the reality which is experienced."

If the difference between nāma, such as seeing which experiences, and rūpa such as visible object that is experienced, is not known, we are bound to take kusala and akusala for self, but they are mere dhammas that arise because of conditions and fall away instantly.

When I listen to a talk by Acharn, enthusiasm (pīti) and happy feeling (somanassa) arise, and these can accompany true appreciation. But, also, I like enthusiasm and happy feeling, and I cling to those very much. It is impossible to disentangle all such different moments of kusala and akusala that are alternating, arising and falling away so rapidly. It is impossible as long as it is not known that whatever appears at the present moment is just a dhamma.

We read in the "Kindred Sayings" (II, 7. The Great Chapter, § 61) that the Buddha spoke about the rapidity cittas arise and fall away. We read:

> "But this, brethren, that we call thought, that we call mind, that we call consciousness, that arises as one thing, ceases as another, whether by night or by day. Just as a monkey, brethren, faring through the woods, through the great forest catches hold of a bough, letting it go seizes another, even so that which we call thought, mind, consciousness, that arises as one thing, ceases as another, both by night and by day."

Citta is called by different names such as mano (mind) or viññāṇa (consciousness). Citta does not become another one when it ceases. This is merely an expression to show how rapidly it arises and falls away.

People sometimes ask why seeing is mentioned first as object of understanding. In the suttas we can also notice that seeing is mentioned first. It is the most common reality and the most intricate reality. Immediately after seeing what is visible, we cling to shape and form and this leads us to thinking of concepts of the world and all the people in it. We take them for lasting and for self. We should learn the difference between seeing visible object and thinking of concepts such as people and things. There are no people and things but thinking is accumulated so that we take them for self. Life is just one moment of experiencing an object.

We also discussed meditation. Someone had strange experiences, such as not experiencing his physical body anymore. Some people were wishing for peacefulness. They thought of peace as a state that is lasting for a while. But each moment of citta passes away immediately. At one moment there may be kusala citta, at another moment akusala citta. It is hard to know the difference. Some cittas are cause, such as kusala citta and akusala citta that can motivate deeds that bring result, and some cittas are result such as seeing or hearing. They experience different objects through the eyes, the ears and the other senses. We can easily mislead ourselves as to the present reality. That is why Acharn reminds us often of the characteristics of seeing, hearing, thinking and all other realities. When we find out that the Dhamma can be verified by considering and testing the truth, there will be more confidence.

Calm was discussed time and again during our discussions. Someone asked what the conditions for calm are in samatha. Acharn said: "What is calm? Who can know it? It is not 'I'. It is a reality arisen because of conditions. It may arise with or without right understanding."

People talk about calm but it is important to know what it is. It is different from the conventional idea of calm. It is a cetasika arising with every kusala citta[2]. Kusala citta and thus also calm can arise with understanding or without it. Calm is a reality, not self, but one is bound to take it for self. When the citta is kusala citta, there is calm of citta and cetasikas, there is no restlessness nor agitation at that moment. There is no infatuation with the object which is experienced. However, it is not easy to recognize the characteristic of calm. The different types of citta succeed one another very rapidly and shortly after the kusala cittas have fallen away, akusala cittas tend to arise. Right understanding has to be keen in order to know the characteristic of calm. If there is no right understanding, we may take for calm what is not calm but another

---

[2]Calm is in Pali passaddhi. It is actually two cetasikas: kāya-passaddhi, calm of the mental body, the cetasikas, and citta-passaddhi, calm of citta.

reality. For example, when we are alone, in a quiet place, we may think
that there is calm while there is actually attachment to silence.

There are likely to be misunderstandings about calm. Someone may
think that he is calm when he is free from worry, but this calm may not
be kusala at all. There may be citta rooted in attachment which thinks
of something else in order not to worry. Or people may do breathing
exercises in order to become relaxed. Calm of cetasikas and calm of citta
which are sobhana cetasikas are not the same as a feeling of relaxation
which is connected with attachment.

Those who see the danger of attachment to sense objects may want
to develop samatha in order to be removed from sense impressions. As
was explained many times during the discussions, for the development
of samatha, right understanding is needed that knows what wholesome
calm is and how calm can be developed with a suitable meditation subject. However this understanding is different from right understanding
that knows the present reality as non-self. Those who develop samatha
without developing also right understanding of the eightfold Path can
be temporarily away from sense impressions but they still take calm for
self.

When right understanding of the eightfold Path is developed, calm
also develops and it is understood as non-self. Acharn asked whether
there is attachment to visible object now. One will not know this by
thinking about it; only paññā will really see the danger of attachment.
When there is ignorance of realities, there are conditions to be attached
again and again. Life is so short and, therefore, one should ask oneself what is more valuable: suppressing clinging to sense objects or
developing understanding of realities which will eventually lead to the
eradication of ignorance and all that is unwholesome.

In the Buddha's time, people who had accumulated the inclination
for samatha would develop it, but after hearing the teachings they would
also develop insight, right understanding of realities. They learnt to
understand the present moment, be it akusala or calm, even to the
degree of jhāna, absorption, as a conditioned reality, non-self.

We read in the "Kindred Sayings" (I, Ch I, The Devas, I, § 10, "In
the Forest") that at Sāvatthi, a deva asked the Buddha:

"Those who dwell deep in the forest,

Peaceful, leading the holy life,
Eating but a single meal a day:
Why is their complexion so serene?"
The Blessed One:
"They do not sorrow over the past,
Nor do they hanker for the future,
They maintain themselves with what is present:
Hence their complexion is so serene."
"Through hankering for the future,
Through sorrowing over the past,
Fools dry up and wither away
Like a green reed cut down."

People spoke about benefits they believed there were in meditation. They found that it helped them in the situation of their work, in the relation with their family. They thought that they had more patience and less aversion. They could stand cold and heat much better and they thought that they had more compassion. However, one may still keep on clinging to oneself. One may cling to patience and calm as states that one can possess. Such moments do not stay. Life is only fleeting moments. The Buddha's way to eradicate the wrong view of self and all that is unwholesome is developing understanding life after life and one cannot expect an immediate effect.

In the Tipiṭaka we read time and again that the Buddha spoke about the impermanence of seeing, hearing and all other dhammas. Some people think that this is also taught in other religions. We all know that people do not live forever and that all things in life are subject to change. The Buddha did not teach general ideas about impermanence, but his teaching is very precise. He taught about the reality of this very moment that arises and passes away. He taught for forty-five years about what we did not know before. We take it for granted that we see at one moment and then hear or think at other moments, but we are ignorant of the arising and ceasing of one reality at a time. The Buddha taught that the sense-cognitions and also thinking arise in processes of cittas that arise and fall away, succeeding one another. Seeing is only real when it arises, and this shows that what the Buddha taught is not theory, it pertains to this very moment. What arises and falls away, never to return, can that be anyone?

It is most helpful that Acharn reminds us all the time about this moment of touching, this moment of thinking, the present moment. Direct understanding of these realities can arise by conditions, not by anyone's will. Otherwise there is wrong thinking, because there is the idea of "I", "I am doing", "I am concentrating on the object", "I am being aware". There is no "I". Everything is conditioned from moment to moment. We forget all the time that it is not "I" who is studying the Dhamma, not "I" who is listening, not "I" who learns about realities.

25

What is most valuable in life

Sarah said: "The development of satipaṭṭhāna can be now, no need to wait. Because there is visible object now, there is seeing, hearing, no need to wait, this moment."

I remarked: "Visible object is not the people here around."

Sarah said: "It is so helpful to remember that even at this moment actually, when we think that we are with our friends we are so attached to, it is only visible object which is seen now, sound that is heard. There aren't any people, there aren't any friends seen. What is touched is only hardness or softness, nothing special that is touched. It is only thinking that thinks about the people in this room, the people around the table. Just a moment of thinking that is completely gone. Nothing of value at all in life, except the moments of understanding. We mind so much about pleasant feeling, but it does not last an instant. The visible object does not last, just here or there or in Holland, just visible object that does not last, sound that does not last. Just the same, no matter where or when, it just lasts an instant. So the world becomes smaller and smaller, closer and closer, just what appears now, just one citta at a time".

Nina: "Like Acharn always says to us: 'There is no one there.' But when we hear that, we find it a point we did not get yet."

Sarah: "A reminder: even now only sound is heard and then gone. That is why considering leads to satipaṭṭhāna, to the development of understanding, to the development of the Path. Even at the moment of wise consideration, it is enough. One does not need to think about it that it is so little or that it is not so clear. At that moment, for an instant, it is clear: it is just sound heard, it is just visible object seen. When there is doubt, just doubt, just another passing dhamma, not of any consequence. Begin again and again."

Jonothan: "We can understand what is seen as just visible object and an idea of people and things follows closely after. We do not need to tell ourselves: 'no one there, no one there', because it is not the reality, the situation for us. That is trying to see something we are not capable of experiencing. But what we can experience is what is there, and what is there can be understood as it is. What is not there can't be understood."

Sukin: "When it is said there is no one there, dhamma is there."

It is true, dhamma is there. There are always dhammas arising and falling away. There is no person or being, but there are citta, cetasika and rūpa.

In the texts we read about many classifications of cittas, cetasikas and rūpas, and the only purpose of this is helping people to have more understanding of non-self. They are all elements that arise because of their own conditions and fall away immediately.

People keep on thinking of their problems, but they do not understand dhammas. They do not know that citta and cetasikas perform their functions while there is thinking. When we are absorbed in thinking of persons and situations, we forget that the real world is the world of whatever reality appears through one of the sense-doors or the mind-door. We believe that "we" see, or "we" hear, but in reality there are only different cittas performing their functions. We live as it were in the world of a magician who makes people believe in whatever he does.

We read in the "Kindred Sayings" (III, Middle Fifty, 5, § 95, Foam[1])

---

[1] Translated by Bikkhu Bodhi in "The Connected Discourses of the Buddha".

that the Buddha said:

> "Suppose, bhikkhus, that a magician or a magician's apprentice would display a magical illusion at a crossroads. A man with good sight would inspect it, ponder it, and carefully investigate it, and it would appear to him to be void, hollow, insubstantial. For what substance could there be in a magical illusion? So too, bhikkhus, whatever kind of consciousness there is... it would appear to him to be void, hollow, insubstantial. For what substance could there be in consciousness?"

The commentary to this sutta states:

> "Consciousness is like a magical illusion (māyā) in the sense that it is insubstantial and cannot be grasped. Consciousness is even more transient and fleeting than a magical illusion. For it gives the impression that a person comes and goes, stands and sits, with the same mind, but the mind is different in each of these activities. Consciousness deceives the multitude like a magical illusion."

We may at times become discouraged, realizing that understanding is so little. But even one moment of understanding is valuable. It is accumulated so that it can arise again. In this way understanding grows. As Sarah said: "One does not need to think about it that it is so little or that it is not so clear. At that moment, for an instant, it is clear."

I used to think, "I have so little understanding and so much ignorance". It seems very humble but we have to realize that this can be conceit (māna), we may be clinging to the importance of self. Sarah reminded me: "It is thinking about oneself, rather than considering dhamma as āyatana (sensefield) or khandha, as different realities conditioned at each moment."

We know that we should learn that whatever is experienced are only conditioned dhammas. Meanwhile we get involved in long stories about people and things which seem to stay. With lobha, dosa, moha and wrong view. But we should remember: it does not matter what arises, it is conditioned already. This is very important. We cannot and do not try to change it. That is the way to learn what dhamma is. It takes a long time.

The thinking, mostly akusala, arises, and we should learn to see it as only a conditioned dhamma. We take thinking for "my thinking". But even such inclination can be known as a dhamma.

Some people want to follow a method and do everything slowly in order to have more mindfulness. Acharn would always help people to return to the present moment, saying:

"Understand what appears right now. At the moment of hearing, there is no seeing. They arise because of different conditions. In a day there are only different realities arising and falling away. There is touching now, hardness appears, not what is seen. Just begin: that which is seen is a reality, but nobody in it. Begin to understand whatever appears little by little. Just hearing without considering is not pariyatti."

Acharn reminded us very often, saying: "Be truthful to the truth." We should carefully consider these words. The truth of life is seeing that appears now, or attachment, unhappy feeling, conceit, whatever appears now. We would rather that akusala realities do not arise, but they are the truth. To be truthful to the truth means developing understanding of whatever appears in order to know it as just a conditioned dhamma, not "I". Actually, when we are truthful it does not matter what arises since it is conditioned and nobody can change it.

We read in the "Kindred Sayings" (III, The Middle Fifty, § 59, The Characteristic of Nonself)[2] :

> Thus have I heard. On one occasion the Blessed One was dwelling at Bārāṇasi in the Deer Park at Isipatana. There the Blessed One addressed the bhikkhus of the group of five thus: "Bhikkhus!"
>
> "Venerable sir!" those bhikkhus replied. The Blessed One said this:
>
> "Bhikkhus, form[3] is nonself. For if, bhikkhus, form were self, this form would not lead to affliction, and it would be possible to have it of form: 'Let my form be thus; let my

---

[2] Translated by Bhikkhu Bodhi in "The Connected Discourses of the Buddha".
[3] Rūpa, physical phenomena.

form not be thus.' But because form is nonself, form leads
to affliction, and it is not possible to have it of form: 'Let
my form be thus; let my form not be thus.'

"Feeling is nonself... Perception is nonself... Volitional
formations are nonself... Consciousness is nonself. For if,
bhikkhus, consciousness were self, this consciousness would
not lead to affliction, and it would be possible to have it of
consciousness: 'Let my consciousness be thus; let my consciousness not be thus.' But because consciousness is non-
self, consciousness leads to affliction, and it is not possible
to have it of consciousness: 'Let my consciousness be thus;
let my consciousness not be thus.' "

Nobody can alter the five khandhas, all conditioned realities, and
have them according to his wish.

One of our friends who attended the sessions in An Villa, had just
heard that her mother passed away. She continued to listen to the
Dhamma but the next day she had to leave earlier to go home. She was
reading one of my travel reports "The Cycle of Birth and Death" I had
written just after my husband's passing away. At that time I began to
understand more that the world of ultimate realities, citta, cetasika and
rūpa and the world of ideas and concepts are quite different. We cling
to dear people but actually what we take for a person are only passing
realities. The company of dear people gives us pleasure and when they
have passed away we lament our lack of this pleasure.

We dwell in our thoughts for a long time on the loss we suffered; many
moments of citta think with sadness but these are all gone immediately.
There are only conditioned dhammas arising and falling away.

Life is very short and we should know what is most important: developing understanding of the reality appearing now. Acharn reminded
us:

"Most important is to understand this moment. Otherwise it is
gone, gone without understanding. Each moment in life is gone, by
conditions. Without conditions, nothing can arise. Seeing cannot arise
without eyesense. Just learn in the beginning to understand the reality,
understand that it is conditioned. By how many conditions, in order to
know that it can never be yours. It is only reality that is conditioned to

arise, no one can stop its arising. Like now, no one can stop the arising of seeing. So there is no you. Learn to understand each moment as not me."

When we learn about the different processes of citta that succeed one another extremely rapidly it becomes clearer that each moment is "gone" very rapidly. We have read about processes of citta in the textbook but it is useful to consider them again and again. Seeing arises in a process of cittas and all of them experience visible object. It is preceded by eye-door adverting-consciousness, cakkhu-dvarāvajjana-citta, which just adverts to visible object that has impinged on the eye-door. It is followed by seeing which sees visible object, a vipākacitta, the result of kamma. This is followed by two more vipākacittas, the receiving-consciousness, sampaṭicchana-citta, that does not see but still experiences visible object while receiving it, and the investigating-consciousness, santīraṇa-citta. Then the determining-consciousness, the votthapana-citta, arises, an ahetuka kiriyacitta (inoperative consciousness without roots) that "determines" the object. It is only one moment of citta that will be followed by seven kusala cittas or akusala cittas performing the function of javana, "going through the object". There is no self that determines whether there will be kusala cittas or akusala cittas, this depends entirely on accumulated conditions. Very often akusala cittas with ignorance and attachment arise. The sense-door process is followed by a mind-door process of cittas after there have been bhavanga-cittas (life-continuum) in between[4]. Also in the mind-door process kusala cittas or akusala cittas arise.

When sound appears, hearing arises in another process of cittas, in the ear-door process. It seems that sound can be experienced at the same time as visible object, but the eye-door process must have fallen away when sound is heard. This shows that processes of cittas follow upon each other extremely rapidly.

Cittas succeed one another without interval. The next citta cannot arise if the preceding citta has not fallen away. Because of the unbroken continuity of cittas, past lives condition the present life and the present life conditions future lives. Kusala cittas and akusala cittas fall away

---

[4]They do not experience an object through one of the six doorways, and they do not arise within processes of cittas. They are vipākacittas and they just keep the continuity in a life. They experience the same object as the rebirth-consciousness.

immediately but the good and bad qualities are accumulated from moment to moment, from life to life, and, thus, there are conditions for the arising again of kusala citta and akusala citta. There is no self who can cause the arising of kusala citta and akusala citta.

Cittas arising in processes arise in a certain order and nobody can change this order. For example, seeing that arises has to be followed by two more vipākacittas that also experience visible object; these cittas cannot experience sound or any other object.

The processes of cittas experiencing an object through the eyes, the ears, the nose, the tongue, the bodysense and the mind-door proceed extremely rapidly from birth to death, and very often the objects are experienced with ignorance and attachment. Thus, countless moments are "gone" with ignorance and in this way we keep on accumulating ignorance. Before we realize it, our life has come to an end. Considering the way processes of cittas proceed all the time can be a condition to develop understanding of the present reality. This does not mean that one has to act in a specific way in order to know the present object; then one is taken in again by the idea of self. Acharn explained that people just want to keep the "I", not to abandon the "I".

I am very grateful for all the explanations and reminders given by Acharn, Sarah, Jonothan and other friends. I found the questions posed by our Vietnamese friends very helpful, they made me consider more the realities of daily life.

Listening and reading alone are not sufficient, one should consider deeply the truth. Acharn said that it is a long way and that it is to be followed with detachment. As she reminded us time and again: most important is understanding this moment. This is the beginning of understanding the truth of life.

Understanding, paññā, can be classified in many ways. The following way demonstrates the different levels of understanding:

- understanding based on hearing, suta-maya-paññā,

- understanding based on considering, cinta-maya-paññā,

- understanding based on mental development, bhāvana-maya-paññā.

This was one of our subjects of discussion. The Pali term "suta" means what is heard; we have to listen again and again, a few times is not sufficient. The words "everything is dhamma" that we often hear sound very simple, but we really have to consider the truth. Listening can condition considering the truth so that there will be more understanding. Realities can be considered in daily life, no matter where one is. One should not think that being with many people or performing one's daily tasks is a hindrance to considering realities. There is no self who considers the truth, it occurs by conditions.

Dhamma is what appears now. The reality that appears cannot be selected. It may be unwelcome, such as strong attachment, great sadness or worry. It does not matter what appears, it is non-self, uncontrollable. We should not forget the words "it does not matter what appears". It is not sufficient to merely think that it is not self. Considering over and over again can be a condition for paññā based on mental development (bhāvana-mayā-paññā), the development of paññā which understands directly the characteristics of realities that appear. At first understanding is not yet firm enough to see them as mere conditioned dhammas. Only the direct understanding of realities can gradually lessen the inclination to take realities for self. Finally it will lead to the eradication of the wrong view of self.

Part V

The Shortness of Life

26

Preface

Achan Sujin and other friends were invited to Vietnam by Tam Bach and other Vietnamese friends for a two week sojourn at the end of October 2016. Sarah and Jonothan were assisting Achan untiringly and with great enthusiasm during her Dhamma explanations. Friends from Thailand, Canada, Australia, Taiwan and myself joined this journey. In Vietnam, Tran Thai made the travel and accommodation arrangements for all of us.

The Dhamma discussions took place in Hanoi. There had been Dhamma sessions before with Acharn Sujin in Hanoi and at that time there were fewer attendees than at this time when the number of listeners had grown; now there were about eighty of them. The listeners became more and more interested to understand the present reality. Among the audience were three monks, many 'nuns', that is to say, women who wear robes and observe eight precepts, and many lay followers. Some had come with their parents. Tam Bach translated into Vietnamese the English Dhamma discussions and a team of Vietnamese friends translated the questions from the audience into English. We were also invited to the mountainous region of Sapa where the discussions were more informal and personal.

Before going to Vietnam, I spent a few days in Bangkok, at the Peninsula Hotel. The King of Thailand, King Bhumibol Adulyadej, had just passed away and a period of national mourning was announced, which had been extended to a year. Every day the daily newspaper, the Bangkok Post, was dedicated to all the achievements of his Majesty. He truly was a man of the people, visiting all parts of the country to meet people personally in order to see in which ways he could solve their problems. With dedication and self-sacrifice, he set up many projects to raise their quality of life. He assisted the hill-tribe villagers who lived in very difficult circumstances. He made people replace opium crops with alternative crops such as peaches and apples. His Majesty spent several years in hospital because of ailing health and also during that time he only thought of the interests of his people.

In Hanoi we usually had sessions of about six hours a day and in addition one of the monks wanted to discuss the conditions[1] for the dhammas that arise. Also during previous sessions in Saigon we had discussed some of the conditions and now he was very interested to understand the way they condition dhammas that appear in daily life.

During the sessions Achan reminded us time and again that we should carefully study each word of the Buddha's teachings. People are inclined to speak about concentration and calm, but first one should consider the meaning of these terms. Otherwise one talks about these subjects without understanding what they exactly are.

---

[1] In the seventh book of the Abhidhamma, the Patthana, twenty-four classes of conditions have been taught.

27

What is Life?

At the moment of seeing what is visible, life is seeing. At the moment of hearing sound, life is hearing. At the moment of smelling odour, life is smelling. At the moment of tasting flavour, life is tasting. At the moment of experiencing tangible object through the body sense, life is tactile consciousness. At the moment of thinking, life is thinking. We find our experiences most important, but we forget that each moment of experience is extremely brief. It arises because of its proper conditions and then it falls away immediately. We cling to all objects that are experienced through eyes, ears, nose, tongue, bodysense and mind, through these six doorways. We cling to them and take them for things that exist, that belong to us.

Throughout our discussions we were reminded that realities that appear are impermanent and non-self, anattā. There is no self or person that coordinates all the different experiences through the senses. When seeing arises it sees visible object, and it is not a self or person who sees. Hearing is again another experience and it is not a self or person who hears. Each moment of experience is actually a moment of

179

consciousness, in Pali: citta.

Before hearing the Buddha's teachings, we only paid attention to the outward world around us, to all the objects that presented themselves. We did not realize that nothing could appear if there were no citta that experiences objects.

There are many different types of cittas and only one citta arises at a time, experiencing one object. Each citta is succeeded by a next one, from moment to moment, from life to life. It seems that we see people and things, but seeing only sees visible object that impinges on the eyesense; persons or things cannot impinge on the eyesense. Very soon after seeing has fallen away, we think of persons and things and this shows how fast cittas arise and fall away and succeed one another. The thinking of people and things could not occur if there were no seeing, but seeing and thinking do not occur at the same time. The fact that there is not one type of consciousness that stays but many different types of cittas succeeding one another helps us to see that there is no self who could direct or manipulate realities. They all arise because of their own conditions and they fall away immediately. Acharn repeated very often: "There is no one".

We can acquire intellectual understanding of the reality that appears at this moment, but this is not the same as the direct experience of the truth. To show us that it takes a long time to develop intellectual understanding up to the level of direct understanding and the full realization of the truth, Acharn said that we are under the water, at the bottom of the ocean. It will take aeons before we rise up out of the water. From life to life we take realities for something permanent.

One afternoon I had a conversation with three friends from Taiwan, with Vincent, his older brother Yung and Maggie. I said to them:

"Now there is seeing, it is not I who is seeing but it is citta that sees. It falls away immediately. It is there for a very short time. Nobody can make seeing arise. That shows that it is anattā, non-self. If there were no eyesense and visible object, all that is visible, there could not be seeing. Hearing is again another experience, a different citta. This is not book knowledge, but it occurs right now. Hearing could not arise if there would not be sound and earsense. It falls away immediately, it is there for a very short time. After hearing has fallen away, there is another citta: a citta that thinks about the meaning of what is heard.

Each citta falls away and is succeeded by a following citta, there is no gap in between. It is like this from moment to moment, from birth to death.

There are many different types of citta: some are good or wholesome, kusala, some are unwholesome, akusala, some are neither. Citta does not arise alone, it is accompanied by several mental factors, cetasikas. Some cetasikas are good or wholesome, some are unwholesome and some are neither. They all arise because of conditions and they condition the citta they accompany. The citta that thinks is sometimes accompanied by cetasikas that are akusala, sometimes by cetasikas that are kusala.

When the cetasika anger, dosa, accompanies the akusala citta, anger falls away together with the citta, but the inclination to anger is accumulated in the citta and it can be a condition that anger arises again. Anger, or aversion, is one of the three unwholesome cetasikas that are roots. The other two are attachment and ignorance. They are called roots because a root is the foundation of the citta. Besides the akusala cetasikas that are roots, there are many other akusala cetasikas, but each akusala citta is rooted in ignorance and attachmant, or in ignorance and aversion, or in ignorance alone. We have not only accumulated aversion, but also attachment. They arise time and again after seeing, hearing and the other sense-cognitions. We are taken in by pleasant objects and at such moments also ignorance of realities arises.

Attachment to pleasant objects experienced through the eyes, the ears, the nose, the tongue and the bodysense and attachment to people is actually attachment to the self. We think of ourselves most of the time. When understanding has been developed more, we shall realize that whatever arises is a conditioned dhamma. Dhammas arise, nobody can make them arise and they fall away.

There are three wholesome or sobhana cetasikas: non-attachment, non-aversion and understanding or wisdom. Each kusala citta is rooted in non-attachment and non-aversion and it may or may not be accompanied by understanding or wisdom. When there is a moment of understanding, it arises with the citta and falls away with the citta. But understanding can be accumulated and then there are conditions for it to arise again and again. I am inclined to think: 'I understand', but it is understanding that understands."

Maggie asked: "Does citta know or does paññā know?"

Nina: "Citta knows or experiences an object but it is different from paññā that understands the true nature of the reality that is the object of citta. Panna can be accumulated and it develops little by little.

What are realities? Citta, cetasika and rūpa are realities of our daily life. Citta and cetasika are nāma, mental realities that experience an object, and rūpa are all those realities that cannot experience anything. Intellectual understanding of the reality that appears now is a foundation for direct understanding."

Question: "How can intellectual understanding condition direct understanding?"

Nina: "When we listen and consider what we hear, intellectual understanding develops and then it can condition direct understanding."

Maggie's question: "It is all for the purpose of liberation from the cycle of birth and death. I will then renounce (worldly life) and become a nun."

Nina: "It all has to be step by step. Do not forget this moment, we cannot think of the end of the cycle yet. The idea of 'doing something' is already wrong."

Question: "What is the difference between conceit, mana, and wrong view of self, ditthi?"

Nina: "They cannot arise together. Ditthi is wrong view, whereas when there is mana, you find yourself important, thinking, 'Here I am'. It is compared to the waving of a banner."

Question: "They are attached to self?"

Nina: "But each in a different way. They cannot arise together. Only the arahat (who has attained the fourth and last stage of enlightenment) has eradicated conceit, mana. The sotāpanna (who has attained the first stage of enlightenment) has eradicated wrong view but not conceit. When you compare yourself with someone else, you may think: 'I am better, equal or less.' The sotāpanna does not have any idea of 'I exist' but he can still think that his khandhas are better than the other's khandhas."

Question: "What is the present reality?"

Nina: "We can ask ourselves: can it be directly experienced and through which doorway - through the eyes, the ears, the nose, the tongue, the bodysense or the mind-door? Can its characteristic be directly experienced, without naming it? Then we know that it is a reality. Seeing appears time and again. We can call it seeing or give it another name, but its characteristic is always the same. It experiences visible object."

Citta is different from cetasika, it is just the faculty of knowing an object, it knows or cognizes an object. It does not like or dislike or understand the nature of the object. Cetasikas condition citta and citta conditions cetasikas. When we come to know that there are many conditions for each reality that arises, it leads to detachment from the view that they are permanent and self.

Feeling accompanies every citta and we take it for self. There are happy feeling, unhappy feeling and indifferent feeling. When the feeling is unhappy and we wish it to be happy, we can see that we cannot control feeling. It has its own conditions for its arising. This shows us that it is beyond control, or anattā."

In Hanoi there were several young people among the audience who asked questions about the way Dhamma could help them in daily life. They asked how the understanding of seeing, for example, could be of use in their social life.

Seeing is an ultimate reality, different from conventional ideas. Before hearing the Buddha's teachings, we only knew the conventional world of people and of different circumstances. We did not know that life really is a moment of experience like seeing, hearing or thinking. Acharn explained many times that seeing is a reality and that there is no one who sees, that only seeing sees. Seeing arises because there are eyesense and visible object, it arises because of several conditions and then it falls away. How can that which falls away be controlled by a[1] self? Seeing is a mental reality, in Pali nāma. Eyesense and visible object are physical realities, in Pali rūpa. They do not experience anything.

What we take for people are nāma and rūpa. We may wonder why a person is always bad-tempered? His accumulated inclinations are the condition for him to behave in this or that way. Understanding of conditioned realities leads to more patience when we are in the company of

---

[1] Conditioned realities can be classified as five khandhas or aggregates: physical realities are rūpa-khandha, and four groups of mental realities are: feeling, vedana-khandha, remembrance, sanna-khandha, the other mental factors besides feeling and remembrance which are saṅkhāra-khandha, and all cittas, vinnana-khandha.

others. When we understand that we all have different accumulations, we shall become more tolerant of someone else. Acharn said: "We can become an understanding person." When there is more understanding of our own accumulations, we will also understand the other persons in our surroundings, in our relationship such as married life. Through the Buddha's teachings, we will have more understanding of accumulated tendencies, wholesome and unwholesome. They condition the citta arising at the present moment.

We all have different likes and dislikes and this is conditioned by accumulations of different tendencies. When we were in a restaurant in a village in Sapa, we had a Dhamma discussion after our lunch. After the discussion, loud music was being played. Vincent and I did not like this music and I was inclined to ask to have it less loud. Vincent's wife was a concert pianist and, therefore, he likes classical music and I like soft Baroque music and classical music. This is clinging, and all clinging is actually clinging to oneself. We noticed that most people liked the music, they were applauding time and again. Through the Dhamma, we can learn more about the clinging to ourselves in the different circumstances of life. The preference for certain objects and the clinging to these is caused by attachment to oneself. More understanding will lead to patience and tolerance when things do not turn out the way we wish.

At this moment there are seeing, hearing or thinking. There can be only one moment of citta that experiences an object. Acharn reminded us that seeing cannot hear or think, and that hearing cannot see or think. These words sound simple, but they remind us to consider the truth again and again.

Acharn said: "There is always the idea of 'I see someone'. That which is seen is nobody, nothing at all. Consider in order to begin to understand the truth of whatever the Buddha taught. This does not mean only listening without considering the truth of that which is heard. Without seeing, can there be the idea of something? Without any reality at all, can there be the idea of 'I'? But what is taken for I is not permanent at all. Is that not wrong understanding about life, about moments of seeing and hearing? As long as seeing is not directly experienced, it is not possible to eradicate the idea of 'something' in it." We may have expectations to have less defilements through the understanding of the Dhamma, but then we are clinging to an idea of self who wants to become a better person. The Buddha's Path is the development of more understanding of whatever reality appears at the present moment. Understanding should be developed with detachment. If we have expectations, we forget that whatever arises, be it wholesomeness, kusala, or unwholesomeness, akusala, has specific conditions. The wholesome and unwholesome tendencies that have been accumulated in each citta can, at a given moment, condition the arising of kusala citta or akusala citta. Most of the time akusala citta arises.

If we believe that a self can avoid akusala, we forget that akusala is conditioned and that it is impossible to push away what has arisen already. We can learn that akusala citta is just a conditioned reality, not self. This is the way to follow the right Path. The Buddha taught that all realities that arise are just conditioned dhammas, non-self.

Our friends from Taiwan believed at first that having long retreats in a meditation centre would help them to have less akusala. But after listening to the discussions we had in Vietnam, they realized that there is no self who can control cittas and that right understanding of realities can eventually lead to the elimination of akusala after countless lives. Maggie came to understand that attachment and anger are normal, that they are conditioned. If they would not arise, how could one understand them? What arises at the present moment can be understood by paññā. When there are conditions for attachment, it arises and then its characteristic can be understood.

One of the listeners in Hanoi was wondering how the understanding of realities like seeing could help him in his social life. He said that when he was planning his diverse activities in his social life, he could not avoid taking account of a self. Our activities in social life have to be planned, and we have to think of other people. But it is beyond control whether or not our plans come true. We never know the next moment and whatever we experience is dependent on several conditions. We may plan to meet someone else at a certain time and place, but due to an accident this may not be according to our plans. We talked about success for someone who is in business. Acharn remarked that he also has to die. The duration of one's lifespan is dependent on kamma, it is beyond control. It is important to know the true nature of realities like seeing, hearing or thinking which occur now. Otherwise we shall never understand their conditioned nature and their impermanence.

We should not change our lifestyle or behaviour in order to develop right understanding of realities. Understanding is to be developed naturally in daily life.

But understanding can be a condition to become more patient and metta, unselfish love, can arise more often instead of attachment to people.

The Buddha spoke time and again about all realities occurring in daily life. We read, for example, in the Kindred Sayings (IV) § 32, Helpful (2):

> "I will show you a way, brethren, that is helpful for the uprooting of all conceits. Do you listen to it. And what, brethren, is that way? Now what think you, brethren, is the eye permanent or impermanent?"
>
> "Impermanent, lord."
>
> "What is impermanent, is that weal or woe?"
>
> "Woe, lord."
>
> "Now what is impermanent, woeful, by nature changeable, is it fitting to regard that as 'This is mine. This am I. This is my self?"
>
> "Surely not, lord."

The same is said about all objects experienced through the six doors, about contact through these doorways and all the sense-cognitions.

We should not just believe these words but carefully consider what appears now. Like seeing, there is seeing now. This is the only way to find out about the Truth of the Buddha's teaching.

28

Kamma and its Result

Our present life is part of an endless series of lives in the cycle of birth and death. When this life has come to an end, it is followed by a next life and after that there are countless other lives. Even so, before this life there were countless past lives. Acharn reminded us many times that this life was once the future life for the past life. This life will be the past life for the coming life, just as today will be yesterday for tomorrow. Yesterday, today and tomorrow follow upon each other and what is past is forgotten very soon. This shows how short each life is. We do not remember our past life, where we lived and whether or not we were married. Remembering that the present life, to which we attach so much importance, is only a minuscule part of the cycle of birth and death is helpful when we lose a dear person through death.

Patacara had lost all her family including her recently born son. She went to the Buddha and his gathering quite mad and without dress. The Buddha taught her the impermanence of life and she was able to develop understanding and finally reach arahatship. She spoke to other women who had suffered loss.

187

We read in the Therigatha (Canto VI, Fifty, Patacara' s Five Hundred) that Patacara said:

> "The way by which men come we cannot know;
> Nor can we see the path by which they go.
> Why mourn then for him who came to thee,
> Lamenting through thy tears: 'My son! my son!'
> Seeing thou knowest not the way he came,
> Nor yet the manner of his leaving thee?
> Weep not, for such is here the life of man.
> Unasked he came, unbidden went he hence.
> For ! ask thyself, again whence came thy son
> To bide on earth this little breathing space?
> By one way come and by another gone,
> As man to die, and pass to other births
> So hither and so hence - why would ye weep?"

A question was raised during the discussions about the last moment of this life and the first moment of the next life. There is no person who travels from this life to the next life. When the last citta of this life, the dying-consciousness (cuti-citta), has fallen away, it is immediately succeeded by the next citta which is the rebirth-consciousness (patisandhi-citta) of the following life. There is no gap between these cittas. It is just like now when each citta is succeeded by the next citta. Actually, also now there is momentary birth and death of each citta that arises and falls away. Life lasts as long as one citta and this is extremely short.

The Buddha taught about life at this moment, what life is now. Acharn said: "Life does not belong to anyone, it is only one moment of experiencing an object. It is extremely short. There should be more understanding that there is no one, only conditioned realities."

We read in the Kindred Sayings (I, Mara Suttas, § 9, Life Span 3) that the Buddha said:

> "Bhikkhus, this life span of human beings is short. One has
> to go on to the future life. One should do what is wholesome
> and lead the holy life; for one who has taken birth there is

no avoiding death. One who lives long, bhikkhus, lives a hundred years or a little longer."

Then Mara, the Evil One, approached the Blessed One and addressed him in verse:

"Long is the life span of human beings,
The good man should not disdain it.
One should live like a milk-sucking baby:
Death has not made its arrival."
[The Blessed One:]
"Short is the life span of human beings,[1]
The good man should disdain it.
One should live like one with head aflame:
There is no avoiding Death's arrival."

Then Mara the Evil One... disappeared right there.

Acharn reminded us: "What is there from moment to moment? What has arisen just a moment ago? It has all gone immediately. Life is nothing. From nothing there is something and then again nothing, completely gone. After seeing, there is the idea of I from birth to death. Each life is conditioned to be born and die. Today will be yesterday of tomorrow."

Before seeing arose, there was nothing, no seeing, and then, when there were the right conditions, it could arise just for a moment and then it was gone, it became nothing.

We attach so much importance to joyful events and we dislike sorrow, but they all arise because of conditions and they do not last. We would like to experience only pleasant objects but this depends entirely on conditions. It is unavoidable that unpleasant objects are experienced: we all are subject to disease and to loss of what is dear to us.

It is kamma that produces birth in different planes of existence. Nobody can choose his birth. The term kamma is generally used for good and bad deeds, but kamma is actually cetana cetasika, volition or intention. Cetana arises with each citta and hence it can be kusala, akusala,

---

[1] I am using the translation of Ven. Bodhi.

vipaka or kiriya. Cetana directs the associated dhammas and coordinates their tasks (Atthasalini, Book I, Part IV, Ch I, 111). There are two kinds of kamma-condition: conascent kamma-condition and asynchronous kamma-condition. Cetana which arises with each citta directs the associated dhammas to accomplish their functions; it conditions these dhammas by way of conascent kamma-condition, sahajata kamma-paccaya. Cetana which accompanies kusala citta and akusala citta directs the tasks of the associated dhammas and it has the function of activity in good and bad deeds. In this last function it produces the results of good and bad deeds.

Kusala kamma and akusala kamma are mental, and, therefore, they are accumulated in the citta from moment to moment. When cetana motivates a good deed or a bad deed, the citta falls away, but cetana or kamma is accumulated. It is unknown which of the accumulated kammas will produce rebirthconsciousness. Rebirth as a human is a happy rebirth, the result of kusala kamma, because understanding can be developed during that life if there are opportunities for listening to the Dhamma. Rebirth in higher planes, heavenly planes, is a happy rebirth. Rebirth as an animal or in a Hell plane is an unhappy rebirth or the result of akusala kamma. Some kammas produce their results in the same life in which they were committed, some in the next life, some in later lives.

Kusala kamma and akusala kamma through body, speech and mind can be of different degrees. Kamma is not always a 'completed action' (kamma patha). There are certain constituent factors which make kamma a completed action. For example, in the case of killing there have to be: a living being, consciousness of there being a living being, intention of killing, effort and consequent death (AtthasalinI, I, Book I, Part III, Ch V, 97). If one of these factors is lacking, kamma is not a completed action. Akusala kamma or kusala kamma which is a completed action is capable of producing rebirth that may be unhappy or happy.

There were several questions during the discussions on mano-kamma, kamma or cetana, performing its function through the mind (mano), and people wondered when mano-kamma would be a completed action. Sarah explained what mano-kamma is and whether it can be kamma patha.

Cittas that experience objects through the sense-doors and the mind-door arise in different processes of cittas. Seeing, for example, sees visible object through the eye-door. But seeing is not the only citta that experiences visible object, it arises in a process of cittas. There are several other cittas that experience the same visible object: they do not see, but while they experience visible object, they perform their own functions. Soon after seeing has fallen away it is succeeded by several cittas, usually seven, that are either kusala cittas or akusala cittas, which have the function of 'javana', 'running through' the object in a wholesome or unwholesome way. The intention or cetana that accompanies those cittas is mano-kamma, but it is not a completed action. As to the kusala cittas or akusala cittas arising in a mind-door process, it depends on the intensity of the cetana accompanying them whether they are kamma through the doors of body, speech or mind that is accomplished kamma, kamma patha. When attachment to a pleasant sound or flavour arises now, it is first experienced through the relevant sense-door and then through the mind-door. It is manokamma, it does not harm anyone else.

Kamma can also be of the degree that it harms another person. As Sarah explained, wrong views are only akusala kamma patha when they lead to deeds and speech, not just the views by themselves. There is mano-kamma whenever there are kusala or akusala cittas which are not said to be bodily or vocal kamma. However, unless all the conditions are completed, it is not kamma patha capable of producing rebirth. Akusala cetana in the mind door processes may be of a strength to condition bad deeds when they are planned or thought about, not just impulsively done. So if the wrong view conditions such deeds or speech, it is mano-kamma patha.

It helps to have less misunderstanding about what kamma is and to appreciate that mano-kamma is very common, to know that even now after seeing or hearing, there are kusala cittas or akusala cittas immediately. None of them is self and most of the time it is not of a strength to be kamma patha which can condition rebirth.

Acharn reminded us several times that the Buddha's teaching is not theory, not book knowledge. Understanding has to be developed of the reality appearing at this moment, so that it will be understood as not self. She said:

"Is there kamma now? Do we have to find out through which door-way or what kind of kamma is there? At this moment it is 'I' who is thinking about kamma so how can there be the understanding now of kamma itself as not self?

It is not like 'what kind of kammas are there in the book', but how to understand it now as not self and by then one can see, without saying it out, what kind of kamma it is. At this moment of speaking, it has to be known that without citta there can never be speaking. What conditions the words which are spoken? It depends on citta. When it is akusala citta it conditions harsh words, bad words, hurting the other. At that moment it is not necessary to classify whether it is the kamma through speech which is vaci-kamma or mano-kamma... The most precious moment is to understand the moment which is conditioned as not self."

Sarah explained: "Akusala kamma patha, no matter through which doorway it is committed, is the one that hurts or harms someone else, but if we try to work out exactly whether this or that is kamma patha, there will not be right understanding of it. Someone gave the example in the discussion about covetousness when you don't take what belongs to someone else but you really wish to have it - and then people want to know whether it is kamma patha. But why is one so concerned about it whether it is kamma patha? Usually it's because one is concerned about oneself, thinking, 'Will I get bad results in another life' or something like this. We cannot know all the details of the Buddha's wisdom, but whether kamma is kamma patha depends on the intensity and whether it harms the others at that moment."

Kamma is the condition for the experience of pleasant objects and unpleasant objects through the senses. We may believe that other peo-ple or the outward circumstances of our life are the cause of sorrow, but the real cause is kamma that produces results in the form of sense impressions. Seeing, hearing, smelling, tasting and body-consciousness may experience a pleasant object or an unpleasant object. Cittas arise and fall away so rapidly that we cannot know whether the object that was experienced was pleasant or unpleasant. It is not necessary to find out. There can be wise attention or unwise attention to whatever is experienced and this is dependent on conditions, it is beyond anyone's power. At this moment, seeing arises and falls away, and it is followed by thinking that arises and falls away. Even so, in the past there was seeing, followed by thinking. In the future, there will again be seeing and all other sense-cognitions, followed by thinking.

When we hear an unpleasant sound, we may have aversion and then the citta is akusala citta accompanied by dosa, aversion. When we hear a pleasant sound, we may have attachment and then the citta is akusala citta accompanied by lobha, attachment. All akusala cittas are accompanied by ignorance. When right understanding is being developed of the realities that appear, there are conditions for wise attention. We may realize that no matter what object is experienced through the senses, pleasant or unpleasant, it is only a conditioned dhamma.

29

Attachment

Whatever arises because of conditions has to fall away immediately. It is not worth clinging to what is impermanent by nature, what is dukkha (unsatisfactory). As paññā develops, it is understood more clearly that life is only one moment of experiencing an object. This is a condition for courage to develop understanding of whatever appears now, be it pleasant or unpleasant, wholesome or unwholesome. It is the only way to understand that realities are beyond control, anattā. Before we heard the Buddha's teachings, we did not have a precise understanding of what attachment is. We knew in general that one is attached to children, members of one's family or friends. Through the Dhamma we learn that there is attachment time and again on account of what is experienced through the eyes, the ears, the nose, the tongue, the body sense and the mind-door. Very often attachment and ignorance arise after seeing has fallen away, but we do not know it. Ignorance covers up the truth of realities. Attachment has been accumulated from life to life. It is accumulated in each citta that arises and falls away and that is why it can arise so easily. It always finds an object.

195

We discussed attachment to persons, which can cause a great deal of disturbance in life. Acharn explained: "But actually it is not the force of that person to condition attachment, but the attachment here has been conditioned for a long, long time and it is so great, so that when there is the right moment and the right object, it is there and paññā (understanding) can understand. In the beginning, paññā cannot see the danger of attachment but it begins to see that it is not self. That is the main point. No matter how great attachment is, it falls away. The self just regrets having it but paññā does not let go of it."

When paññā has not been developed to a higher degree, it cannot let go of it. Only those who have reached the third stage of enlightenment, the stage of the non-returner, anagami, have eradicated attachment to sense objects. Only the arahat has eradicated all kinds of attachment.

Sarah said: "One always clings to something or someone because of not understanding reality. We think this is 'my problem - I'm so attached to people', but actually it is not 'my problem'. They are just moments of thinking with attachment that fall away instantly and they don't last at all. Just moments of attachment and thinking long stories because of saññā (memory) and clinging to the stories and ideas - taking them for someone or something. But even such moments of clinging do not last."

Nina: "Thinking again and again all the time - it is so disturbing."

Acharn: "Panna begins to see that it is wasting of time, because there is nothing, only the object of attachment. It can arise any time."

Nina: "Panna is too weak to see that, too weak."

Acharn: "We do not mind and just develop understanding. Paññā will work its way."

Sarah: "If we mind that there is clinging or are disturbed by the clinging, then it is just more disturbance about the disturbance. More self - 'I don't like this, I don't want this kind of thinking'. Thinking and attachment are conditioned and fall away anyway, so there is no point in minding and thinking that it shouldn't be like that."

Acharn: "The object of attachment does not last at all. Only thinking and at that moment there can be attachment to other things instead of that because it is accumulated in the citta. Nothing can take it away - only paññā can purify it little by little. Only that, so be happy. What-

ever happens is just a moment and it does not last... only a reality which
has fallen away completely and is no more."

Nina: "I don't know yet that it is just a moment."

Acharn: "By understanding, little by little."

Sarah: "Never mind! Even if there is no understanding now, moments of ignorance - they are just passing realities. So, it doesn't matter
if there is a lot or a little understanding, attachment or disturbance or
moments of kusala - they are all gone instantly. When we think we
are so attached to people, actually it is visible object and sound and so
on that there is so much attachment to and that is why there is thinking about them again and again. It is not 'my disturbance' but just
common, ordinary realities. It is like that for everyone."

Acharn: "Paññā accumulates so little at a time but it is so great
when it has accumulated more and more. It will come."

Sarah: "No need to think about it - how much or little. Let it just
perform its function and do its job, otherwise if one is thinking about a
lot or a little understanding, one is disturbed again, attached again.

One thinks of attachment to others but one is most attached to oneself. One thinks 'Oh, no understanding, very little understanding', and
this is all attachment to oneself. As soon as it matters, there is the idea
of self. There is nothing to be concerned about or upset about, attachment is very common. The problem is that one thinks 'my attachment
is so special'. "

People go to Acharn with different problems concerning their relationship with others, in the family, with their partner, in their work.
Acharn always asks: "Is there seeing now?" She brings us back to the
present moment, because without understanding of the present reality,
problems cannot be solved. There is no I who sees, seeing sees. Seeing
arises because of conditions and it cannot be manipulated. This shows
us the nature of anattā. There is no one there. Thinking thinks of a
problem and the problem becomes very great and important. But it is
only in our thinking. Thinking is also a conditioned reality, and it is
not 'I think'. The thinking thinks. When things in life are not the way
we would like them to be, we are inclined to wish to control our life.
That is attachment and with attachment problems will not be solved.
We think of long stories instead of realizing that whatever happens is
beyond control. The realities of our life are only citta, cetasika and

rūpa, no person who can be master of situations and events. They just arise for a moment and then fall away.

We may not realize how extremely brief one moment of citta is. When we see, it seems that we immediately see people, but then seeing has fallen away and thinking has arisen already.

It is helpful to consider again and again the following verse of the "MahaNiddesa" quoted in the "Visuddhimagga" (VIII, 39):

> Life, person, pleasure, pain - just these alone
> Join in one conscious moment that flicks by.
> Ceased aggregates of those dead or alive
> Are all alike, gone never to return.
> No [world is] born if [consciousness is] not
> Produced; when that is present, then it lives;
> When consciousness dissolves, the world is dead:
> The highest sense this concept will allow' (Nd.1,42).

Life, person, pleasure, pain: What is life? It is all that appears through the five senses and the mind-door. When seeing arises, life is seeing; when hearing arises, life is hearing; when thinking arises, life is thinking. When we think of a person, he seems to exist, but what we take for a person are only impermanent nāma and rūpa, fleeting phenomena. Pleasure and pain are impermanent: in our life happy moments and sad moments alternate, they appear one at a time. We attach great importance to our experiences in life, to our life in this world, but actually life is extremely short, lasting only as long as one moment of citta. As we read:

> No [world is] born if [consciousness is] not
> Produced; when that is present, then it lives;
> When consciousness dissolves, the world is dead:

When we are thinking about the world and all people in it, we only know the world by way of conventional ideas. It seems that there is the world full of beings and things, but in reality there is citta experiencing different dhammas arising and falling away very rapidly. Only one object at a time can be cognized as it appears through one doorway. Without the doorways of the senses and the mind, the world could not appear.

So long as we take what appears as a 'whole', a being or person, we do not know the world.

If there were no citta, nothing could appear, but since citta arises at each moment, realities appear. We are reminded of the brevity of all experiences, including thinking with worry about our problems. The real cause of problems is not in the outside world nor in other people, it is in the citta. People wonder what they should do in difficult situations, in their dealings with other people. They ask: "What next?" But who knows the next moment? This depends entirely on conditions which are beyond control. Because of our clinging to the idea of self, we create our own problems and we believe that we can act in this or that way to solve our problems. Development of right understanding of one reality at a time as it appears at this moment is the condition for one to be less taken in by concepts and ideas of the conventional world with all the problems and worries. One begins to see the world in the ultimate sense: citta, cetasika and rūpa. That is the world that is real, that is the world that should be understood more and more.

When we were at the airport, about to leave Vietnam and go back to Thailand, Acharn spoke about attachment. She said that we should not be afraid of it. We should not mind having it, or try to force ourselves not having it. It arises because there are conditions for it and it falls away immediately. It is only a dhamma and when paññā is more developed, it can realize its characteristic. Now we are mostly thinking about ideas which are not real and there is likely to be the idea of 'my attachment'. We are afraid of having attachment, but the reason for being afraid of it is that we take attachment for self. Even not wanting to have attachment is attachment already.

We had a discussion with the listeners about the way how to solve problems. Someone suggested that this could be with therapy. Acharn asked: "Is there a problem now? What is the cause of problems?" The Dhamma is not like a therapy. The cause of problems is that we are thinking of self, that we relate problems to ourselves. All that is arising now is only a conditioned dhamma, not self, and nobody can make it arise or do anything about it. When we listen to the Dhamma, there can be a little more understanding. The development of understanding is with ups and downs but we can see that even a little more understanding is beneficial. We cannot expect an immediate result of listening and considering the Dhamma. When there is any expectation, we cling to an idea of self. We can accept that the development of paññā is just step by step.

Sarah said that one learns to live easily and naturally while developing understanding instead of trying to change our life with the wrong idea of self. She said: "It is like letting go of a big burden. The happiness of understanding is different from the happiness with clinging."

Acharn quotes from the teachings time and again that the development of understanding should be with courage and gladness. She told us to be happy about the reality that appears. She said: "Be happy. Whatever occurs is just a moment and it does not last. It is only a reality that has fallen away completely and is no more." We should be grateful that the Buddha taught that whatever appears is only a conditioned dhamma, impermanent and not self.

Is there seeing now? It does not see a person, it sees only visible object for an extremely brief moment. While realities are considered in the right way, there is no worry, no disturbance at that moment.

The Buddha spoke time and again about seeing, hearing, all the sensecognitions and all objects experienced by them.

We read in the "Kindred Sayings" (IV, 32, Second Fifty, § 60, Comprehension):

> "I will show you, brethren, a teaching for the comprehension of all attachment. Listen to it. What is that teaching?
>
> Dependent on the eye and the object arises eye-consciousness.
>
> The union of these three is contact. Dependent on contact is feeling. So seeing, the well-taught Arian disciple is repelled by the eye, by objects, by eye-consciousness by eye-contact and by feeling. Being repelled by them he lusts not for them. Not lusting he is set free. By freedom he realizes 'Attachment has been comprehended by me' ".

The same is said about the ear and sounds, the nose and scents, tongue and savours, body and tangibles, mind and mind-states.

The Buddha explained that the objects that are experienced, the types of consciousness, cittas, the feelings arising on account of them, are all conditioned.

He spoke separately about all the six doors. The aim is to understand anattā, to become detached from the ideas of person, self, situations, things. Understanding leads to detachment.

We see here that there is Abhidhamma in the suttas. We read about what is real in the ultimate sense, different from stories about persons and things we think of all day long.

The conditions for the experience of visible object, for seeing are entirely different from the conditions for the experience of sound. Eye-sense and visible object are conditions for seeing. Earsense and sound are conditions for hearing.

The more we understand about conditions, the less we cling to a self who could cause the arising of seeing or hearing.

In the Abhidhamma texts details are given about the different processes of cittas experiencing one object. All with the aim to cling less to the self, to understand anattā.

The cittas of the eye-door process, of the ear-door process, of all processes succeed one another very rapidly so that it seems that we can experience more than one object at a time.

We should distinguish between the world of thinking of concepts, of persons, things, situations, from the world of realities that can be experienced one at a time. We mostly live in the world of concepts, imaginations, but we can begin to know the difference. This cannot be accomplished immediately, since we accumulated ignorance and attachment from life to life.

30

Conditioned Dhammas

One day, when we were having lunch, Acharn explained to Vincent, our friend from Taiwan, about realities. Vincent was working hard all the time, translating into Mandarin all the Dhamma conversations held during the sessions for his brother and for Maggie.

We usually think that we see people and do not realize that seeing just sees visible object, not a person or thing. While we were eating a salad with tomatoes, Acharn said:

"How could there be an idea of something without visible object? Visible object is a reality, it is not a thing like a tomato, it is just that which can impinge on the eyebase. It arises and falls away. Attachment and ignorance arise and attachment wishes to understand, but it covers up the truth. Why did he teach visible object? If he had not, there would be something in it all the time.

It would not appear as it is and it would be impossible to let go of the idea of someone. The eyebase is a condition for the arising of seeing. Without it, it would be impossible to see. Each citta experiences an object, whenever it arises it experiences an object."

Then the term saṅkhāra dhamma, conditioned dhamma, was discussed. We should study each word of the teachings, otherwise we talk about what we do not know. Whatever arises because of conditions and appears is saṅkhāra dhamma. Understanding this is the beginning of paññā. Paññā eradicates ignorance.

Vincent asked whether saṅkhāra is a concept.

Acharn said: "We do not talk about concepts. What appears through the eyes?"

Vincent answered: "White colour, but this is already thinking."

Acharn: "We talk about citta, the faculty that experiences. It does not have the function of like or dislike. The table has no quality to experience. You think of saṅkhāra but there is no understanding of its meaning. What appears now?"

Vincent: "Sound."

Acharn: "If sound had not arisen it could not appear. Whatever appears has arisen because of conditions, not by anyone's will. The eyebase cannot condition hearing. It is a condition for seeing. Does it arise?"

Vincent: "Yes."

Acharn: "It is saṅkhāra dhamma, a conditioned reality. At this moment of seeing, we do not have to think of a flower or another thing. There is just that which is seen. This is the way to let go of the idea of someone or something in it. There is nothing mixed in it at all. Smell is smell, sound is sound. Is sound sankhara dhamma?"

Vincent: "Yes."

Acharn: "Is hearing sankhara dhamma? Is thinking saṅkhāra dhamma?"

Vincent: "Is concept not saṅkhāra dhamma?"

Acharn: "We do not talk about concepts, just about absolute realities. That is why we have the words paramattha dhamma (absolute or ultimate reality) and abhidhamma (subtle dhamma or dhamma in detail). We begin with the word dhamma: whatever is real. We know that there are so many different kinds of realities. There are realities that can experience something and realities that cannot experience anything."

Acharn then explained that there are nāma, realities that experience something, and rūpa, realities that cannot experience anything. There is nobody, no one, no permanent self. The word saṅkhāra is used to indicate that there is no one, only dhammas. She explained that by talking and discussing one will have more understanding. She said that discussing is a blessing, since it brings more understanding. Otherwise one reads the texts but one does not know how much understanding there is. She then spoke about meditation centres.

Acharn: "It is useless to go somewhere and meditate. Then one does not have understanding of the reality at this moment. What is saṅkhāra dhamma? Whatever arises by conditions. Without conditions nothing can arise. That is why it cannot belong to anyone. It is not anyone. All dhammas are anattā. When you go somewhere, is that atta or anattā?"

Atta means self, one's actions may be motivated by the idea of self, or by anattā, the understanding of non-self.

Vincent answered: "Atta."

Acharn: "No understanding of anattāness when one thinks: 'I would like to do this or that'. If there is no atta, why do you go there? If there is right understanding, it is now, right understanding of that which appears. What is dhamma?"

Vincent: "What is real."

Acharn: "Can atta make it arise? Atta cannot bring about right understanding. That is the reason one goes to a quiet place, but it cannot be the right Path; it is motivated by ignorance and attachment. Here we are talking about Dhamma. What brings you here is listening to the Dhamma."

Vincent: "So, that kind of desire is not-attachment. There is the opportunity to listen."

Acharn: "One knows what can bring less attachment: right understanding."

While we were having our Dhamma conversation at the lunch table, preparations were going on for Khun Deng's birthday. Acharn said to her: "May you be happy" and then went on immediately with the Dhamma explanation. Khun Deng found this the best way to celebrate her birthday. There were songs for her and a birthday cake was being shared out. She went to Acharn and said that she had appreciated so much the simile of the closed fist Acharn had given her. When a fist is closed, we do not know what is in it, but when one opens it, one sees that there is nothing. Even so, what we take for our life are realities that arise and fall away. There is nothing or nobody there.

We read in the commentary to the "Satipatthana Sutta":

The character of contemplating the collection of primary and derived materiality is comparable to the separation of the leaf covering of a plantain-trunk, or is like the opening of an empty fist.

As to primary and derived rnpas, these are the four Great Elements of solidity, cohesion, temperature and motion, and the derived rūpas of taste, odour, smell, nutrition and other rnpas. They arise and fall away all the time. The body does not exist, what we take for our body are only fleeting rnpas.

Acharn: "It is not easy to understand that there is no one at all. What is there when there is no one? What is the reality at this very moment?"

Vincent: "Nāma and rūpa."

Acharn: "We may name it, but it takes a long time, from life to life, to understand what is real now. Each word of the Buddha should be considered, because it represents a reality, just one characteristic at a time. Only when there is a great deal of listening to the Dhamma, considering it and wise reflection, understanding can begin to develop. Now it is intellectual understanding but it can become firmer and firmer."

Intellectual understanding of the reality that appears at this moment, in Pali pariyatti, is the foundation for the development of direct understanding of realities, in Pali patipatti. This again can eventually lead to the direct realization of whatever reality appears, pativedha.

People had questions about sati, mindfulness of realities, that is developed in satipaṭṭhāna. Paññā that is accompanied by sati of this level is actually patipatti, which is often translated as practice. This translation is misleading since it suggests a self who is acting in a specific way.

There are many misunderstandings about mindfulness or awareness. Some people think that this means knowing what one is doing, such as walking or applying oneself to tasks in the house or at work. Sati is a sobhana cetasika, a beautiful mental factor, that accompanies every kusala citta. It is non-forgetful of kusala. It can be of many levels and degrees. Sati of the level of dana arises when one is generously giving gifts. Sati of the level of slla arises when one abstains from harsh speech or when one is helping others. Sati of the level of samatha, calm, is non-forgetful of the object of calm. Sati of the level of satipaṭṭhāna is mindful of the reality appearing at the present moment. It accompanies paññā so that it can know this reality as only a conditioned dhamma that is not self or mine. When there is an opportunity for kusala, one may be lethargic and lazy, thinking of one's own comfort and pleasure. One is forgetful and lets the opportunity go wasted. However, when sati arises, it is nonforgetful of kusala and does not let the opportunity go wasted.

Some people wish for the arising of sati and they do not see that sati also is a conditioned reality that arises because of its own conditions. Acharn spoke many times about the conditioned nature of seeing, because there is seeing time and again, also right now. What has arisen is real and what has not arisen is not real. She would speak about seeing time and again to bring people back to the present moment instead of paying attention to abstractions, ideas which are not realities. If there is correct understanding of seeing at this moment, one can leam the meaning of conditioned reality that is beyond control. Then it will be clearer that also sati is beyond control.

It is difficult to be aware of one reality at a time that appears without thinking of the word. One has to get used to their characteristics, each one is different.

When there is no understanding of what appears, there is attachment, because it seems to be permanent. What is the object of attachment that appears and disappears? Actually, there is clinging to that which is no more. When there is understanding of what appears, like seeing right now, it is the beginning of understanding that it is just a conditioned reality.

The Buddha taught details so that people would have more understanding of conditioned realities. Acharn reminded us: "There is no method at all. It is dependent on right understanding when it has been sufficiently developed to condition direct awareness of seeing right now. Before hearing the teachings, hardness was experienced at the moment of touching with the idea of 'something' all the time, with the idea of I or 'mine'. Softness appears all the time but there is no understanding. Nobody can change it."

Acharn explained about conditioned realities: "How can there be less attachment to seeing right now? The Buddha taught the conditions for the arising of seeing. Otherwise one would think that just opening one's eyes is a condition for the arising of seeing. That is wrong understanding. Seeing experiences that which is now appearing. Without the accompanying cetasikas, seeing could not arise."

The accompanying cetasikas are conditions for seeing. Contact, phassa, is a cetasika that contacts visible object so that seeing can see it. One-pointedness or concentration, ekaggata cetasika, is the condition that seeing only experiences visible object and that there is no thinking of other things at that moment. Memory or saññā marks or remembers the object that is seen. Even so, sati could not arise without the accompanying cetasikas. It needs non-attachment, alobha, as a condition. It also needs concentration, so that it is mindful of one nāma or rūpa. It needs calm that accompanies every kusala citta.

Some people believe that there should be calm first before right understanding of a reality can arise. They take a feeling of relaxation, or not being disturbed by noise, for calm. Calm as it is understood in conventional sense is quite different from the reality of calm, passaddhi. This is a cetasika that accompanies every kusala citta. It can only arise when there are the right conditions for kusala and nobody can cause its arising. When one is generous, there is already calm with the kusala citta. When one studies the Dhamma with kusala citta, there is already calm accompanying the kusala citta. If one thinks that one should go to a quiet place in order to have calm, it is wrong understanding. One clings to an idea of self who can induce calm.

Nāma and rūpa appear one at a time and each one of them has its own characteristic. These characteristics cannot be changed. Seeing, for example, has its own characteristic; we can give it another name, but its characteristic cannot be changed. Seeing is always seeing for everybody, no matter an animal sees or any other living being sees. It has to be known as only a dhamma. Concepts are only objects of thinking, they are not realities with their own characteristics, and, thus, they are not objects of which right understanding is to be developed. Thinking is a reality, there is no self who thinks. Sometimes when there is thinking of beings there can be understanding at that moment, one may realize that it is just thinking.

Only one reality at a time can be experienced by citta and, thus, mindfulness which accompanies the kusala citta can also experience only one object at a time. Since we are so used to paying attention to 'wholes', to concepts such as people, cars or trees, we find it difficult to consider only one reality at a time. When we know the difference between the moments of thinking of concepts and the moments that only one reality at a time, such as sound or hardness, appears, we will gradually have more understanding of what mindfulness is. It can only arise when there is no expectation.

The following sutta emphazises the importance of listening and discussing the Dhamma in order to have more direct understanding of realities.

We read in the "Gradual Sayings" (Book of the Fours, Ch XV, § 7 Seasons):

> "Monks, there are these four seasons which, if rightly developed, rightly revolved, gradually bring about the destruction of the asavas. What four?
>
> Hearing Dhamma in due season, discussion of Dhamma in due season, calming in due season, insight in due season. These are the four.
>
> Just as monks, on a hilltop when the sky-deva rains thick drops, that water, pouring down according to the slope of the ground, fills up the clefts, chasms and gullies of the hillside; when these are filled, they fill the pools; when these are filled, they fill the [1] lakes; when these are filled, they fill the rivulets; when these are being filled, they fill up the great rivers; the great rivers being filled fill the sea, the ocean; - just so, monks, these four seasons, if rightly developed, rightly revolved, gradually bring about the destruction of the asavas."

---

[1] There are four kinds of asavas: the canker of sensuality (kamasava) the canker of becoming (bhavasava) the canker of wrong view (ditthasava) the canker of ignorance (avijjasava)

31

Understanding this Moment

Acharn reminded us: "When there is no understanding, attachment arises to what appears; it seems permanent. The truth is that the object of attachment appears and disappears very rapidly. There is clinging to what is no more. Seeing arises and falls away but ignorance cannot understand that. So it takes what is seen or seeing as 'something'. Seeing a moment ago is gone completely. Thinking about it is gone immediately."

Acharn explained that anattā, the truth of non-self, can only be understood by paññā, not by trying so hard to make paññā arise.

Vincent remarked: "But citta is so fast."

Acharn said: "No one can stop the rapidity of the succession of cittas. There cannot be selection to have this or that as object of awareness. Realities roll on very fast. Life is the stream, the flux of realities arising and falling away by conditions."

People were asking how there can be direct understanding of realities. The answer is: only when paññā has grown to a higher level with direct awareness of whatever reality appears. This will take many lives, but intellectual understanding of what appears now, thus, pariyatti, can condition understanding of the level of patipatti, direct understanding of realities.

Some people believe that they have to concentrate on nāma and rūpa in order to develop direct understanding of realities. But, what is concentration? As Acharn often said, we have to study each word of the teachings in order to understand the true meaning. People like to have concentration but they do not understand what it is. Coming back to this moment, is there concentration now? Someone thought that concentration helps a great deal to understand the present moment. Acharn asked again:

"Is there concentration right now? At the moment of seeing, is there concentration? All realities are unknown. We are only talking about the story of them. Citta experiences only one object at a time, and it is the function of ekaggata cetasika, concentration, to cause citta to focus on that one object."

There are many misunderstandings about concentration. It arises with every citta. When it accompanies akusala citta, it is wrong concentration, and when it accompanies kusala citta, it is right concentration. It is a conditioned dhamma and nobody can cause its arising.

One of the listeners said that there was quite a revolution in his way of thinking when he gave up wrong ideas about the eightfold Path. He sees now that understanding should be developed in a natural way and that he should not try to focus on particular realities.

If we try to concentrate or if we think, "I am concentrated", we cling to an idea of self who has concentration and then we follow the wrong Path. When we think that we can do something to develop understanding, it is wrong practice. One should consider realities more that appear now in daily life so that understanding can develop naturally.

Someone asked how one can reach the stage of patipatti, the development of direct understanding, and whether meditation is necessary to reach it. She wished for enlightenment.

Sarah answered: "Bhavana is the development of understanding. Let us speak about understanding now. It does not mean practice. No I who can do anything. Hearing about the realities that arise in a day leads to a little more understanding of what pariyatti means. There can be bhavana right now, there is no need to wait for another time or place.

When one thinks of going to follow a method, it is thinking. There can be understanding of thinking."

The person who asked questions about meditation had an idea of wanting to experience emptiness. Sarah explained:

"It seems that there is just emptiness, nothing there, no citta, no object. That is moha, ignorance. It is not possible for the citta that arises not to experience an object. The object is a reality or a concept. It is not nothing."

Sarah then explained, if someone has an idea of having no object but being able to have concentration lasting a few hours, experiencing emptiness, that it does not bring him closer to the Buddha's teachings. It will induce people to take the wrong Path, it is not a condition for understanding conditioned dhammas. Following the wrong Path is so dangerous. If one listens, like now, one will realize that dhammas are anattā, each one impermanent and unsatisfactory (dukkha).

Acharn repeated very often that realities such as sound, hearing or tangible object are experienced in darkness. Only at the moment visible object is experienced by seeing, the world is light. But when visible object has fallen away, the world is dark. It seems that the world of light lasts but this is an illusion. Visible object impinges again and again on the eyesense and seeing and the other eyedoor process cittas follow. But there are numerous other processes of cittas in between. This shows us how rapidly cittas are arising and falling away in succession. When Acharn said that hearing experiences sound in darkness, she reminded us that only one object at a time can be experienced. She reminded us of the rapidity of the stream of realities.

The Buddha taught about cittas that experience objects through the doors of the senses and the mind, arising in different processes of cittas. Cittas arise and fall away in succession extremely rapidly. When we consider his teaching more deeply, it will help us to see that nobody can interfere with these processes, that they are beyond control. All realities are anattā.

Each of the sense-cognitions experiences an object through the appropriate doorway. There is not only one citta that experiences visible object, or one citta that experiences sound, but each of the sense-cognitions arises in a series or process of cittas succeeding one another and sharing the same object. They all cognize the same object, but they each perform their own function.

Seeing is preceded by the eye-door adverting-consciousness, which adverts to visible object. It does not see but it merely turns towards the visible object that has just impinged on the eyesense. This citta is an ahetuka kiriyacitta (inoperative citta without hetus, roots), it is not akusala citta, not kusala citta and not vipakacitta. Seeing, which is an ahetuka vipakacitta, is succeeded by two more ahetuka vipakacittas which do not see but still cognize visible object that has not fallen away yet. They perform a function different from seeing while they cognize visible object. Visible object is rūpa and it lasts longer than citta. These cittas are receiving-consciousness (sampaticchana-citta), that receives visible object and investigating-consciousness (santlrana-citta), that investigates the object. The investigating-consciousness is succeeded by the determiningconsciousness (votthapana-citta), which is an ahetuka kiriyacitta. This citta is followed by seven cittas performing the function of javana, which are in the case of non-arahats kusala cittas or akusala cittas. There is a fixed order in the cittas arising within a process and nobody can change this order.

The five-sense-door adverting-consciousness (panca-dvaravajjana-citta) turns towards the object through one of the five sense-doors. It is named after the relevant sense-door, such as eye-door adverting-consciousness or ear-door adverting-consciousness.

There is no self who can determine whether the determining-consciousness will be succeeded by kusala cittas or akusala cittas. Cittas arise and fall away succeeding one another extremely rapidly and nobody can make kusala citta arise at will. Kusala or akusala performed in the past is a condition for the arising of kusala or akusala at present.

When the sense-door process of cittas is finished, the sense object experienced by those cittas has also fallen away. Very shortly after the sense-door process is finished, a mind-door process of cittas begins, which experience the sense object which has just fallen away. Although it has fallen away, it can be object of cittas arising in a mind-door process. The first citta of the mind-door process is the mind-door adverting-consciousness (mano-dvaravajjana-citta) which adverts through the mind-door to the object which has just fallen away. The mind-door adverting-consciousness is neither kusala citta nor akusala citta; it is an ahetuka kiriyacitta. After the mind-door adverting-consciousness has adverted to the object, it is succeeded by either kusala cittas or akusala cittas (in the case of nonarahats), which experience that same object.

When visible object is experienced through the mind-door, the cittas only know visible object, they do not pay attention to shape and form or think of a person or a thing. But time and again other mind-door processes of cittas follow which think of people or things and then the object is a concept, not visible object. The experience of visible object conditions the thinking of concepts of people and things which arises later on. It seems that while we are seeing we can think already about what is seen, but in reality seeing and thinking arise in different processes. Since cittas succeed one another so rapidly, it seems that they last.

How much understanding is there now of visible object as visible object? Right understanding has not been sufficiently developed so as to become detached from the idea of self. There should be listening to the Dhamma, considering what one hears and understanding of what is now appearing. Thinking always follows seeing, hearing and all the other sense-cognitions. What is thinking? It is different from seeing but only when understanding is more developed their different characteristics can be directly known.

We may only 'think' that seeing is not self but the actual moment of that which sees is not known yet. When there is more understanding, there will be less attachment to realities as self. We should have confidence in right understanding, it can understand what was not known before. As long as seeing is not directly known, it is impossible to give up the idea of something in it. There can be more confidence that whatever happens, whatever we do only lasts for an extremely short moment.

People are often wondering what the conditions are for right understanding and right mindfulness of the eightfold Path. The condition for right awareness is right understanding from hearing, considering. Paññā is not developed sufficiently to know that there is no one in visible object. We mostly live in the world of ignorance; there is no understanding of what is true and real. Considering realities is a precious moment.

On my last day in Thailand I attended the morning session in Thai at the Foundation. The subject discussed was the real purpose of monkhood. The following sutta was duscussed:

Gradual Sayings, Book of the Tens, Ch IV, § 1, Upali and the Obli-
gation. Upali asked the Buddha what the purpose of the Vinaya was.
The Buddha explained that this was:

"For the excellence of the Order,
for the well-being of the Order,
for the control of ill-conditioned monks
and the comfort of well-behaved monks,
for the restraint of the cankers in this same visible state,
for protection against the cankers in a future life,
to give confidence to those of little faith,
for the betterment of the faithful,
to establish true dhamma,
and to support the discipline."

Khun Unnop stressed that the second point was most important: the
well-being of the Sangha. Often there is wrong understanding about the
meaning of monkhood. Young men take ordination for a short while, to
please their parents and without any understanding. People give money
to monks and they accept it, but this is wrong. Monks have left the
home life and should not accept money or enjoy the idea of it. They
should see the danger of being in the cycle of birth and death and their
life should be directed towards freedom from the cycle, to be reached at
the attainment of arahatship. The monk has only two tasks: the study
of the scriptures and the development of insight. Nothing else. The
study of the scriptures is not in order to gain theoretical knowledge, but
to understand the reality of the present moment. Acharn adapted most
of her radio programs to explain the purpose of monkhood.

I met Khun Samnuang Sucharitakul, who came very cheerfully in a
wheelchair. She had recently turned a hundred years. She used to get
up at night for a few hours to transcribe Acharn' s talks in Thai, so
that these could be printed as books which were beneficial for many. It
enabled me to translate several of these books into English.

At the Foundation[1], during the English session, we discussed the
accumulation of akusala. By listening to the Buddha's teachings, there

---

[1]Dhamma Study and Support Foundation. This is the centre where all sessions
with Acharn Sujin take place each weekend.

can be more understanding of attachment (lobha), aversion (dosa) and ignorance (moha) which are of many degrees. They arise because of conditions, they have been accumulated from life to life. Whenever there is attachment, we think of ourselves. Some degrees are very harmful such as wanting to steal something, and some are not harmful for others. We can learn to see the danger and disadvantage of all degrees of akusala.

We are attached to friends and family members but it is good to know that we are actually attached to ourselves when we like the company of dear people. It was emphasized several times that it is so common and that we should not consider it as our special problem or find it important.

The discussions held during these weeks were most beneficial to all of us. Sarah and Jonothan added many useful points to Acharn's explanations of dhammas that arise in daily life. I am very grateful for all those reminders. It was emphasized in many ways that understanding should be developed naturally. One should not change one's lifestyle or give up one's job to study Dhamma with the purpose to have kusala citta with understanding more often. Then clinging to the idea of self will not be eradicated.

Acharn had said before many times that paññā was not developed sufficiently so as to condition direct understanding of realities. We may repeat these words but at first they may not be very meaningful. Now, after all our discussions, it became somewhat clearer that only a higher level of paññā can condition direct awareness and understanding of the present reality. We cannot act in any way to cause the arising of a higher level of paññā, except persevering in listening and considering what we hear. Seeing and thinking that appear now can be understood as just conditioned dhammas, but it will take a long time, even many lives, before this is clearly understood. Gradually there will be more confidence in the growth of paññā. How could one interfere with realities that arise and fall away extremely rapidly?

Acharn asked: "Life is so very short. What is the best moment in life?"

The answer is: listening to Dhamma so that we come to know what the truth is in life - whatever reality appears is only a conditioned dhamma, not self.

Part VI

Sharing Dhamma

32

Preface

The Buddha developed all the perfections[1] with right understanding of realities to the greatest extent so that he could become a Sammāsambuddha who teaches the truth of realities to the world. His teaching is the most precious gift to us all. He taught in such a way that the listeners could develop their own understanding. It is thanks to the Buddha that we can still listen to the Dhamma and that we can meet for discussions. In this way we can share what we hear with others who are interested in the teachings.

Our Vietnamese friends are very keen to learn and understand the truth of the Dhamma and they use every occasion to listen, consider and discuss the Dhamma. They organise several times a year sessions with Acharn Sujin in different locations in Vietnam. Acharn Sujin's book "Survey of Paramattha Dhammas" and my "Buddhism in Daily

---

[1] The perfections or pāramīs are: generosity, wholesome behaviour (kusala sīla), renunciation, wisdom, energy, patience, truthfulness, determination, loving kindness, equanimity. The Buddha developed these for aeons in order to become the Sammāsambuddha.

Life" were translated into Vietnamese. At this moment Tam Bach is translating my "Conditionality of Life". During this journey she asked many questions on the different conditions, paccayas, in order to facilitate her translation. They are a very active group of friends who are truly dedicated to make known the Dhamma.

They had invited Acharn Sujin and her sister Khun Sujit to Vietnam in January 2016 for a ten days sojourn. They sponsored their flight and hotel accommodation. Sarah and Jonothan were assisting Acharn during her Dhamma explanations and friends from Thailand, Canada, Australia and myself joined this journey. In Vietnam Tiny Tam, Tran Thai's wife, made all the traveling and accommodation arrangements for us.

The Dhamma discussions took place in Saigon, in a hall near our hotel. Among the audience were usually two monks, many "nuns", that is to say, women who wear robes and observe eight precepts, and many lay followers. Tam Bach translated into Vietnamese the English Dhamma discussions and a team of Vietnamese friends translated the questions from the audience into English.

Our Vietnamese friends took great care of all our needs and they were most inventive in taking us to different restaurants for luncheon. Once I had a bad cough, and they prepared a drink called "birds' nest" with great loving care. It proved to be very effective, even after a few days.

Throughout our journey Acharn reminded us not to move away from the present object. Whatever is real appears now. Seeing is a conditioned dhamma, it cannot be a person who sees. I am grateful to hear again and again what she repeats because the development of understanding takes a long time to become well established.

33

The World

What is the world? We live in the world of persons, of self, of different things. Before hearing the Buddha's teachings we did not really understand what the world is. Because of ignorance of the world we cling to our possessions, our family and friends. In truth the world is citta (moment of consciousness), cetasika (mental factor accompanying citta) and rūpa (physical phenomena). Seeing is a citta, experiencing visible object, just for a moment and then it falls away. Thinking is another citta that thinks of persons and different things like a table or tree. Thinking may be unwholesome, akusala, and then it is accompanied by ignorance and other mental factors, cetasikas, that are unwholesome such as attachment or aversion. Or thinking may be wholesome, kusala, and then it may be accompanied by kindness, compassion or understanding of realities. There could not be seeing without eyesense which is a physical reality, rūpa. Also what is seen, visible object, is a type of rūpa which conditions seeing by being its object.

We cling to our body and we believe that it belongs to us. However, what we take for body is in reality different rūpas that arise and fall

away. They arise because of different conditioning factors and they are
beyond control.

Citta, cetasika and rūpa arise just for a brief moment because of
their proper conditions and then they fall away immediately. When seeing arises, only visible object is experienced and both seeing and visible
object do not last, they fall away immediately. When hearing arises
sound is experienced and both hearing and sound fall away immediately. There cannot be seeing and hearing at the same time; only one
citta arises at a time and experiences one object through one of the six
doorways of eyes, ears, nose, tongue, bodysense and mind-door. Thus,
actually, there are six worlds, appearing one at a time: the world of the
experience of visible object, of sound, of odour, of flavour, of tangible
object and the world of thinking.

Because of ignorance and clinging we have to reborn again and again.
So long as there is birth there have to be old age, sickness and death.
During life we have to experience a great deal of sorrow. The Buddha
taught the end to rebirth by the development of right understanding of
all realities that appear. During the discussions there was reference to
the "Rohitassa Sutta".

We read in the "Gradual Sayings", Book of the Fours, Ch V, §5,
"Rohitassa", that the deva Rohitassa asked the Buddha:

"Pray, lord, is it possible for us, by going, to know, to see,
to reach world's end, where there is no more being born
or growing old, no more dying, no more falling (from one
existence) and rising up (in another)?"

The Buddha answered that that end of the world is not by "going"
to be reached. Rohitassa said that formerly he was the hermit Rohitassa
of psychic power, a sky walker. The extent of his stride was the distance
between the eastern and the western ocean. Rohitassa said:

"Though my lifespan was a hundred years, though I lived
a hundred years, though I traveled a hundred years, yet I
reached not world's end but died ere that."

He praised the Buddha saying, how well it is said by the Exalted
One that the world's end is not by going to be reached. The Buddha
said:

"Nay, your reverence, in this fathom-long body, along with its perceptions and thoughts, I proclaim the world to be, likewise the origin of the world and the making of the world to end, likewise the practice going to the ending of the world.

Not to be reached by going is world's end.
Yet there is no release for man from Dukkha
Unless he reaches world's end. Then let a man
Become world-knower, wise, world-ender,
Let him be one who lives the divine life.
Knowing the world's end by becoming calmed
He longs not for this world or another."

Through the development of right understanding of mental phenomena (in Pali: nāma) and physical phenomena (in Pali: rūpa) one can become a world-knower, wise, a world-ender. The objects of right understanding are not far away, they are "this fathom-long body, along with its perceptions and thoughts", thus, whatever mental phenomena and physical phenomena appear in daily life. For him who has completely developed understanding of the world at this moment and eradicated all defilements there will not be any rebirth, no more world at any time.

Acharn emphasized time and again that realities such as seeing, visible object, hardness or sound appear all the time in daily life and that understanding of them can be developed very gradually. One does not have to go to a quiet place and concentrate on realities. She reminded us that intellectual understanding of what appears now, pariyatti, can gradually condition direct understanding, paṭipatti, and this again conditions paṭivedha, the direct realization of the truth. Many times she said that each word of the Buddha points to the truth and leads to detachment. Study of the teachings is not for speculation or memorizing but for the understanding of this very moment.

In Saigon there were about a hundred listeners every day. They listened with great interest and many questions were raised. The topics that were discussed were the meaning of non-self, anattā, the perfections, free will and fatalism, meditation and many other subjects. Every day, before the morning session, a discussion was held in a smaller group with venerable Bhikkhu Silavamsa. He was first ordained as a Mahāyana monk and then he became a Theravada monk. He read my

"Letters on Vipassanā" and became interested to listen to Acharn's explanations and attended Dhamma discussions with her since 2013. He wanted to study all twenty-four classes of conditions for realities as laid down in the "Paṭṭhāna", the seventh book of the Abhidhamma. But the study of conditions should not just be book study, theoretical knowledge. We cannot find out by how many conditions, paccayas, this moment is conditioned. Acharn always referred to understanding this moment of reality that arises. Seeing is conditioned by visible object and eyebase; without these rūpas, seeing could not arise. Visible object and eyebase are different realities which have different conditions for their arising. The Buddha taught the conditions for the realities which arise so that people could understand more deeply the truth of non-self, anattā. Whatever arises because of conditions cannot be directed by a self, it is beyond anyone's control. Every day we discussed some aspects of the conditions which pertain to our daily life. Acharn emphasized the importance of deeply considering the meaning of the conditions for the realities that arise at this moment.

The texts we read about conditions always pertain to this moment. Whenever seeing arises there must be that which is seen, visible object. Visible object is object-condition for seeing, but we do not have to name it object-condition. We can come to understand this condition by understanding the reality appearing at this moment. Many times Acharn reminded us that life is very short and that what is most valuable is understanding this moment. Learning about conditions supports the understanding of seeing and hearing as not self. It depends on the individual's accumulated understanding to what extent he can penetrate the truth of the different conditions.

Problems we have in daily life were also discussed and as Sarah stressed many times, the real problem is our own thinking with defilements. Instead of developing understanding of what is real at this moment, we continue to think of difficult situations and persons and we worry a great deal. Then we live in a dream world. Sarah said that there is always something to worry about, that there is no end to it. Not the circumstances or other people are the cause of our problems, the only problem is our unwholesome thinking arising now.

Sometimes we had to walk in the dark and this caused fear to me since I walk with difficulty. One night I had to take extremely high steps to get into a friend's car and then I was surprised to see Acharn sitting in the car already. She spoke to me about my thinking of fear in the dark and thinking that this would be my last trip, always thinking of "self". She reminded me that I have to build up courage, otherwise I will take fear with me from life to life.

The greatest courage is perseverance with the development of understanding of whatever appears now, no matter what the circumstances of our life are. We may come across the greatest difficulties and problems, but there are always seeing, visible object, hearing or attachment with different characteristics to be known.

Sarah had a conversation with Glen, Ann's husband, about life. She spoke about basic notions of Dhamma and she repeated this conversation when we stayed in Thailand, in Kaeng Krachan. Some people may not think that it is important to know more about realities such as seeing or hearing but Sarah explained the relevance of having more understanding of the realities of our life. She said:

"We believe that we see people and things, but actually just that which is seen, visible object, is experienced. Immediately after that there is thinking about people, chairs and trees. This is thinking, not the experience of that which is seen, visible object. The question is whether life just continues as usual with ignorance, or whether we are interested to understand a little more about life. What we usually find most important is our family, our work or our possessions, for example. What is the purpose of having more attachment to what we find important in life? For some of us what is most important of all is having more understanding about the truth of life. When people are dreaming and wake up it is very clear that it was a dream world, a fantasy world, not real. The dream seems so real, but it is just fantasy, an illusion. What about now? What about the dream we are having at this moment? When driving along the road one thinks that one sees a lake, but when one gets closer one knows that it was just a mirage. Also now we are living in a world of mirages and fantasies. As soon as we see people, trees and different things it is the world of mirages and fantasies."

As Sarah said, when we are dreaming our experiences such as seeing seem very real. But actually, at such moments there is no seeing, there is not visible object impinging on the eyesense. When we are asleep our eyes are closed and while dreaming we are just thinking of different ideas.

Even so, when we are awake we believe that we are seeing when seeing
has fallen away already and we are just thinking of different things, of
people. Seeing is one extremely short moment of citta and after it has
fallen away many other types of citta arise. We take for seeing what is
actually thinking of mirages.

Sarah explained:

"Only visible object is seen now, only sound is heard. We think
that we hear the sound of birds, of traffic, sound in the microphone.
Immediately there is an idea of people and things, all the time. Actually,
only sound is heard. There is just the experience of one world at a time,
through eyes, ears, nose, tongue, bodysense and mind and that is all.
It seems that 'I' have such experiences, that I am seeing or hearing,
but who is the 'I' that is seeing or hearing? It is just one moment of
experience followed by moments of thinking. We can learn that what
we take for 'I' is a mirage, an idea. There is just a moment of seeing,
experiencing that which is seen and then thinking about it. Different
realities, each one arising because of its own conditions. This is life,
different moments of experience arising because of different causes or
conditions which no one can control or make arise at will.

It is not a matter of the terms, the details or the books, but it
is about what can be tested now at the moment of touching what we
take for a table. Just hardness that appears now. Just touching of
hardness. We may be thinking of a table, but that is not the reality
that is experienced. When there is an idea of table we are back to the
world of ideas. Images are not real, they are mind-created. One may
think of the brain, but who could control the brain? That is a scientific
outlook, not the present moment."

Acharn said about the brain:

"We are told that the brain experiences. What is seen are different
colours. We hear the word brain and think about its function but it
cannot experience anything at all. When it is touched it is hard and
hardness cannot experience anything at all. We can see a picture of it,
but when it is seen, visible object cannot experience anything. Brain
is that which cannot experience or know anything. It cannot know, it
cannot do anything at all."

Brain is conventional truth one may think of, and it is different from
what is real in the absolute sense: the physical phenomena or rūpa and

the mental phenomena or nāma that appear one at a time at the present moment.

Acharn explained: "This is what we are interested in: to learn more, to have less selfishness, less clinging to the self, the ego, the 'I', because it harms. All unwholesome realities harm oneself and the other. We cling to 'I', everything must be to our liking, from moment to moment. We search for pleasure from that which is experienced, from every doorway, from seeing, hearing, smelling, tasting and the experience of tangible object. Do you think that attachment is wholesome?"

Glen answered: "Attachment is harmful, but it is human."

Acharn said: "That is the right answer. It is there, it is natural. It is conditioned, no one can do anything about it. It is conditioned to arise and fall away, like all conditioned realities. Each reality has its own characteristic and its own function."

We were often reminded that the development of understanding has to be natural. Whatever reality arises cannot be changed, there were conditions for its arising. It has fallen away already when we think about it. It is valuable to hear again and again about basic dhammas, about what life really is from moment to moment. It is different from what we used to believe before hearing the Buddha's teachings. We learn that what we take for 'I' are citta, cetasika and rūpa only. No self sees, but seeing sees, just by conditions. This is life.

34

The Meaning of Anattā

The Anattā Lakkhaṇa Sutta is the Buddha's second sermon. We read in the "Kindred Sayings" (III, Kindred Sayings on Khandhas, Elements, Middle Fifty, § 59) that Buddha said in the Deerpark in Vārāṇasī:

> "Body, brethren, is not the Self. If body, brethren, were the Self, then the body would not be involved in sickness, and one could say of body: 'Thus let my body be. Thus let my body not be.' But, brethren, inasmuch as body is not the Self, that is why body is involved in sickness, and one cannot say of body: 'Thus let my body be. Thus let my body not be.',"

He said the same about the four nāma khandhas[1] of feeling, perception (saññā), the activities (saṅkhārakkhandha) and consciousness. We

---

[1] All conditioned realities can be classified as five khandhas or groups: one is rūpakkhandha, the khandha of physical phenomena, and four are nāmakkhandhas, citta and cetasikas. Saṅkhārakkhandha are all cetasikas apart from feeling and saññā, remembrance.

then read:

> "Now what think you, brethren. Is body permanent or impermanent?"
>
> "Impermanent, lord."
>
> "And what is impermanent is that weal or woe?"
>
> "Woe, lord."
>
> "Then what is impermanent, woeful, unstable by nature, is it fitting to regard it thus: 'this is mine; I am this; this is the Self of me'?"
>
> "Surely not, lord."
>
> "So also it is with feeling, perception, the activities and consciousness. Therefore, brethren, every body whatever, be it past, future or present, be it inward or outward, gross or subtle, low or high, far or near- every body should be thus regarded, as it really is, by right insight- 'this is not mine; this am not I; this is not the Self of me.',"

He then said the same about the four nāma khandhas. We read:

> "So seeing, brethren, the well-taught Ariyan disciple feels disgust for body, feels disgust for feeling, for perception, for the activities, feels disgust for consciousness. So feeling disgust he is repelled; being repelled he is freed; knowledge arises that in the freed is the freed thing[2]; so that he knows: 'destroyed is birth; lived is the righteous life; done is my task; for life in these conditions there is no hereafter.' "

After this sermon the five disciples who were from the beginning with the Buddha became arahats.

During our discussions one of the listeners said that the meaning of anattā is: nothing, no reality. He thought that it means that in the past, present and future there is no reality. Jonothan asked him whether there are dhammas now. The meaning of anattā cannot be understood merely by thinking about it. We should have more understanding of

---

[2]There is the knowledge that the mind is liberated.

the dhammas that are arising at this moment. Seeing that arises at this moment is not self, it is seeing that sees. Nobody can make seeing arise. When understanding of the level of pariyatti develops, thus, intellectual understanding of the present reality, the meaning of anattā becomes clearer very gradually. We cannot expect to fully understand the meaning of anattā after a few years or even after one lifetime of listening to the Dhamma and considering it. But very gradually one can become closer to understanding of whatever appears now. Otherwise we are lost in words and ideas.

Someone else remarked that if all kusala and akusala arise because of conditions we cannot do anything. Some people believe that this would lead to fatalism, to being subject to fate. Acharn answered that what we take for "I" are different realities arising because of different conditions. In other words, also wholesomeness and unwholesomeness are cittas accompanied by cetasikas, not self. It makes no sense to hold on to the idea of someone who can do something to have more kusala. People believe that if there is no free will, responsibility for one's actions is denied. Volition or intention is a mental factor, a cetasika, cetanā cetasika, accompanying every citta. It is conditioned. When there are conditions for kusala citta, cetanā is also kusala and when there are conditions for akusala citta cetanā is also akusala. Right understanding of realities can condition more kusala in one's life.

That may be a beginning of the development of the perfections. In our life there is usually akusala citta and akusala citta cannot understand any reality. When kusala citta arises there are no attachment, aversion or ignorance. The perfections which are actually kusala through body, speech or mind, support right awareness and right understanding of realities. Kusala without understanding is not a perfection. Firm and keen understanding of whatever appears now needs the perfection of truthfulness (sacca) and this can condition detachment from the idea of self. When the truth is known that there is no person, that there are only conditioned elements, there is a degree of detachment that develops along with understanding. Also the perfection of determination (adiṭṭhāna) and the other perfections are needed. One has to be firmly determined not to move away from the present object since the understanding of seeing or visible object that appears now is the only way to understand that there is no one there.

The perfection of patience is indispensable for the development of understanding. Acharn said: "Not just be patient towards cold and heat, but understand even such moments as not self who is patient." There can be patience when we experience an unpleasant object, but also when the object we experience is pleasant there can be patience. When attachment arises on account of a pleasant object there is no patience.

Very often there is the idea of "I am patient". For example, we were enjoying ourselves sitting in a restaurant outside, but there was mostly seafood which I cannot eat because of an allergy. But I found myself very patient, not complaining eating plain rice. Sarah said that we have a conventional idea of patience. When there is the perfection of patience there has to be the understanding that it is not I who is patient.

When listening to the Dhamma and considering it one should not be impatient and expect clear understanding of realities very soon. Acharn explained that when one has heard about right understanding that can penetrate the true nature of reality, there may be attachment and ignorance trying to attain this goal. That is not detachment from wanting to experience it. There are so many traps of attachment and that is why life continues in the cycle.

Robert Kirkpatrick came to visit us in Saigon with his wife and two young children, Ryan and little Nina, a baby of five months old who was named after me. Acharn was so kind to give us all an opportunity for Dhamma discussion in the evening after the usual morning and afternoon sessions. The discussion was held in Robert's room. Ryan was sweetly playing with his toy cars and now and then he needed attention and the approval from his father. He was no longer the only child and his lovely little sister received a lot of attention. This happens to adults as well. We like to have other people's attention and to be approved by them. At such moments we cling to the importance of self, there is conceit. Without the Buddha's teaching we would not know when there is conceit.

Acharn explained that when intellectual understanding of the level of pariyatti has become firm it can condition right awareness of the level of satipaṭṭhāna. There is not any idea of "I prepare, I will do" but right awareness arises unexpectedly by conditions. It is most important to remember that understanding is anattā and that it develops because of conditions. We should not turn away from the present object and look for a specific method to cause understanding to grow.

One of our friends remarked: "The more we hear, come to the sessions and hear new terms, the more we become agitated by intellectual understanding." Acharn answered: "It indicates that it is 'you' who studies, there is no understanding of realities as not 'you'. It brings about the idea of 'shall I do this, shall I do that'. That is the wrong study of Abhidhamma because it does not eliminate the idea of self. How deeply rooted it is."

She explained that only the Buddha's words can condition right understanding, not one's own thinking or the guidance of someone else. There can be very firm confidence in the teachings. Realities arise by conditions and fall away again. Even doubt is real, it is not self. Usually we have an idea of my doubt, but paññā can see it as it is. She said: "It does not matter what reality arises, it is conditioned. That is the way to let go of the idea of self; by understanding that particular object, right then."

People often wonder what they should do to have more wholesomeness in their life and more understanding. It is important to remember that there is no doer, no person who can do anything at all. Only citta accompanied by cetasikas can perform functions. These are fleeting phenomena, they fall away instantly. When we think of them they have fallen away already, so, how can they be a self that is doing or acting? Intellectually, this can be understood, but realizing the truth at the present moment when citta, cetasika or rūpa appears that is another matter. We are so used to take them for "self" or "mine", and this wrong idea cannot be eliminated soon. Intellectual understanding of seeing now, hearing now, thinking now can become firmer and then it can be a condition for satipaṭṭhāna, direct awareness of whatever appears. There should be no selection of the object of mindfulness, the object is just whatever appears by conditions. We cannot select seeing as object of mindfulness, maybe at a given moment there is a condition for hearing, and only one reality at a time can be object of mindfulness. It is totally unexpected what reality appears, we never know the next moment: it may be kindness or selfishness. In this way the truth of anattā can become a little clearer: there is no doer, there is no one who makes such or such dhamma arise.

Kusala cittas and akusala cittas alternate all the time and we may
wonder how we can know when there is kusala citta and when akusala
citta. When we rejoice in other people's kusala, kusala citta arises, but
in between also akusala cittas arise when we are attached to them. A
kind and generous friend brought us several times at luncheon a special dessert. We appreciated her kindness but also akusala cittas with
attachment arose. Acharn remarked: "Everything is dhamma." We
are likely to forget this and we take kusala citta and akusala citta for
self. When we find it important to have kusala citta instead of akusala
citta we cling again to the idea of self. Everything is dhamma, non-self.
Whatever arises is conditioned.

Jonothan remarked that the teaching is about the understanding
of the presently arisen dhammas. It does not matter whether there is
attachment or not, also attachment can be object of awareness and right
understanding. We should not limit the dhammas that can be object
of awareness. Instead of just wanting to have more kusala in a day
one should have more understanding of whatever dhamma arises at the
present moment.

During the discussions several questions about samatha or the development of calm were raised. Acharn explained that we should consider
what true calm is: being away from akusala. In samatha calm is developed to a high degree so that jhāna can be attained.

Calm suppresses the hindrances[3] and it is opposed to restlessness,
uddhacca.

The aim of samatha is to be free from sense impressions that are
bound up with defilements. Right understanding is necessary for the
development of calm, there has to be precise understanding of the characteristic of calm so that it is known when kusala citta with calm arises
and when attachment to calm arises.

There is also calm in the development of insight. Acharn explained
that every moment of kusala is calm, there are no attachment, aversion
or ignorance. Every kusala citta is accompanied by the cetasika calm,
passaddhi[4]. When there is right understanding of nāma and rūpa, the

---

[3]The hindrances (nīvaraṇa) are the defilements of sensuous desire, ill will, sloth
and torpor, restlessness and worry, doubt.

[4]Actually, there are two cetasikas which are passaddhi: calm of body (kāya passaddhi) and calm of mind (citta passaddhi). Calm of body pertains to the mental

six doors are guarded at that moment and there is true calm. When one has not heard the Buddha's teachings, one knows about good and bad deeds, but there is no precise understanding. There is no understanding of realities as non-self. One may take for calm what is not calm and cling to a conventional idea of calm which is actually a feeling of relaxation with attachment.

People are inclined to believe that there is awareness, sati, when one observes what one is doing. Sarah said that the idea of observing is not sati that naturally arises. No one can stop akusala citta from arising. Through more understanding of dhammas as anattā there will be less the idea of observing or selecting an object of awareness.

At the end of the sessions one of the nuns spoke very well on the development of right understanding. She used to think that she could attain nibbāna during this life, but now she realized that the development of understanding is bound to take a very long time. She had understood that one should not cling to terms, but truly understand characteristics of realities. She appreciated the Dhamma she had heard and she had understood that the conditions for understanding are listening and wise consideration of what one hears.

---

body: And here 'body' means the three (mental) aggregates, feeling, perception and formations, see Dhs.40.

35

Diverse Topics of Discussion

"This life was the future life of last life, and it will be the past life of the next life." Acharn repeated this many times during our journey in order to remind us that we are at this moment in the cycle of birth and death. We cling to our family and friends, but they will not follow us to the next life. We find our life very important, but this life will be past life very soon, since each life does not last long. Then we will not remember who were our dear ones.

During all the discussions in Vietnam and also in the different locations in Thailand where we stayed, questions were raised about life and death, kamma and its result, conditions for kusala and akusala, the development of calm and of insight. In all her answers, Acharn would help the listeners to understand the present reality. She said many times that each word of the Buddha's teachings leads to right understanding of reality now.

She said that we should even understand one word: "dhamma", and she explained: "Dhamma is a reality, but it is no one. At the moment of seeing it is a dhamma. At the moment of hearing it is a different

dhamma. By different conditions it arises and falls away, there is no
self, no one at all."

Whatever is real is dhamma. Time and again a dhamma appears
through one of the senses or the mind-door. Whatever appears now is
a reality that is conditioned. Otherwise it could not arise at all. Paññā
of the level of pariyatti can begin to understand the characteristic of
whatever appears, and there is no need to name it. Pariyatti is not book
study. Realities work their own way by themselves, no one can make
them arise. When this has been understood we are less inclined to cling
to a collection of things, a whole, or a being, like before. Understanding
leads to detachment.

There are two kinds of reality: the reality that experiences an object
or nāma and the reality that does not know anything, or rūpa. Seeing
experiences an object, it is nāma, whereas visible object does not know
anything, it is rūpa. When seeing arises there is also visible object but
they have different characteristics and these can be known one at a time.
This cannot be realized in the beginning, but when paññā is more developed it can distinguish their different characteristics. Understanding
of the level of pariyatti is not sufficient yet to understand directly just
one reality at a time.

Acharn reminded us time and again: "Study one reality at a time,
until one sees it as not self. We may say: 'seeing is a reality', but that is
not enough. We should be careful in considering what is heard: 'Seeing
sees what?' It takes time to get used to the fact that what appears is
not self. It is only a dhamma that can impinge on the eyebase and that
arises and falls away. When we think: 'I see someone or something' the
understanding is not enough."

When we cling to the idea that a flower is seen, a table is seen, we
have to listen to the Dhamma and consider the truth again and again
in order to have less ignorance. The Buddha and his great disciples
recognized different people and saw different things such as a mountain
or table, but they had no wrong view, they clearly distinguished between
ultimate realities and conventional truth or concepts that can be objects
of thinking.

People usually think of life and death in conventional sense. However, the Buddha's teachings lead to the understanding of what is real in
the ultimate sense: citta, cetasika, rūpa and nibbāna. Everything else is

241

conventional truth, not ultimate truth. The last moment of life is a citta, the dying-consciousness, cuti-citta. It depends on kamma when it is time for the arising of the cuti-citta and nobody can prevent its arising. It is immediately followed by the rebirth-consciousness, paṭisandhi-citta, of the next life. The dying-consciousness and the rebirth-consciousness are both results of kamma, vipākacittas. Kusala citta and akusala citta may have the intensity to motivate deeds, kusala kamma and akusala kamma through body, speech or mind. Kamma is actually the cetasika volition or cetanā. When it is kusala kamma or akusala kamma it can produce result, vipāka. Kamma can produce vipāka in the form of rebirth-consciousness and in the course of life by way of pleasant and unpleasant experiences through eyes, ears, nose, tongue and body-consciousness.

Kusala kamma and akusala kamma are mental and, thus, they can be accumulated from one citta to the next citta and so also from past lives to the rebirth-consciousness of this life. All the kammas that have been accumulated and are carried on to the rebirth-consciousness have the potential to produce their appropriate results in the following lives. The rebirth-consciousness is followed by other cittas, bhavanga-cittas or life-continuum. These cittas are also vipākacittas produced by the same kamma that produced the rebirth-consciousness and they experience the same object as the rebirth-consciousness. We do not know what that object is, it is not experienced through any one of the six doorways. They arise throughout life at those moments that there is not the experience of objects through one of the six doorways by cittas arising in processes of cittas, such as seeing, hearing or thinking. Thus, they arise time and again in between the different processes of cittas. They also arise in deep sleep, when we are not dreaming. They keep the continuity in the life of an individual.

Seeing is vipākacitta and it arises in a process of cittas. It is preceded and followed by other cittas that do not see but nevertheless experience visible object while they perform other functions. A rūpa such as visible object lasts longer than citta, it is experienced by several cittas arising in a process. Seeing is only one moment of experiencing visible object and it falls away immediately. Very shortly after it has fallen away kusala cittas or akusala cittas that experience the same visible object arise and fall away very rapidly. They experience it with wholesomeness or unwholesomeness and this is conditioned by the wholesome or unwholesome inclinations that have been accumulated from one citta to the next one. When that sense-door process is over it is followed by a mind-door process which experiences visible object through the mind-door and later on there are other mind-door processes which think about the visible object.

During our life the experience of pleasant objects and unpleasant objects alternate: gain and loss, fame and obscurity, praise and blame, bodily wellbeing and pain. These are among the "worldly conditions" the Buddha spoke about. The moments of vipāka are extremely brief and when we think of the source of our experiences, they are already gone. The moments of thinking are no longer vipāka, but usually akusala cittas and these are conditioned by the accumulation of akusala in the past. This type of condition is different from kamma that produces vipāka[1]. When someone else speaks in a harsh way to us, we are inclined to blame that person and we take the unpleasant experience for "mine". Then we do not think wisely about cause and result. In the ultimate sense there are only conditioned realities that just arise and appear very shortly. Kamma produces hearing which is vipāka, and thinking with akusala citta is caused by our accumulated defilements. There is no person who inflicts sorrow upon another person and no person who experiences it. There are only conditioned realities arising and falling away.

Cittas arising in a process do so in a specific order while they perform each their own function. The citta that adverts to an object that presents itself arises before seeing or another one of the sense-cognitions, and kusala cittas or akusala cittas arise later on in that process. One may wonder what the use is of knowing such details. The Buddha taught proximity-condition, anantara-paccaya of cittas, meaning that cittas succeed one another: when one citta falls away it is immediately succeeded by the next one. He also taught contiguity-condition, samanantara-paccaya, meaning that cittas succeed one another in a fixed order that cannot be altered. This clearly shows the nature of

---

[1]Kusala kamma or akusala kamma that produces later on its appropriate result, vipāka, is one type of condition, kamma-condition. Wholesome and unwholesome inclinations that have been accumulated can condition the arising of kusala citta or akusala citta later on and that is another type of condition: natural decisive support-condition, pakatūpanissaya-paccaya.

anattā of cittas, they cannot be directed or controlled. There isn't anybody who is master of the cittas that arise and could change the order of their arising.

We are in the cycle of birth and death right now. Vipākacitta arises by way of an experience through one of the sense-doors, and then defilements are likely to arise. These may motivate kamma and kamma produces vipāka. Again defilements will arise and motivate kamma that produces vipāka. In this way the cycle goes on and on. All this occurs now, anywhere, at any time.

Many times Acharn said that we should not cling to names and terms, but that we should understand the characteristics of realities that appear. Citta is the faculty of experiencing an object and it is assisted by at least seven cetasikas that accompany it, such as feeling, remembrance (saññā), one-pointedness (ekaggata cetasika). When we read about cetasikas such as energy or effort (in Pali: viriya), we may think of their meaning in conventional sense, and then misunderstandings may arise. We believe that a self can make an effort to have more kusala and right understanding. We should remember that the cetasika viriya may arise with many cittas though not with all cittas, not with seeing and the other sense-cognitions and a few other cittas. Thus, effort may be kusala, right effort, or akusala, wrong effort. When we make an effort to have kusala citta, we are likely to cling to an idea of self who wants to direct cittas. Without knowing it we may take wrong effort for right effort. When understanding of the present reality is developed more, it is paññā that will know when citta and cetasikas are akusala and when kusala. We cannot find out by thinking about it. Several times we were warned not to try to work things out, then there is just thinking with an idea of self behind it.

We learn from the texts that some cetasikas are roots, hetus. Ignorance (moha) attachment (lobha) and aversion (dosa) are three akusala hetus. Understanding (paññā or amoha), non-attachment (alobha) and non-aversion (adosa) are three sobhana hetus, beautiful roots. A root, hetu, is the foundation of akusala citta or kusala citta. Ignorance accompanies every akusala citta. Acharn explained the roots with examples from daily life in order to help us to know their characteristics when they appear. They are not just classifications in the textbook and we should remember this whenever we read about the different cittas, cetasikas and rūpas. She said:

"We are attached to what is completely gone, but because of moha, ignorance, it seems to last. Each word of the Buddha pertains to right understanding of realities. Akusala hetus and sobhana hetus are opposites. At this moment of not understanding realities there is moha. A moment of understanding is not self but paññā cetasika. The subtlety of the teachings is that they are all about now. Otherwise it would be useless to listen, there would only be different words. What we take for the world are only citta, cetasika and rūpa. It is not you who understands but paññā cetasika. Each reality is different at each moment. Moha takes realities as a whole, such as a flower. Without seeing colours can there be a concept of flower?

When there is right understanding there is some detachment from ignorance and clinging. Life is like a dream, the world of people, 'I' and things. Actually, there is no one, only realities arising and falling away in succession...

There is seeing; it is citta, it is accompanied by cetasikas. Learn to understand that it is not 'I', that it is citta. There can be conditions for direct experience, paṭipatti. Without pariyatti this is impossible. The Buddha did not tell anybody to gain it. He taught to understand what appears now, as it is. If this is not known how can there be paṭipatti. If paññā is not fully developed there will never be the realization of the four noble Truths, paṭivedha. Who knows what has been accumulated from aeons ago up until now."

Most of the time there is forgetfulness of realities instead of the development of understanding. We have accumulated so much ignorance and forgetfulness.

Sarah gave us some good reminders about forgetfulness of realities. She said: "There is forgetfulness and it is just a dhamma, falling away instantly. There is not my understanding or my forgetfulness. If we think: 'How can I have less forgetfulness' there is more attachment. It can be known when it appears as just a conditioned reality in daily life. We always follow the objects of desire and how ridiculous is this, because they fall away instantly. Like this morning, we were clinging to visible object, clinging to sound, but they have fallen away, just to be forgotten. Like now, who can remember them. Usually there is so much attachment to pleasant feeling, and we are disturbed by unpleasant feeling. Attachment is so common, it is not a matter of trying not to have it, trying not to be forgetful. But we should just understand what appears at this moment."

We all have defilements that we would rather suppress instead of knowing them as conditioned dhammas. The sotāpanna, the person who has eradicated wrong view and wrong practice, knows all the defilements that arise as only a dhamma, non-self. It may be ignorance, forgetfulness, subtle or strong lobha or conceit, māna. Their characteristics can only be known as they arise and appear at the present moment. If we do not realize as they are the defilements that arise, they will never be eradicated. Paññā can only investigate attachment when it has arisen. Paññā of the level of satipaṭṭhāna understands attachment little by little.

36

The Benefit of listening

The understanding of anattā begins with listening, considering, investigating the present reality. If the Buddha had not taught the truth of realities we would not know that seeing is not self, hearing or thinking are not self. We can never listen and consider enough. Acharn repeated what she had said before about the three kinds of gocara[1], resorts or objects: upanissaya gocara, the object that is a strong support; arakkha gocara, the object that is a protection; upanibandha gocara, the object that one can depend on.

Upanissaya gocara is the object that is a strong support; there should be considering, understanding right now. Seeing is not self. Without

---

[1] Gocara is resort or pasture. The Visuddhimagga, I, 49-51 mentions three kinds: resort as support, as guarding and as anchoring. Proper resort as support, upanissaya, is a good friend "in whose presence one hears what has not been heard, corrects what has been heard, gets rid of doubt, rectifies one's view, and gains confidence: or by training under whom one grows in faith, virtue, learning, generosity and understanding." As to proper resort as guarding (arakkha), here the Visuddhimagga gives an example of the bhikkhu who is restrained. As to proper resort as anchoring (upanibhanda), this is the four foundations of mindfulness.

247

visible object and eyebase there is no seeing. The explanations of dhammas, realities, can be a strong support to hear more, consider more, develop understanding, so that it will be a protection, arakkha gocara, from akusala, from ignorance and attachment. Acharn said about upanibhanda gocara, resort as anchoring:

"This is not going away from reality right now, not going astray to such or such story. But what is there now?"

We are often absorbed in stories, conventional realities, with attachment or worry. We think of the future, of what will happen to "self" in the future. Then we forget that whatever pleasant or unpleasant experiences we have is conditioned by kamma of the past. We think with defilements and if we had not listened to the teachings we would not know that whatever problem we have in life is caused by our own defilements. Acharn explained about understanding ultimate realities:

"Seeing arises and falls away, without understanding at all. It has to be direct understanding with direct awareness of a reality which arises and falls away. If it is not direct how can there be the understanding of the arising and falling away of realities? Seeing experiences just visible object. Where is my hand? Seeing is conditioned. Hardness appears only at the moment of touching, it is gone completely. Each moment there is a reality that experiences an object. There are many things in this room, how many moments of that which experiences are there to condition that which is seen as some 'thing', as images of this or that?"

On account of what is seen we think of many things like persons or trees, but do we realize that there must be countless moments of seeing arising and falling away to condition thinking of concepts? Seeing arises and falls away again and again and visible object appears again and again. This gives us an idea of continuity. In reality, dhammas arise and fall away extremely rapidly and only a sign or nimitta is left of them when they have fallen away already. One unit of rūpa and one citta is not known, only a sign or nimitta of a dhamma is known, as Acharn reminded us time and again. One clings to that which has gone, but only a sign is left. The reality and its nimitta can be compared to a sound and its echo. Saññā, the cetasika remembrance, marks and remembers visible object so that we perceive shape and form and this leads to recognizing different people. We remember a person wrongly as permanent. We hear many things Acharn had said before, but it is most beneficial to hear it again, to consider it again and again. This is the way understanding can gradually grow.

Acharn had spoken before about subtle defilements that arise and that are unknown. It is beneficial to hear about these again since this reminds us how little we know. It reminds us that listening and considering the Dhamma has to continue on so that understanding can grow. There are countless defilements arising that are unknown. The Buddha taught different aspects and different intensities of defilements. He taught about the subtle defilements, intoxicants or āsavas[2]. It seems that after seeing or hearing that arise now nothing else is appearing, but subtle defilements that are unknown are bound to arise after seeing and the other sense-cognitions.

Very soon after seeing has arisen and fallen away there may be a subtle clinging that is unknown. Attachment is bound to arise on account of the experience of all the sense objects, of visible object, sound, odour, flavour and tangible object. Attachment to sense objects conditions rebirth again. Attachment is a danger, but it has to be understood as a conditioned dhamma, not to be suppressed. If it is not known when it appears as only a conditioned dhamma, it can never be eradicated.

After we returned from Vietnam, a side trip to Samir Sakorn was organised the next day by Khun Keowta for a group of Thais and I was invited as well. We stayed for two days in "Ravi Home Resort" and Khun Keowta paid for our whole stay as a gift of Dhamma. We appreciated her generosity. We had a short walk to a pavillion in the middle of nature where we had a copious luncheon. A choir was singing songs for Acharn, anticipating her birthday the next day. The next day films were shown with fragments of her life, there were songs with words of praise and poems were recited in honour of her. In the morning everyone entered the room where she stayed and paid respect to her. Actually, paying respect to her is paying respect to the Dhamma. The best respect we can show is listening to the Dhamma and discussing it. Someone made a touching speech, mentioning that his father listened to Acharn's radio programs and since his father had put on the radio, he could not help listening too from his childhood on. It is so fortunate to be born a human

---

[2]These are: the canker of sensuous desire (kāmāsava), the canker of becoming (bhavāsava),the canker of wrong view (diṭṭhāsava), the canker of ignorance (avijjāsava).

so that we have an opportunity to hear the Dhamma. We cannot be sure to have such an opportunity the next life. He expressed with a song Acharn's merit.

There were several sessions with Dhamma conversations. Acharn explained that most people want to eradicate quickly attachment, lobha, the second Truth. However, first wrong view of self should be eradicated. As long as we take realities for self, defilements cannot be eradicated. When we learn that whatever reality appears is only a conditioned dhamma that cannot be controlled, we shall gradually attach less importance to them.

She also explained that we may cling with wrong view, diṭṭhi, or without wrong view, or with conceit, māna. Clinging without diṭṭhi may arise, for example, when we dress ourselves or when we are eating delicious food. There need not be any wrong view at such moments. When there is conceit we find ourselves important. Conceit may arise because of beauty, possessions, rank or work. Or because of one's skills, knowledge, education or wisdom. There may be the wish to advertise oneself because of these things. We like to be honoured and praised. When we are dissatisfied with the way other people treat us there are bound to be moments of aversion, but there may also be moments of conceit. We find ourselves important and we are disturbed when others do not treat us the way we like to be treated. We tend to have prejudices about certain people, even about our relatives, we may look down on them. We should find out whether we have conceit when we are together with other people. There are many moments of forgetfulness and then we do not notice when there is conceit. A moment of conceit, of upholding ourselves, can arise so easily.

There were a few other trips in Thailand with Dhamma conversations in English. We went to Nakorn Nayok, to a place where we had been before. Vietnamese friends joined us and the sessions were held in their bungalow. They arranged everything for us with great hospitality, setting out the chairs, serving us drinks and snacks. They helped me with great kindness in many ways, when I was tired while walking. We had breakfast and other meals in the restaurant near a waterfall, and Tran Thai made delicious Vietnamese coffee for me.

We also went together with our Vietnamese friends to Kaeng Krachan, the place where Acharn and Khun Duangduen often stay. When we arrived at Kaeng Krachan, Sarah and Jonothan had to undergo a test of patience. Although our bungalows were reserved ahead of time, they were not available since the former occupants did not want to leave. Sarah and Jonothan spoke to the office and waited for a very long time. At last bungalows were assigned to us. I was in a bungalow next to Ann and Glen. One morning Ann helped me walking back from the restaurant which is on a hill, to the bungalow, in one hand holding Glen's breakfast in a covered dish to keep his toast and eggs warm and with the other hand giving me a support while walking.

We had at first sessions outside in the garden but since a cold wind was blowing one of our friends, Khun Bencha, brought shawls for everyone. Later on we continued the sessions in the bungalow of our Vietnamese friends. In the early morning they were already sweeping the place and cleaning up before setting out all our chairs. I came early and could lie down on a long chair enjoying the view of nature outside. Our friends made me feel at home.

During all our discussions we were reminded that book study, remembrance of names and terms, is not the same as understanding the reality that appears at the present moment. Acharn said:

"We better not go far away to other subjects, but what about now? The reality which is seen cannot be the reality which sees it. It takes years, a long time, to realize this. Seeing, the experience, has no shape and form. Attend more to seeing now. Get closer to whatever is now: hearing now, thinking now. Otherwise we are lost in the world of words and thinking. This is the beginning of the development of the perfections, pāramīs: really understanding that there is no one, only different elements. We do not have to call it pāramī, but the understanding begins to develop and this is the beginning of the pāramīs. No matter what kind of kusala arises, when there is no understanding it is not a perfection.

For right understanding to be keen and very firm, it needs the perfections of truthfulness, resolution and the other perfections because there is not enough accumulation of kusala. At the moment of kusala citta there are no attachment, lobha, aversion, dosa, and ignorance, moha. Each moment is conditioned and nobody can change it."

Seeing sees visible object, but they are different realities. Seeing is a mental reality, nāma, and visible object is a physical reality, rūpa. Even so, hearing is nāma and sound is rūpa. Nāma and rūpa have different characteristics, but, as Acharn said, it takes a long time to directly understand these different characteristics. Only paññā that precisely understands the present reality can distinguish different characteristics of realities.

Listening to the Dhamma at this moment and all the moments of considering it are not in vain, but they are accumulated, not lost. The understanding of realities at this moment falls away together with the citta it accompanies, but understanding is accumulated from one citta to the following citta and, thus, there are conditions for the arising of understanding again.

Towards the end of my stay in Thailand a short journey was organized for a group of Thai friends to Chiengmai, Lampun and Chiengrai, in the North of Thailand. Ann, Glen and I joined this group. Acharn explained that paññā can understand sound appearing now. The future has not come yet and what is past has gone. What has fallen away cannot be known. Acharn reminds us time and again to investigate the present moment, since that is the only way to penetrate the truth of nāma and rūpa. Sometimes there are conditions for the arising of sati, sometimes not, nobody can cause the arising of sati. We may enjoy our meal but when sati does not arise there is ignorance of realities such as hardness or flavour which may appear.

I was mentioning that appreciating someone else's good deed is kusala citta, but that also akusala citta arises with attachment to that person. Cittas arise and fall away so rapidly and therefore it is difficult to distinguish between kusala and akusala. Acharn said: "Everything is dhamma is the answer. Not self." I said that I often forget that understanding is not self. Khun Unnop remarked: "The idea of self has not been eradicated yet." When akusala citta arises paññā can know it as a dhamma, not self and this is most important.

Straight after the afternoon session in Chiengmai we went to Lampun, to visit an annex to "Dhamma Home" in Chiengmai. This was the first time for Acharn to visit this place. It was a traditional Thai house that had to be reached by following a path that went high up. Khun Porntip had bought this house to be used for regular Dhamma meetings. We were received with warm hospitality and many different kinds of food were offered to us. First Acharn had a more private conversation with friends who were very interested in the development of right understanding. Then there was a general introduction by everyone who was present, very informal and friendly. We returned late to Chiengmai where we had another session the next morning, and after that we went by car to Chiengrai, to a meditation center we had visited last year. There we were received by the same kind lady we knew from last year. She is a very keen listener to Acharn's explanations of the Dhamma. Acharn said that paññā cannot be developed quickly, that it takes a long time. But we should not be neglectful since life is very short. Khun Unnop remarked that the problem is that it is unknown when there is neglectfulness.

Acharn explained about seeing: "Seeing now is seeing, it is not eyesight or visible object. It is the result of kamma. Pleasant and unpleasant objects are seen, we cannot select any object. We cannot know whether the object that is seen is pleasant or unpleasant, cittas arise and fall away very rapidly." It seems that we see immediately people and things, but that is thinking on account of what is seen, it is not the experience of visible object.

Acharn explained that we have to look into the mirror, and then we shall know when we are in the world of ignorance. It seems that we are really inside the mirror, but when we touch the mirror only hardness appears.

We climbed up a hill where our hostess had a delicious luncheon prepared so that we could enjoy the meal and the view outside. In between we talked about Dhamma.

37

The Four Noble Truths

After the Dhamma sessions in Saigon we went for a few days to Muine, a seaside resort at the Chinese South Sea. Here we discussed the four noble Truths. In his first sermon the Buddha explained the four noble Truths. We read in the "Kindred Sayings" (V, Mahāvagga, Ch II, § 1, Setting in Motion the Wheel of Dhamma)[1]:

> "Thus have I heard. On one occasion the Blessed One was dwelling at Bārāṇasī in the Deer Park at Isipatana. There the Blessed One addressed the Bhikkhus of the group of five thus: 'Bhikkhus, these two extremes should not be followed by one who has gone forth into homelessness. What two? The pursuit of sensual happiness in sensual pleasures, which is low, vulgar, the way of worldlings, ignoble, unbeneficial; and the pursuit of self-mortification, which is painful, ignoble, unbeneficial. Without veering towards either of these extremes, the Tathāgata has awakened to the middle way,

---

[1] I used the translation by Ven. Bodhi.

255

which gives rise to vision, which gives rise to knowledge, which leads to peace, to direct knowledge, to enlightenment, to Nibbāna.

And what, bhikkhus, is that middle way awakened to by the Tathāgata, which gives rise to vision... which leads to Nibbāna? It is this Noble Eightfold Path; that is, right view, *right intention*[2], right speech, right action, right livelihood, right effort, right mindfulness, right concentration...

Now this, bhikkhus is the noble truth of suffering[3]: birth is suffering, ageing is suffering, illness is suffering, death is suffering, union with what is displeasing is suffering; separation from what is pleasing is suffering; not to get what one wants is suffering; in brief, the five aggregates subject to clinging are suffering.

Now this, bhikkhus is the noble truth of the origin of suffering: it is this craving which leads to renewed existence, accompanied by delight and lust, seeking delight here and there; that is, craving for sensual pleasures, craving for existence, craving for extermination.

Now this, bhikkhus, is the noble truth of the cessation of suffering: it is the remainderless fading away and cessation of that same craving, the giving up and relinquishing of it, freedom from it, nonreliance on it.

Now this, bhikkhus, is the noble truth of the way leading to the cessation of suffering: it is this Noble Eightfold Path; that is, right view... right concentration.

'This is the noble truth of suffering': thus, bhikkhus, in regard to things unheard before, there arose in me vision, knowledge, wisdom, true knowledge, and light.

---

[2]Ven. Bodhi and other translators have right intention, but sammā-sankappa is right thinking. Intention is the usual translation of cetanā cetasika, but this is not a factor of the eightfold Path.

[3]This is the translation of dukkha.

'This noble truth of suffering is to be fully understood': thus, bhikkhus, in regard to things unheard before, there arose in me vision, knowledge, wisdom, true knowledge, and light.

'This noble truth of suffering has been fully understood': thus, bhikkhus, in regard to things unheard before, there arose in me vision, knowledge, wisdom, true knowledge, and light."

The same is said about the origin of suffering, its cessation and the Path leading to its cessation.

In the preceding text we see three rounds or phases:

Sacca ñāṇa: 'this is the noble truth of suffering', clear understanding of all dhammas in daily life appearing now that are dukkha. All conditioned realities that are impermanent, are dukkha.

This is pariyatti, but pariyatti is not theory, it pertains to the dhamma that appears at the present moment. Sacca ñāṇa is pariyatti that has become firm so that it can condition direct understanding.

Kicca ñāṇa: 'Now this noble truth of suffering ought to be fully understood'.

Understanding the task (kicca), the development of direct understanding of the characteristics of all dhammas as they appear one at a time through the senses and the mind-door. This is satipaṭṭhāna, and this is the way dhammas will be directly known as impermanent, dukkha and non-self.

Kata ñāṇa: 'Now this noble truth of suffering has been fully understood'.

This refers to the direct realization, paṭivedha, of the truth that is reached when understanding of realities has been developed.

These three rounds pertain to each one of the four noble truths, and, thus, there are twelve modes of the three rounds. Kicca ñāṇa begins when awareness and right understanding is developed of all realities appearing through the six doors. This is the only way eventually to realize the cessation of dukkha.

Acharn often mentioned the levels of pariyatti, paṭipatti and paṭivedha, and the three rounds of sacca ñāṇa, kicca ñāṇa and kata ñāṇa. People may think that after reading the texts it is time for them to practise.

They do not realize that the right conditions are necessary for paññā to develop stage by stage and that is likely to take many lives.

In Muine we discussed the different stages of understanding the noble Truths. Acharn asked us whether the understanding of the first noble Truth, of dukkha, is firm enough. Paññā should know nothing else but what appears now. What else will be the realization of dukkha if it is not understanding of what appears now.

In the sutta quoted above we read about all the different aspects of dukkha, and at the end the Buddha said: "the five aggregates subject to clinging are suffering." The five khandhas are all conditioned realities. They arise and fall away instantly, and, thus, they are dukkha, not worth clinging to. Thus, the first noble Truth of dukkha is not merely bodily and mental suffering, it is the unsatisfactoriness due to the impermanence of all conditioned realities.

Acharn explained: "There should be no trying to understand the four noble Truths, but now is the first noble Truth. The impermanence of this moment is so fast that it seems that nothing arises and falls away. Detach from the idea of 'I' or something permanent. Pariyatti is not hearing or thinking but study of what appears now. There should be more understanding of non-self. There is seeing, but no understanding of seeing. We need hearing more and more so that there are conditions for direct understanding in daily life only, of different elements arising by different conditions."

The succession of dhammas is so rapid that they seem to stay. Acharn said that it seems to us that we see not visible object but people, that we hear words, not sound, because of the continuous arising and falling away of realities. The first Truth is very subtle and there can be wise consideration arising just because of conditions. In other words, there is no self who can make wise consideration arise.

Acharn said that we cling to nothing. What has fallen away is no more, but we still cling to it. We shall not understand what dukkha is if we are ignorant of the reality appearing now. We have to distinguish between what is reality now and what is only a conventional idea or "story". Visible object is a reality, it arises and falls away. On account of what is seen we think of "something", such as a glass or a tree. These are ideas, not realities that can be experienced one at a time through one of the six doorways.

Acharn explained that attachment and ignorance are the cause of
dukkha. We are attached to all objects we experience but we do not
realize when attachment arises. We fall into the trap of lobha time and
again. Whatever arises does so since it is conditioned by ignorance and
attachment. There is not yet direct awareness and direct understanding,
but it is sacca ñāṇa that really understands what causes the arising of
dukkha. The first Truth should be known and the second Truth should
be abandoned.

When intellectual understanding of the level of pariyatti is firm it is
sacca ñāṇa: clear understanding of all dhammas in daily life that are
dukkha. One does not move away from the present object.

Nibbāna is the end of attachment, and there can be firm understanding that there is freedom from conditioned realities that are arising and
falling away and that are unsatisfactory. One can come to understand
that there is an unconditioned reality that is the end to dukkha and one
will have strong confidence that there can be the direct realization of
nibbāna.

There is a way to reach the end of the cycle of birth and death
and that is the development of the eightfold Path, the fourth Truth.
When understanding of the Path has become well established one does
not deviate from the right Path anymore. One does not search for
another practice in order to reach the goal more quickly. The more
understanding grows, the less one clings to a result.

When there is firm confidence in the four noble Truths there can be
a condition for direct awareness and understanding which is the second
round of the four noble Truths, kicca ñāṇa.

Acharn said: "There will be detachment gradually, all the time, at
the moment of understanding. When hearing the Dhamma one finds
it so difficult, but since it is the teaching of the Enlightened One how
can it be easy? But by having confidence there begins to be direct
understanding or satipaṭṭhāna of whatever appears now, by conditions.
The more right understanding grows, the more we see the anattaness
and it becomes firmer and firmer. It is very natural."

I asked whether the understanding of the arising and falling away of
the present reality is already a highly developed paññā.

Acharn answered: "Of what degree, of the level of sacca ñāṇa or of
kicca ñāṇa? Sacca ñāṇa is not kicca ñāṇa."

I asked: "How can arising and falling away be understood on the level of sacca ñāṇa?"

Acharn said: "Is seeing now permanent? Is thinking now permanent?"

I answered that they are impermanent.

Acharn explained that the fact that I said that they are impermanent showed that there is more confidence in the truth.

The second round, kicca ñāṇa, of the four noble Truths is satipaṭṭhāna, direct awareness and understanding of whatever reality appears. When right awareness arises it can be known that it is uncontrollable. It arises unexpectedly, by conditions. Hearing Dhamma at this moment and considering the truth of it is never lost, it is accumulated in the following cittas, on and on, so that there are conditions for its arising again. Like now, we may have a little understanding of explanations about realities, and such moments do not stay. Other cittas arise that experience for example a pleasant flavour we enjoy. We may be absorbed in savoury food. But still, in all those different cittas there is paññā accumulated. Then we listen again to the Dhamma and there is a new opportunity for the arising of understanding. Each time we understand a little more, a little more.

Patience is needed in the development of understanding and one should not be discouraged if paññā does not arise often. If it would be impossible to develop paññā of the levels of sacca ñāṇa, of kicca ñāṇa and even of kata ñāṇa, the Buddha would not teach it.

We read in the "Gradual Sayings, Book of the Twos, Ch II, § 9[4] that the Buddha said:

"Abandon evil, O monks! One can abandon evil, O monks! If it were impossible to abandon evil, I would not ask you to do so. But as it can be done, therefore I say 'Abandon evil!'

If this abandoning of evil would bring harm and suffering, I would not ask you to abandon it. But as the abandoning of evil brings weal and happiness, therefore I say, 'Abandon evil!'

---

[4]I used the translation of Ven. Nyanaponika, BPS Kandy 1970.

Cultivate the good, O monks! One can cultivate what is good, O monks. If it were impossible to cultivate the good, I would not ask you to do so. But as it can be done, therefore I say, 'Cultivate the good!'

If this cultivation of the good would bring harm and suffering, I would not ask you to cultivate it. But as the cultivation of the good brings weal and happiness, therefore I say, 'Cultivate the good!' "

People wonder about the characteristic of sati. Sati or awareness accompanies every citta. It is non-forgetful of the object citta experiences. When we are giving with generosity, the kusala citta is non-forgetful of generosity. When intellectual understanding of the present reality arises, sati is non-forgetful of that reality. When understanding of the level of satipaṭṭhāna arises sati is non-forgetful of the nāma or rūpa that appears. At that moment sati is mindful and paññā understands the characteristic of the present reality.

When people read in the "Satipaṭṭhāna Sutta" that the bhikkhu should be aware while he is standing, walking, sitting or lying down, they take this as a specific practice. However, the Buddha taught that there can be awareness of realities during all one's daily activities very naturally, no matter in what situation. Someone asked when he intends to drink and takes up a glass whether that is mindfulness. At that moment one thinks of a situation and of concepts such as a glass, whereas sati of the level of satipaṭṭhāna is mindful of one nāma or rūpa as it appears through one of the six doorways. It is essential to know when one is thinking of concepts or ideas and when there is mindfulness of one reality at a time. When one touches a glass hardness may appear and this may be known as a kind of rūpa, a physical reality, and then one does not think of a "thing" that stays.

When one has the intention to be aware, there is still the idea of self who wants to know realities. At the moment of right understanding of realities as they appear one at a time there is no one, no world, only the experience and that which is experienced. Paññā abandons attachment to wrong practice.

The reality that experiences an object is quite different from the reality that does not experience anything. Each citta must experience an

262   CHAPTER 37. THE FOUR NOBLE TRUTHS

object, if there were no citta nothing could appear. We have heard this many times, but it always seems new to us, we did not consider this enough. When hardness appears or seeing appears the truth of realities can be investigated so that pariyatti can become firm intellectual understanding, sacca ñāṇa, which can condition direct understanding, satipaṭṭhāna. I am most grateful for all the explanations and reminders of the truth given by Acharn and friends. Those are the greatest treasures one could possibly receive. All the discussions we had are a way of sharing the gift of Dhamma.

Hardness appears at the moment of touching. It is not a table, it is not my hand but it is only a reality: a khanda, an element, an āyatana [5], dukkha ariya sacca, a reality that arises and falls away. All conditioned realities are impermanent and dukkha and all dhammas, including nibbāna, are anattā. What the Buddha taught was not his own invention, he taught the true nature of all realities. He had by his supreme wisdom penetrated the truth and he taught the truth to others. The Sammāsambuddha had realized all by himself, through his enlightenment, the truth of all dhammas.

We read in the "Gradual Sayings," Book of the Threes, Ch XIV, §134, Appearance, that the Buddha said:

> "Monks, whether there be an appearance or non-appearance of a Tathāgata, this causal law of nature, this orderly fixing of dhammas prevails, namely, all phenomena are impermanent. About this a Tathāgata is fully enlightened, he fully understands it. So enlightened and understanding he declares, teaches and makes it plain. He shows it, he opens it up, explains and makes it clear: this fact that all phenomena are impermanent."

The same is said about the truth that all conditioned dhammas are dukkha and that all dhammas are non-self.

The Buddha respected the Dhamma he had penetrated. We read in the "Kindred Sayings" (I, Sagāthāvagga, Ch VI, §2, Holding in Rever-

---

[5]Realities can be classified as āyatanas. The inner ayatanas are: the eyesense and the other senses and citta, and the outer ayatanas are: the sense objects and dhammāyatana, including cetasikas, subtle rūpas and nibbāna. The āyatanas show the aspect of association of realities for the experience of objects.

ence) that the Buddha, shortly after his enlightenment, while staying at Uruvelā, was considering to whom he could pay respect. But he could find nobody in the world who was more accomplished than himself in morality, concentration, insight, emancipation, or knowledge of emancipation. We then read that he said:

"This Dhamma then, wherein I am supremely enlightened –

what if I were to live under It, paying It honour and respect."

Part VII

The Present Moment

38

Preface

A ten days journey to Sri Lanka with English discussions was organized in October 2015 by Sarah and Khun Toey. Preceding this journey we stayed two days in Nakorn Nayok, in Thailand, where we had Dhamma discussions with Tadao from Japan, Ann from Canada, Sukinder and Khun Metta who live in Bangkok, and other friends. I found that it is most valuable to be in the company of good Dhamma friends. I am so grateful for all the good reminders of the truth about realities appearing in daily life. Early morning in the hotel in Sri Lanka Sarah reminded me that all the problems with difficult steps I had to take (very high and very deep), problems with the laundry, the bathroom, stiffness, are nothing compared to the Dhamma we received. I was so glad to hear again and again: "understanding is not yet firm enough, not enough yet." I found it most helpful that Sarah and Jon elaborated on the subjects Achan spoke about and gave us reminders of reality time and again.

I admired Jon's translation from Thai into English of all the details of the Vinaya Khun Sangob gave us, even including technical subjects

267

like the Sima (measurement pertaining to boundaries).

The sessions in Sri Lanka were mostly two hours in the morning and two hours or more in the afternoon. Achan never thinks of her own comfort or rest. That is why she decided, when we were in our hotel in Negombo (near Colombo), to travel during our stay there, to Colombo, which meant four hours in the traffic each day. In Colombo we went to the Buddhist Cultural Center to have Dhamma discussions with monks, sisters and other people. Even after returning to the hotel she would still be with us for Dhamma discussions. I am very grateful for all the reminders she gave about "dhamma now".

39

Concepts and Realities

The aim of the Buddha's teachings is to develop right understanding of the dhamma appearing at this moment and this will lead to detachment from the idea of self and to the eradication of all that is unwholesome.

We read in the "Khuddhaka Nikaya" in the Commentary to the "Basket of Conduct", the "Conduct of Yudanjaya", about the beginning of the development of paññā during the life the Bodhisatta was young Yudanjaya:

> "In his life when the Bodhisatta was Yudanjaya, he was the eldest son of the King and had the rank of the viceroy. He fulfilled every day maha-dana, the giving of an abundance of gifts. One day when he visited the royal park he saw the dewdrops hanging like a string of pearls on the tree-tops, the grass-tips, the end of the branches and on the spiders' webs.
>
> The prince enjoyed himself in the royal park and when the sun rose higher all the dewdrops that were hanging there disintegrated and disappeared. He reflected thus: 'These

dewdrops came into being and then disappeared. Even so
are conditioned realities, the lives of all beings; they are like
the dewdrops hanging on the grass-tips.' He felt a sense of
urgency and became disenchanted with worldly life, so that
he took leave of his parents and became a recluse."

The Bodhisatta realized the impermanence of realities and made this
predominant in accumulating a sense of urgency and disenchantment;
it arose once and then became a condition leading to its arising very
often.

What falls away immediately is dukkha, not worth clinging to. Seeing appearing at this moment is dukkha, it arises and falls away, never
to return. We cling to whatever can be experienced through the senses
and the mind, but actually we cling to what is gone already. What is
gone never arises again.

In Sri Lanka we stayed first in a hotel outside Colombo, in Negombo.
The first afternoon Venerable U Pandita and Kevin, a Vietnamese stu-
dent who is living now in Colombo, visited us. We discussed dukkha,
the first noble Truth and the difference between what is real and what is
an idea or concept. Dukkha pertains to the arising and falling away of
realities and if we confuse reality with concept and do not know the difference we cannot understand the truth of dukkha. The truth of dukkha
refers to realities appearing at this moment.

We may have read texts of the Buddhist teachings about ultimate
realities, dhammas, appearing one at a time through the six doors of
the senses and the mind-door and we have learnt that these are different
from what is real only in conventional sense such as a garden or a person
which are a collection of things or a "whole" of impressions. We have
theoretical understanding of the difference, but Achan Sujin helped us
time and again to have more understanding of the reality appearing
now, at the present moment. In this way we learn to verify the truth for
ourselves. For instance, when we are seeing now, it seems that we see
persons and different things like a glass or a table. Persons and different
things do not impinge on the eye-sense, they are objects of thinking
after seeing. Seeing experiences what is visible object impinging on
the eye-sense. We can come to know the difference between seeing and
thinking very gradually, but it will take a long time since ignorance and

attachment have been accumulated for a long time.

Seeing is not a person, it is a citta (moment of consciousness) that sees. It falls away and is then succeeded by a next citta. Only one citta arises at a time, but every citta is accompanied by different mental factors, cetasikas, which may be wholesome, unwholesome or neither. Our life is a succession of cittas that arise and fall away, succeeding one another. There is no moment without citta. That is why good and bad tendencies are accumulated from one citta to the next one, from life to life.

When we listen to the Dhamma and consider what we hear, there may be a little more understanding of what is real in the ultimate sense. Achan said that we discuss a great deal about seeing and visible object, because otherwise we would be forgetful. The fact whether there is an interest in the Dhamma today is due to what has been accumulated in the past.

An illustration of this fact was given to us by a family in Thailand we met after our short sojourn in Nakorn Nayok, before we travelled to Sri Lanka. We stopped on our way back to Bangkok to visit this family at a place where they sold trees and plants. The grandmother is a garbage collector who happened to listen to one of Achan's radio programs and found that she had never heard before such an explanation of the Dhamma. She gained confidence and collected and sold old bottles to make money for the "Dhamma Study and Support Foundation". Her children were not interested in the Dhamma, but recently they independently from each other happened to see Achan's program on the T.V. and hear on the radio one of her lectures broadcast. They were impressed by her words and from then on they listened regularly. Now a family of three generations, the grandmother, her children and grandchildren have great confidence in the Dhamma they heard. Understanding and interest in the Dhamma does not arise without there being conditions. What has been accumulated in the past can be a condition for understanding today.

Different objects are experienced by citta and if there were no citta, these objects could not appear. We are so absorbed in the objects that present themselves that we are forgetful of citta. Achan explained that what appears now to seeing is a reality, a dhamma. No matter what we call it, it is that which is seen. Visible object impinges on the eye-sense and, after it has fallen away, the impression or sign, nimitta, of visible object is what is left. It seems that visible object lasts for a while, but in reality it arises and falls away. We know that seeing arises at this moment, but we cannot pin point the citta which sees, it arises and falls away very rapidly and another moment of seeing arises. We only experience the "sign" of seeing.

The notion of sign or nimitta can remind us that not just one moment of seeing appears, but many moments that are arising and falling away in succession. Also visible object is not as solid as we would think, there are many moments arising and falling away in succession which leave the sign or impression of visible object. Achan Sujin used the simile of a torch that is swung around. In this way, we have the impression of a whole, of a circle of light that seems to stay. In reality there is no whole.

Visible object that was experienced by cittas of a sense-door process has fallen away; sense-door processes and mind-door processes of cittas alternate very rapidly. Visible object impinges again and again and seeing arises again and again. When their characteristics appear we cannot count the different units of rūpa or the cittas that see, they arise and fall away; the impression or nimitta of what is seen and of the seeing appears.

Achan Sujin said: "No matter whether we call it nimitta or not, it is appearing now. Whatever appears is the sign or nimitta of the dhamma that arises and falls away."

We cling to what appears for a very short moment, but it does not remain. It is the same with saññā, remembrance, a cetasika accompanying every citta. It marks or remembers the object experienced by citta so that it can be recognized later on. There is not one moment of saññā that marks and remembers, but countless moments, arising and falling away. We can speak of the nimitta of each of the five khandhas: of rūpa, of feeling, of saññā , of saṅkhāra-kkhandha (the other cetasikas apart from feeling and saññā that can accompany citta), of consciousness. There are nimittas of all conditioned dhammas that appear at this moment, arising and falling away extremely rapidly.

What is seen is not one reality arising and falling away, it is only the succession, the rapidity of the succession of visible object, and it appears as "something". The nimitta of visible object that arises and falls away in succession gives rise to thinking of shape and form, of a concept of a person or thing.

We do not have to think of nimitta, but it is helpful to know about it: we come to understand that it is not possible to experience just one reality such as one moment of seeing or one visible object. It is of no use to try to catch it, wondering about it whether it is this visible object or that one. It is gone already. The next visible object has appeared already, but its characteristic can be known as just a dhamma. The teaching of nimitta gives us an idea of the shortness a reality appears; it is insignificant, not worth clinging to.

Seeing and visible object are realities, dhammas, but a concept we think of on account of what was seen is not real in the ultimate sense. Realities such as seeing, visible object, hearing, sound, all the sense-cognitions and the sense objects appear all the time and when they appear they can be objects of study. The study of the Dhamma is not theoretical. We may read texts of the Buddha's Teachings and believe that we, while we read them and ponder over them, we already understand them, but that is not so.

Kevin said while he experiences hardness or softness by touch, that he has to think: "This is hardness, this is softness". Otherwise he would forget the Buddha's words.

Achan answered: "When characteristics of realities are experienced, you need not think about words. We can know the difference between thinking about the 'story' of dhammas and the direct understanding of them. Whatever appears, there is no one there."

She reminded us very often that there is no one there. The Buddha taught the nature of non-self, anattā, of realities. There is seeing, but it is not a person who sees, the seeing sees, the hearing hears. Seeing and all conditioned realities are non-self, there is no one who can cause their arising. They are beyond control. We may believe that we see a person, but only what is visible, visible object, is seen, there is no one there.

Seeing is real, it is a dhamma. We have to understand seeing that arises now, who can make it arise? Nobody can have anything at will. It can be said that seeing is a paramattha dhamma[1] and this means that its characteristic cannot be altered. We can give seeing another name, but

---

[1] Paramattha: The highest sense.

its characteristic does not change: seeing experiences what is visible. Or it can be said that seeing is abhidhamma: subtle dhamma or dhamma in detail[2]. When we hear the word abhidhamma we need not merely think of the text; that part of the Tipiṭaka that is the Abhidhamma explains all realities in detail and it pertains to whatever reality appears now. In this sense it can be said that seeing, visible object, hearing, sound, that all realities are abhidhamma.

We are usually living in the world of concepts and we may have no understanding of paramattha dhamma, of what arises because of conditions. It is true that we have to think of people and things all day long, otherwise we could not lead our daily life naturally. We have to know that this is a book, that a table. But the difference between concepts and ultimate realities can be understood.

When there is wise attention to the object that appears now, understanding of realities can grow very gradually. But it takes a long time not to move away from the present object. That is why Achan reminded us many times of the different phases of understanding: pariyatti, which is not theoretical understanding but intellectual understand ing of the present object; patipatti which is direct understanding of whatever appears; and pativedha, the direct realization of the truth. Pariyatti can condition direct understanding and this again conditions pativedha.

Moreover, there are three rounds of the understanding of the four noble Truths that can be discerned: sacca nana, the firm understanding of what has to be known and what the four noble Truths are; kicca nana, understanding of the task, that is, direct awareness and understanding, Satipaṭṭhāna[3] ; kata nana, understanding of what has been realized, the direct realization of the truth[4].

When pariyatti has become firm and more accomplished it is sacca nana. Then one does not move away from the dhamma appearing right now and turns to other practices in order to understand the truth. Sacca nana is the firm understanding of the fact that every dhamma that arises

---

[2]The prefix "abhi" is used in the sense of "preponderance" or "distinction". "Abhidhamma" means "higher Dhamma" or "Dhamma in detail".

[3]Satipaṭṭhāna is the development of right understanding of mental phenomena and physical phenomena appearing at the present moment.

[4]See Kindred Sayings V, Kindred Sayings about the Truths, Ch 2, § 1, The Foundation of the Kingdom of the Dhamma.

is conditioned.

After our discussion with the venerable U Pandita and Kevin, in Negombo, they had to return to Colombo, which meant for them about two hours or more in the traffic. Achan decided that it would be better to visit them instead in Colombo for the next three days. There were sessions in the "Buddhist Cultural Center" in Colombo where monks, sisters and other people listened and showed their interest by their questions. In spite of the many hours we spent in the bus Achan was never tired to have Dhamma discussions. She always encourages us not to think of ourselves and our own well-being, and then we do not mind when we are in difficult circumstances. Whatever experiences arise, they are all gone immediately.

Sarah often reminded me, even early morning before breakfast in the hotel, that what really matters is the development of understanding of the dhamma appearing at this moment. She said that we have so much confidence and interest in the Dhamma that we travel a long way to hear the Dhamma. While we see its benefit we do not think of hardship, "my pain" or "my problems".

In the Buddhist Cultural Center questions were raised that pertained to science and psychology, and people tried to find a common ground for Buddhism and science. However, science belongs to the world of conventional realities and its aim is different from the Buddha's teachings. We all know conventional realities and we need not to be taught about them. When we are thinking about the world and all people in it, we only know the world by way of conventional truth. It seems that there is the world full of beings and things, but in reality there is citta experiencing different dhammas arising and falling away very rapidly. Only one object at a time can be cognized as it appears through one doorway. Without the doorways of the senses and the mind the world could not appear. So long as we take what appears as a "whole", a being or person, we do not know realities. The Buddha teaches realities, dhammas that are real in the ultimate sense and that can be directly experienced. A medical doctor specialized in brain diseases had questions about memory, believing that this was stored in the brain. Achan explained that memory, saññā, is a cetasika, mental factor, that accompanies every citta and that it arises and falls away all the time. It marks each object experienced by the citta it accompanies so that it can be recognized later on. When we recognize something or someone saññā performs its function.

With all her answers Achan tried to help the listeners to understand the present reality, such as seeing, visible object, feeling or thinking. We had heard this very often, but every time it seems as if it is new. We are forgetful of realities and that is why we found it beneficial to listen again and again to her explanations about seeing now.

She said: "The seeing that now sees is not 'I'. Life is the experience of one object at a time. There is always the idea of 'I see, I hear, I think'. There are only different realities, no one at all.

Self is trying so hard to understand realities, but without the right conditions it is impossible."

Even when we do not think of a self who is seeing, there is still a notion of "I see". It is so deeply engrained. Achan often said that understanding is not yet sufficient to be detached from the idea of self. Patience is needed because it takes a long time for understanding to develop. The term pariyatti was often discussed. It is understanding of what appears at this moment. We may feel hot and then we usually have a notion of "I" who feels hot. We live in the world of concepts, instead of understanding what is reality. But sometimes one characteristic of reality such as heat or bodily feeling may appear. Then we begin to understand the reality of the present moment and even at this level there can be some detachment from taking heat or feeling for self or mine. Without pariyatti there will not be conditions for right awareness and right understanding of the Eightfold Path[5]. Pariyatti, when it is firmly established, conditions patipatti. Patipatti is often translated as practice but there is no one who practices. When people hear the word practice they are inclined to think of doing specific things in order to attain enlightenment. However, it is a level of paññā that directly understands the dhamma that appears at the present moment. It is of the level of Satipatthāna. It can only arise when there are the right conditions, it is not under any one's control.

---

[5]The eightfold Path are the cetasikas of right understanding, right thought, right speech, right bodily action, right livelihood, right effort, right mindfulness and right concentration. They develop together so that realities can be seen as impermanent, dukkha and anattā.

Achan often reminded us that there cannot be patipatti when understanding of the level of pariyatti has not been sufficiently developed.

40

One path

One of the listeners in the Buddhist Cultural Center had doubts about
the truth of the Abhidhamma. He was thinking about the history of
the text and thought that it was of a later date. Achan answered:
"Whatever appears is Abhidhamma. Is it 'I' who sees?"

In other words, Abhidhamma is not theory, we can come to understand what Abhidhamma is if there is wise attention to the present
reality. The text of the Abhidhamma teaches that there is no person,
no self, only citta, consciousness, cetasika, mental fators accompanying citta and rupa, physical phenomena. There is an unconditioned
dhamma, nibbāna, but this can only be experienced through the attainment of enlightenment. In our daily life citta, cetasika and rūpa
appear all the time. Seeing is not self, it is only a conditioned dhamma.
Nobody can cause its arising.

For most people Achan's explanations were new and they found
it hard to grasp immediately what she said. Sometimes her answers
are short, but deep in meaning. Therefore, it was most helpful that
Sarah elaborated on Achan's words in answering questions. Sarah and

279

Jonothan assisted all the time during the sessions in adding more explanations to Achan's words.

Realities are different from concepts that can be objects of thinking but are not real in the ultimate sense. Achan would time and again speak of seeing and explain that seeing is real. We are seeing all the time but we know so little about it. Instead of giving theoretical explanations about realities and concepts Achan would speak about what appears at the present moment in order to help the listeners to understand what is real. At the moment of seeing there is no idea of a human, a bird or "I". There is just a conditioned dhamma and no one makes it arise. The citta that sees falls away but it conditions the following citta to succeed it.

Some monks from Bangladesh showed great interest and one of them asked why the Buddha had spoken about groups of rūpa, kalapas.

Rūpas do not arise singly, they arise in units or groups. What we take for our body is composed of many groups or units, consisting each of different kinds of rūpa, and the rupas in such a group arise together and fall away together.

There are four kinds of rupa, the four "Great Elements" (Mahabhuta rūpas), which have to arise together with each and every group of rūpas, no matter whether these are rūpas of the body or rūpas outside the body. The types of rūpa other than the four Great Elements depend on these four rupas and cannot arise without them. They are the following rūpas:

the Element of Earth (pathavldhatu) or solidity, appearing as hardness or soft ness,

the Element of Water (apodhatu) or cohesion,

the Element of Fire (tejodhatu) or heat, appearing as heat or cold,

the Element of Wind (vayodhatu) or motion, appearing as oscillation or pressure.

Every day we experience a great variety of sense objects, but they are, in fact, only different compositions of rūpa elements. When we touch a cushion or chair, tangible object may appear, such as hardness or softness. We used to think that it was a cushion or chair which could be experienced through touch. When we are more precise, it is hardness or softness that can be experienced through touch. Because of remembrance of former experiences we can think of a cushion or chair and we know that they are named "cushion" or "chair". This example can remind us that there is a difference between ultimate realities and concepts we can think of but which are not real in the ultimate sense.

The Buddha taught about the groups of rūpa and each rūpa that arises is conditioned by the other rūpas in that group. It is entirely dependent on conditions and there is no body who could cause its arising. The Buddha taught the nature of anattā of each dhamma. Visible object is always accompanied by the four great Elements and by other rūpas arising in a group. There have to be at least eight rūpas in each group. Apart from the four Great Elements these rūpas are visible object, odour, flavour and nutritive essence. Visible object arises in every group of rūpas, but only visible object impinges on the eyesense, the other rūpas of that group do not. We believe that we see a person but a person cannot impinge on the eyesense. However, there could not be an idea of "person" if visible object did not impinge on the eyesense and there would not be seeing.

Rūpas are classified as twenty-eight, but seven types appear all the time in daily life. They are: visible object, sound, odour, flavour, and three kinds of tangible object which are solidity (appearing as hardness of softness), temperature (appearing as heat or cold) and motion (appearing as motion or pressure). The Element of Water or cohesion cannot be experienced through touch, it can be experienced only through the mind-door.

All the texts of the Tipiṭaka, including the Abhidhamma, are not meant merely for intellectual study or memorizing, they are directed to the development of direct understanding of realities. The classifications in the texts of the Abhidhamma of cittas, cetasikas and rūpas are an exhortation to develop understanding of whatever reality appears at this moment. This is the development of the eightfold Path leading to the eradication of all defilements.

The Abhidhamma teaches about different cittas: cittas that are kusala, wholesome, akusala, unwholesome, vipaka, result of kamma, or kiriya, inoperative, not kusala, akusala or vipaka. A citta never arises alone, it is accompanied by several cetasikas, mental factors. Some cetasikas accompany every citta, such as remembrance (sanna) or feeling. Some accompany only akusala citta or only kusala citta. Each citta cognizes an object, that is its function. Akusala cetasikas or beautiful cetasikas that accompany it cause the citta to be akusala or kusala. When we are attached to people we are inclined to believe that it is self who is attached. However, it can be understood that attachment (lobha) is only a cetasika that is conditioned to accompany akusala citta at a particular moment. We were attached in the past and, thus, this inclination is accumulated from one citta to the next citta so that attachment arises again.

Our life is an uninterrupted series of cittas arising in succession. That is why good and bad qualities are accumulated and carried on from moment to moment.

We read in the text of the "Path of Discrimination" (Patisambhidamagga, Ch 69, 585) more about the meaning of accumulation:

> "Here the Perfect One knows beings' biases, he knows their underlying tendencies (asayanusaya nana), he knows their behaviour (carita), he knows their dispositions (adhimutti), he knows beings as capable and incapable. . . "

The Commentary to the "Path of Discrimination" (the "Saddhammappakasinī") gives explanations about the knowledge of beings' biases and underlying tendencies:

> "As to the term anusaya, bias, they explain this as dependence, abode or support on which beings depend. This term denotes the disposition to wrong view or to right view that has been accumulated. It denotes the disposition to all that is unwholesome, such as clinging to sense objects, or the disposition to all that is good, such as renunciation that has been accumulated.

> The defilements that lie persisting in beings' continuous stream of cittas are called anusaya, latent tendencies. This term denotes the defilements such as clinging to sense objects that is strong."

Thus, anusaya, latent tendency, refers to unwholesome inclinations that lie dormant in every citta. They do not arise but they can condition the arising of akusala citta. Anusaya refers to both wholesome and unwholesome inclinations that have been accumulated and can condition the arising of kusala citta or akusala citta.

There were ignorance and clinging in past lives and these have been accumulated from life to life and that is why there are conditions for their arising time and again. However, in listening to the Dhamma and truly considering it, there may be a little more understanding of realities. A moment of understanding is never lost, it is accumulated in the citta so that it can arise again and grow very gradually.

We should understand first what is dhamma, before we can understand kusala and akusala dhammas. As Achan often said, kusala is not a person, akusala is not a person. It is dhamma, only a reality. Generosity (alobha) may arise and this is a cetasika that accompanies kusala citta. It arises and then falls away with the citta. It cannot stay and it does not belong to a self. Evenso, aversion that arises is a cetasika that may accompany akusala citta. It cannot stay and does not belong to a self.

Seeing and hearing arise time and again. These are vipakacittas, results produced by past kusala kamma or akusala kamma. Kamma is accumulated from one citta to the next citta and it can produce its appropriate result later on.

Our world seems to be full of people, but there are only two kinds of reality: mental phenomena or nāma and physical phenomena or rūpa. Citta and cetasika are nāma, they experience an object, whereas rūpa does not know anything. Visible object and eyesense are rūpas that are conditions for seeing, they do not know anything. At each moment of life there is citta, accompanied by cetasikas. What we call body are groups of rūpa, arising and falling away. If there were no citta, the body could not move.

One of the monks said that there are different Paths for different people. He emphasized good behaviour in family life as essential for lay people. Achan said that all the teachings point to right understanding. Kusala sīla is the wholesome behaviour of citta. Sīla before the Buddha's time was different from the sīla he taught.

Achan said: "Not killing is what everyone can say, not only a Buddha. He taught that there is no one, no self, at any time. All dhammas are anattā . With regard to not killing, there is no "I" at all, only wholesome mental factors. There is no one. There are seven anusayas: sensuous desire, aversion, wrong view, doubt, conceit, craving for existence and ignorance. There may be wrong understanding, taking realities for self, from life to life. All the teachings are about understanding realities as not self. Ignorance, moha, and aversion, dosa, kill, not a self. His teachings are different from others' teachings. Morality with understanding is his teaching. One should not just follow his words, but develop one's own understanding."

An illustration of the fact that sīla with understanding is the Buddha's teaching we find in the "Vyagghapajja Sutta" (Gradual Sayings, Book of the Eights, Ch VI, §4 8). We read that Vyagghapajja visited the Buddha and asked for an instruction leading to happiness in this life and in a future life. First the Buddha explained the conditions for worldly progress using conventional terms expressing situations in everyday life. He spoke about abstaining from debauching, drunkenness, gambling and from friendship with evil doers. After that he spoke about the conditions for spiritual progress: the accomplishment of faith (saddha-sampada), the accomplishment of virtue (sīla-sampada), the accomplishment of charity (caga-sampada) and the accomplishment of wisdom (paññā-sampada). The accomplishment of faith is confidence in the Triple Gem and this points to right understanding. When right understanding is being developed confidence in the Buddha who taught the truth about realities is ever growing. The accomplishment of sīla is abstaining from killing, stealing and the other akusala kamma the abstention of which is contained in the five precepts. The sotapaññā who does not believe in a self who is abstaining, will never transgress these five precepts. He really has the accomplishment of sīla. Even so the sotapaññā who has eradicated all stinginess has the accomplishment of caga. Caga in its widest sense is actually relinquishment, giving up, renunciation from all akusala.

As to the accomplishment of wisdom, we read:

> "Herein a householder is wise: he is endowed with wisdom that understands the arising and cessation (of the five aggregates of existence); he is possessed of the noble penetrating insight that leads to the destruction of suffering. This is called the accomplishment of wisdom."

The Buddha taught that all dhammas, including sīla, are anattā. Whenever kusala sīla arises we should understand that it does so because of the right conditions and that there is no self who can make an effort for kusala sīla. If one thinks that one should accumulate more sīla so that later on there will be more understanding of realities, this is not according to the Buddha's teachings. When kusala citta does not arise, akusala citta arises very often. Right understanding sees the danger of akusala. One can begin not to neglect any kind of kusala, be it even of a slight degree. There can be more conditions for kindness, compassion and helpfulness. Sīla accompanied by right understanding can lead to enlightenment. There is actually only one Path, the development of right understanding of realities.

Questions about samatha, the development of calm, were raised. Someone thought that samatha had to be developed before vipassanā. Achan explained that one should know what calm is. If one expects or wishes to be calm it is attachment and there is no understanding. For both samatha and vipassanā right understanding is indispensable. Understanding has to know when the citta is kusala and when akusala, lest one mistakes akusala for kusala. One may believe that one is calm whereas in reality there is attachment. One may be attached to being in a quiet place without any noise. True calm (passaddhi) arises with every sobhana citta. When one assists someone else with kindness or one abstains from harsh speech, there is calm with the kusala citta. When someone develops samatha there are specific subjects of meditation, such as recollection of the Buddha, the Dhamma and the Sangha, or death. Paññā in samatha has to be very keen so that it is known how true calm is to be developed with a meditation subject.

Mindfulness of breathing, anapanasati, is a subject that is often misunderstood. One may believe that by concentrating on breath calm can arise. We should first know what breath is. It is rūpa, conditioned by citta. Rūpas of the body can be conditioned by four factors: by kamma, by citta, by nutrition and by temperature. Breath is conditioned by citta. It is very subtle and very easily one may take for breath what is not breath. The rūpa that is breath is different from breath as we use this word in conventional language. Even when we are holding our breath as we say in conventional language, citta still produces the rūpa that is breath. Citta produces breath from birth to death.

One may believe that samatha is developed by concentrating on a meditation subject. Concentration can also arise with akusala citta; it focusses on an object in an unwholesome way. Paññā has to know when it is akusala and when kusala. When some one tries very hard to concentrate on a meditation subject, there may be attachment instead of calm.

The word meditation often leads to misunderstandings. In Pāli the word bhavana is used and this means developing. There is samatha bhavana and vipassanā bhavana which are different ways of development and have a different aim. Before the Buddha's time samatha was developed by those who saw the disadvantage of clinging to sense objects. They developed calm to a high degree in order to become free from sense cognitions and from being involved in sense objects. vipassanā is taught only by the Buddha. It is clear understanding of whatever reality appears at the present moment. This understanding eradicates ignorance and wrong view.

Throughout the discussions Achan would frequently remind us never to move away from the present object. She would explain whatever can be understood right now.

We think of a self who is seeing or hearing, but seeing and hearing should be understood as not self. Ignorance and wrong view are deeply engrained and that is why each reality is taken as "I". Understanding has not been developed sufficiently so as to abandon the idea of self.

There is much to learn and consider so that understanding can very gradually develop. One may like to understand anattā now, to experience directly the arising and falling away of dhammas, but that is impossible. Only paññā can realize the truth, there is no one who can do anything. Achan said: "The opportunity to listen to the Dhamma is not easy to find, it depends on conditions. Who knows what will happen the next moment or tomorrow? This moment of hearing the teachings can be accumulated little by little. Confidence in the teachings is more valuable than anything else in the world. The most precious thing in life is a moment of understanding. The teachings are very subtle and, therefore, more words of explanation and more consideration are necessary, otherwise there are conditions for forgetfulness of realities. Paññā can begin to see the danger of not understanding reality as it is, since ignorance will condition more and more akusala."

41

Living Alone

Sometimes we may feel lonely, but Achan reminded us time and again that there is no one who lives alone, that there are only different realities arising and falling away. We have heard this many times, but when we are in a difficult situation, such as the experience of the loss of a dear person, we tend to forget that in truth life is only one moment of citta experiencing one object that presents itself through one of the senses or the mind-door. When seeing, life is seeing that experiences only visible object, not a person. When hearing, life is hearing experiencing sound. When thinking of a person life is thinking, and the object of thinking is a concept, the concept of a person, and each of these moments falls away immediately.

Huong, one of our friends, wanted to join us in Negombo, but while she travelled she lost her friends in Vietnam twice since they had missed the plane. She did not know the right address and sent an Email to the Dhamma Study Group after she had moved into a hotel in Negombo. Sarah happened to check Emails very early in the morning and saw Huong's post. She did not hesitate and immediately took a taxi to fetch

287

Huong at her hotel. It was all by conditions that Huong could meet us. Huong's mother had recently passed away and Huong was going through a difficult time because of her loss. Achan said:

"The thinking is gone, everything is gone, each moment. Understanding is not sufficiently developed to see that whatever appears is dhamma. There is an idea of 'my mother', but even what is taken for mother is dhamma, and thinking about her is dhamma. Whatever appears, whatever arises is a dhamma. What we take for some thing or someone are in reality different dhammas...

We should not forget that whatever appears, whatever arises must be a dhamma only, one dhamma at a time...It's only a reality. That's why we learn about reality to understand reality as not self, otherwise there must be 'I'. When there's 'I', there's 'my Mom', Right? But when we talk about realities, we begin just to learn that whatever we take for someone or something are in reality different dhammas."

Developing understanding of realities does not mean that we do not think of persons anymore, but we learn to discern the difference between what is real in the ultimate sense and what is a "story" we may be thinking of.

When we feel lonely because of the loss of a dear person, unhappy feeling arises. But feeling does not last, it falls away immediately. We continue holding onto our feelings and sad thoughts, and we think of ourselves as being alone. It is natural that we think of dear persons with attachment though we understand intellectually that there is no one there.

Achan said: "There is no one there, only seeing arises and it sees. There is no one at the moment of hearing, no one who hears."

Sarah remarked: "The development of understanding is learning to live alone, each moment. That is the nature of dhamma: always arising alone, falling away alone. From the moment of birth until the moment of death we are alone, there is never any one there. Citta arises on its own by conditions. No matter the circumstances, no matter how difficult they are, we have to remember that citta is always alone, at each moment."

After five days in Negombo we travelled by bus for about five hours to our next destination: Nuwara Eliya. This is located in the mountains, past Kandy. The hotel was at 1800 meter altitude. We passed tea plantations on the green hills and waterfalls. Our guide explained that in Sri Lanka nature is well protected and no more trees are to be cut. If someone would cut a Jackfruit tree he can await five years in prison. Our bungalow type hotel was situated high above terraces full of flowers. We had Dhamma sessions in the morning and in the afternoon. It was the rainy season but in the morning we could sit outside for our discussions. Achan went out together with some of our group for a morning walk and Sarah told me that the talk was about flowers and plants all the way. This is natural, daily life. There should be no selection of objects that are experienced. At another moment Achan asked people about the food they would eat and explained that we should not avoid talking about these things. We enjoyed the Singhalese breakfast with the traditional "egghoppers", pan cakes with an egg. If we believe that there cannot be awareness when talking about such subjects we go the wrong way. Thinking is real, but it is gone immediately.

Our friends Vince and Nancy also came over for the sessions. We have known them for a long time. Vince spoke about Lodewijk, my late husband, with great appreciation and kindness. He asked me full of concern whether it was not a great change for me to live alone. I reacted later on to his question when the owner of the bungalow, Rajid, attended our sessions. We discussed about realities and the importance of knowing whatever appears at the present moment. This is the way leading to the understanding that there is no self, no person, only mental phenomena and physical phenomena arising and falling away. It is not easy to see that this truth concerns our daily life and, therefore, I returned to Vince's question about my reaction to Lodewijk' s death in order to help Rajid to see the relevance of Dhamma to daily life. I explained that we learn from the Buddha's teachings that even when a person is still alive there are just fleeting phenomena, only citta, cetasika and rūpa that arise and pass away instantly. Through the Dhamma our outlook on life can very gradually change and we can learn to live alone, even when we have a loss. Citta is always alone, each moment.

Sarah said that the Dhamma is the best medicine but that it is not always easy to take this medicine. We hear about realities appearing now and that there is no person. We have to consider this, we cannot understand the truth immediately. It takes more than one life, but this does not matter. It is good that we begin to listen and consider. Understanding can only grow very gradually. It is useful to have discussions and remind one another of the truth.

I said that although I understand intellectually that a person does not exist, I still find it difficult to accept that Lodewijk, after passing from this life and going on to an other life, does not care for me anymore. Achan said that after dying-consciousness has arisen and fallen away and rebirth-consciousness has arisen, there is for the reborn being no more attachment to a particular person. Lodewijk cared for me in the past and I have some idea that he can still care for me. Achan asked me whether I remember my past life? It is helpful to consider that this life is only one short period in the innumerable lives of the past and the lives yet to come. Thinking with attachment is very natural, but there are only dhammas. Dying-consciousness is succeeded by rebirth-consciousness and then there is a new life, a new story.

She reminded us: "We have to understand whatever appears. It is conditioned, no body can control it, no matter pleasant or unpleasant experiences occur. When it is gone, it is gone. But we think that an experience is there all the time. From nothing to something to nothing, never to arise again. One characteristic of reality appears and then it does not ever appear again. It seems that the world continues to be the same, but actually it never is the same. Whatever occurs is only once in the cycle of birth and death, and then never again. This is the truth. It seems that seeing continues all the time, but there are countless moments of seeing. There is the succession of the arising and falling away of realities, appearing through six doorways all the time."

In the "Kindred Sayings" (Ch III, Kosala, Persons, § 2 Grandmother) we read that King Pasenadi visited the Buddha. The Buddha asked him why he had come at this hour of the day. The King said:

> " 'My grandmother, lord, is dead. She was aged and full of years; long her span of life, long her life's faring. She has passed away in her 102th year.
>
> Now, my grandmother, lord, was dear to me and beloved. If I had been offered the gift of a priceless elephant [or that her life might be preserved], I should have chosen that my grandmother had not died; nay, I would have given the elephant away to save her life. I would have done no less had I

been offered, or did I possess a priceless horse, or the choice
of a village, or a province.'

'All beings are mortal; they finish with death; they have
death in prospect.'

'That is notably and impressively said, lord...'

'Even so, sire, even so... Even as all vessels wrought by the
potter, whether they are unbaked or baked all are breakable.
They finish broken, they have breakage in prospect.

All creatures have to die. Life is but death.
And they shall fare according to their deeds,
Finding the fruit of merit and misdeeds:
Infernal realms because of evil works;
Blissful rebirth for meritorious acts...' "

Wholesome deeds, kusala kamma, is accumulated and can produce
a happy rebirth or pleasant sense impressions during life. Whereas evil
deeds, akusala kamma, is accumulated and can produce an unhappy
rebirth or unpleasant sense impressions during life. A wholesome deed or
unwholesome deed committed in a past life can produce its appropriate
result even after aeons. It is never lost but it is accumulated in the citta
and passed on from moment to moment.

We usually think of death as the end of a lifespan, but in reality
there is birth and death at each moment of citta that arises and passes
away. A moment of seeing that arises now falls away instantly, never to
return. What we take for life are only fleeting realities.

Huong asked me whether I have attachment now to my late husband.

I answered: "It depends on the citta at a particular moment whether
attachment to my late husband arises. There is no attachment to thinking of him all the time, when seeing, or when having fun and laughing.
There is only one citta at a time, experiencing one object. We may think
of a whole situation of being sad, missing a dear person, but that is only
a moment of thinking. It seems to last, but that is not according to re
ality. There are only seeing, hearing, other sense-cognitions or thinking
and they are all gone immediately."

The teachings are very subtle and the truth of there being no person
cannot be penetrated immediately. We may understand intellectually

that there is no person, no self, but, as Achan emphasized many times, there are not yet sufficient conditions for direct understanding and direct awareness of the truth. If we wonder about it how to have more conditions there is no understanding of dhamma at all, Achan said. We hear the word anattā and think about it, but there is no direct understanding of a reality that appears as only a dhamma. We have to be truthful to what is real now.

Achan said many times: "What is seen cannot be anything at all, this is the way to have less attachment."

What is seen, visible object, is only a type of rūpa that arises, impinges on the eye- base and then falls away. It is present for an extremely short moment, but we think about it for a long time, clinging to what has gone already. It seems that we see people, but they are not there, they are only objects of thinking, not of seeing. There is no one there, no person, that is the truth of anattā.

Visible object is an element, this means: devoid of self. It is a conditioned element, it is conditioned by the four great Elements that always arise together with it. The composition of these Elements is different at different moments: sometimes heat is more intense or it may be less, or hardness is more intense or it may be softer, and this causes the visible objects that are seen to be different. It seems to us that visible object can stay, but since it is conditioned, it falls away, it cannot stay.

Achan said: "We talk about what appears, about seeing, hearing, smelling, but there is no understanding of these realities as not 'I' at all. Then there is no paññā. Every one knows 'I see, I hear, I think', but at this moment there is seeing and seeing is conditioned. Little by little paññā begins to understand that it is not 'I'. But it is not developed enough to give up the idea of self at all, no matter how many times we hear about this, for years, or our whole life. It depends on paññā and sati. Even at the moment of kusala there is sati, but sati is not apparent. So how can paññā see sati as sati which arises with kusala citta, when it is not apparent. But when paññā develops on and on there are moments of understanding reality, not only stemming from hearing, but sufficient to directly understand the nature of it as just a reality. Very naturally."

42

Treasures

The subject of pariyatti was often discussed. We are bound to have misunderstandings about pariyatti and take for pariyatti what is only thinking about the teachings. Achan said: "At the moment of understanding reality as not self, that is pariyatti."

Sarah remarked: "That is what is meant by not moving away from the present object." We should not mind when there is only thinking about the teachings, because whatever has conditions for its arising arises.

One may wonder whether there is just thinking about realities at a particular moment or whether there is pariyatti. Sarah said to me: "Behind such thinking there is strong clinging to self, to 'my understanding' and wanting to know how I can have result. Such thinking occurs when it is not understanding dhamma as anattā at this moment."

We read in the "Dhammapada" (vs 76):

"Should one see a wise man, who, like a revealer of treasures,
points out faults and reproves, let one associate with such

293

a wise person; it will be better, not worse, for him who associates with such a one."

Being an ordinary person (puthujjana), I am full of ignorance, wrong view and clinging. I often do not see when these defilements arise. Even when I do not think: this belongs to me, this is myself, I am still full of the idea of me, me, me. As soon as I open my eyes and seeing arises, there is still the idea: I see, even when I do not say so or think so, it is there. When a good friend reminds me of my ignorance and wrong view I am just grateful, otherwise I would not know about them. I receive a treasure.

There may be a subtle trying to have awareness or to catch realities. Effort or viriya is a cetasika that arises with many cittas. We may believe that we do not try to have awareness. But there is a very, very subtle trying that is unknown to us. We wish to avoid akusala, we wish to have more understanding and not to be full of ignorance.

At such moments there is a subtle trying. Paññā may come to know such moments.

Sarah said: "It is self trying. The most precious moment is understanding the anattāness of realities, not just want to have understanding. This is the way to have less attachment."

We had a discussion about sati and I mentioned that there is sati with each kusala citta. Sati of the level of thinking. Our discussion was as follows:

Achan: "Thinking about I, all about I."

Sarah: "It is all about the 'story' of sati."

Nina: "At the moment of kusala citta?"

Sujin: "It is true, but you do not need to talk about it."

We often think about the "story" or concept of realities instead of understanding their characteristics. Achan explained that when there are the right conditions for sati it is aware and at that moment there is no thinking about realities, no need to talk about sati. It arises unexpectedly, nobody can plan it. We talk so much about sati and about what level it is, and then we cling to an idea of "my sati". Or we may think that we are not yet ready for sati of the level of Satipaṭṭhāna. Also at such moments we are clinging to the idea of self who is not yet ready. If we do not mind whatever reality arises, even if it is a very unwholesome thought, and it is understood as just a conditioned dhamma, it is pariyatti. If friends would not remind me of the truth, I would go around life after life, not knowing about clinging to the self, to my thinking. Thus, these are rare gems to receive in the cycle of birth and death.

If paññā of the level of pariyatti has not been developed, there are no conditions for the arising of direct understanding of realities. Pariyatti is not reflecting about words and their meaning. Achan often asked us: "Is there seeing now?" It is a reminder that there is seeing at this very moment, not an object we merely think about. What appears must be a reality, it is conditioned. If there were no conditions it could not appear. By understanding this, it is of the level of pariyatti. As understanding develops there will be detachment from taking things as a whole, as a being.

Pariyatti is understanding of what appears, but it is not yet direct understanding. Achan said: "The understanding of realities is pariyatti, it is not understanding merely what this word pariyatti means. It is understanding of reality appearing now.

It is the understanding of any moment, it is not thinking. It is not remembering the words of the texts. We can think about them, but pariyatti is the firm understanding of realities. Without pariyatti one goes the wrong way. Pariyatti is the understanding of realities which will condition direct understanding. If it is not firmly established it can never condition patipatti, Satipaṭṭhāna. Pariyatti is not listening and thinking. The moment of understanding the truth of reality is pariyatti. We do not have to pinpoint whether there is intellectual understanding or direct understanding. Right now we talk about seeing, visible object, hearing, thinking, but it is not as clear as when paññā is developed to the degree that it can directly experience these realities."

It seems that we understand what dhamma is, but when it arises, there is no understanding. More intellectual understanding of what appears now, pariyatti, will condition patipatti. Intellectual understanding knows just the "story" but it is not direct understanding.

The development of understanding should be very natural, there is no need to go to a special place or assume a special posture. One should not select a specific object for sati and paññā. Achan often said: "no one can do anything". This is not an excuse to be indolent. It is a warning not to cling to an idea of having sati and paññā by engaging in specific actions. Then we fall into the trap of lobha and wrong view. It is difficult to go against the current of the accumulated lobha, ignorance and wrong view. The Buddha's teachings can condition less attachment to the object that appears.

Very gradually it can be learned that not a self sees but that seeing sees, that there is no thing, no person in visible object. There is no person, only citta, cetasika and rūpa. As Achan reminded us, who understands the teachings of the Buddha will listen more, consider more and leave it to anattā, because the development of understanding is conditioned. If one tries to have it, it is not anattā. What arises in the world is two kinds of realities: the reality that experiences and the reality that does not experience anything. We should discern the true nature of nāma and of rūpa but we do not have to call them nāma and rūpa. Confidence can become firmer, confidence that there is a way to know directly realities, not merely by thinking about them.

Right understanding has to be developed together with the "perfections", paramis, [1] which support right understanding. In the Commentary to the "Cariya Pitaka", in the introduction (Nidana Katha) we read about four ways of development which indicate that paññā has to be developed during innumerable lives. They are:

The complete development of the entire range of the Perfections, sabbasam-bhara-bhavana.[2]

Development without interruption, nirantara-bhavana. The development of the Perfections throughout the minimum period of four asankheyya (incalculable period) and a hundred thousand aeons, or the medial period of eight asankheyya and a hundred thousand aeons or the maximum period of sixteen asankheyya and a hundred thousand aeons, without a break of even a single existence.

Development for a long time, cirakala-bhavana, the development of the Perfections for a long duration which is not less than the minimum period of four asankheyya and a hundred thousand aeons.

---

[1]The perfections or paramis are: generosity, morality, renunciation, wisdom, energy, patience, truthfulness, determination, loving kindness, equanimity. The Buddha developed these for aeons in order to become the Sammasambuddha.

[2]Sambhara can mean requisite or ingredient.

Development with respect, sakkacca-bhavana, the development of Perfections with seriousness and thoroughness.

Earlier Achan had given some additional explanations and Sarah rendered these as follows:

Sabbasambhara-bhavana refers to how kusala 'ingredients' are conditions for the development of understanding. Without kusala, there is just akusala all day. Any kusala, however small, should be developed. Without right understanding, it won't be known or developed.

Nirantara-bhavana refers to the fact that understanding does not develop at once, but over lifetimes to come with continuous development. It doesn't matter how long.

What is important is that the understanding about anattā is firmly established. Nirantara means without interval, in the sense of continuously, forever. The development of understanding takes great patience for a long time, with no thought of being engaged with a particular practice in order to have a result more quickly. This is the only way to be freed from being enslaved by attachment.

If there is desire for results or impatience with the path, it shows that understanding is not firmly established.

When people read about development without interruption, continuously, nirantara-bhavana, misunderstandings may arise. This does not mean that there has to be mindfulness and understanding all day long, without interruption. Nobody could force the arising of mindfulness, it is anattā. One should be firmly established in anattā as Achan said.

Achan explained: "Understanding should not be only once but since all realities are anattā, not under one's control, no one can try to force having it all day impossible. So this means not just in this life, but in whatever life to come, one is firmly established in anattāness. If there is the idea of 'atta', it is against the teachings, the Truth, that's why it's very subtle. Take courage to really understand what is now, not 'I try to have awareness'. It doesn't mean to have awareness continually, it means no matter in what life anytime."

Cirakala-bhavana is the understanding of how long it takes before there is understanding of what the Buddha said. There is no doubt about what had to be known and realized by the previous followers of the Buddha.

Sakkacca-bhavana[3] refers to the respect for each word of the Teachings. When respectfully understood, there are conditions for more understanding and less ignorance.

When we read about the incalculable periods it can remind us that paññā has to continue to develop lifetime after lifetime in order to understand the reality appearing at this moment. When we begin to see that clinging to self is deeply rooted we can understand that the development of paññā together with all the perfections must take innumerable lives.

We read in the commentary to the Cariyapitaka about the means by which the perfections are accomplished, and it is said that they should be performed perseveringly without interruption, and that there should be enduring effort over a long period with out coming to a halt halfway. We may become discouraged when we do not see a tangible result of the development of understanding. Then we are thinking about self, about "my lack or progress", instead of developing understanding of whatever reality appears at the present moment. We are falling into the trap of lobha, as we were reminded several times during our journey.

There is lobha time and again, even while studying the teachings or listening to Dhamma. One should understand the nature of anattā, also at such moments. Achan said: "When we are talking about what appears, attachment may arise and then reality does not appear as it is. Attachment covers up the nature of anattā, so that one does not know that seeing and that which is seen are not anyone at all."

The perfections should be developed now, at this moment. There should be patience and determination to begin to understand realities that appear, they should be investigated very carefully. We need truthfulness to investigate all realities of daily life. It takes time to really understand and follow the teachings. We need the perfection of patience, khanti, energy or courage, viriya, truthfulness, sacca and determination, aditthana. Without patience paññā cannot grow. We need the perfection of equanimity to face the worldly conditions such as gain and loss, praise and blame, without being disturbed by them. When understanding becomes firm we have more confidence in the Buddha's words. Whatever experiences through the senses occur, pleasant or unpleasant, they all have conditions for their arising. We shall be less

[3]Sakacca means having honoured, respected.

inclined to think of our own well being. Many conditions are necessary for the development of paññā, there is no self who can do anything.

We need energy and courage, viriya, to listen again and again to the Dhamma. When we are convinced that hearing true Dhamma and right understanding are the most valuable in our life we appreciate the opportunity for listening we still have in this human plane. We do not need to think of the perfections or enumerate them, they are any kind of kusala though body, speech and mind.

We may not like having akusala citta, but when there are conditions it arises. Nobody can change it. If we are not courageous enough to develop understanding of akusala we shall forever be ignorant of akusala cittas that are bound to arise, even in between moments of doing generous deeds. We cling to a notion of self who performs kusala and forget that each citta is impermanent and non-self.

When akusala citta arises we can verify how much understanding there is. Do we try not to have akusala? We may be looking for different ways in order not to have it.

Achan explained: "I do not think, 'defilements are so ugly', they are just realities. There should be understanding of them. People want to get rid of all defilements but they do not have any understanding of them. Why should our first objective not be right understanding? I do not understand why people are so much irritated by their defilements. One is drawn to the idea of self all the time, while one thinks about it whether one has less defilements or more. There is no understanding but merely thinking of kusala and akusala as 'ours'. So long as there is ignorance there must be different degrees of akusala. We should just develop understanding of whatever real ity appears. At the moment of developing understanding one is not carried away by thoughts about the amount of one's defilements, wondering about it how many defilements one has or whether they are decreasing. Just be aware instantly!"

Time and again Achan reminded us of the development of understanding at any moment: "Like now, there's seeing, hearing, thinking. That's all. Whatever arises by conditions just understand it. Usually it's the object of ignorance and attachment, but it can be the object of right understanding and detachment when there's more and more understanding. Just live by conditions. You cannot change it, you cannot make any thing arise at all, whatever is there. Best of all is understanding it not wanting more or less or this or that."

Paññā has to be developed together with all the perfections so that it can eradicate the wrong view of self and all other defilements. Because of the accumulated ignorance we do not realize that we cling to the idea of self, that we have the idea that we see, we hear, we think. Paññā will see more and more how deeply engrained the clinging to self is.

The following sutta illustrates how common clinging to self is. We read in the "Kindred Sayings" (I, Kosala, § 8, Mallika) that King Pasenadi of Kosala said to Queen Mallika:

> "Is there, Mallika, anyone more dear to you than yourself?"
>
> Mallika answered: "There is no one, great king, more dear to me than myself. But is there anyone, great king, more dear to you than your self?"
>
> The King answered: "For me too, Mallika, there is no one more dear than myself."
>
> We read that the Buddha recited the following verse:
>
> "Having traversed all quarters with the mind,
> One finds none anywhere dearer than oneself.
> Likewise each person holds himself most dear;
> Hence one who loves himself should not harm others."

The commentary to the "Verses of Uplift"(Udana)[4] , which has the same sutta (Ch V, Sona, I) explains that if one wants happiness for oneself, one should not harm, including even a mere ant or other insect. When one harms others one will experience the result of akusala kamma. This is the law of kamma.

---

[4]Translated by Ven. Bodhi.

43
Clear Comprehension

We may come to see that the Dhamma we hear and study is of the highest value in life. During this journey and also on many occasions we could listen to the Dhamma; we acquired a better understanding that the object of right understanding is any reality that appears at this moment. This is the only way to have less ignorance.

We discussed "clear comprehension", sampajanna, which is classified by way of four aspects. This classification as we find it in the Commentary to the Satipaṭṭhāna Sutta[1] and in the "Fruits of the Life of a Recluse" (Dialogues of the Buddha, Chapter 2), reminds us of the purpose of developing right understanding and of the suitable means in order to reach the goal, so that we have less delusion about the objects of right understanding.

The four aspects of clear comprehension are:

clear comprehension of purpose, satthaka sampajanna,

clear comprehension of suitability, sappaya sampajanna,

clear comprehension of resort, gocara sampajanna,

---

[1] Translated by Soma Thera in the "Way of Mindfulness".

clear comprehension of non-delusion, asammoha sampajanna.

When we begin to read the text in the commentary about these four kinds of sampajanna we may believe that it all pertains to the life of a bhikkhu, to the ways he should behave and do what is suitable. He should not go to crowded places, that is not suitable for him. We read how he should walk, wear his robes, eat. All the time he should not be forgetful of the four ways of clear comprehension.

Here we read about situations described by conventional terms. But the commentary also points to ultimate realities. Sometimes the truth is explained by way of conventional terms, sometimes by way of ultimate realities. We should remember that sīla is the behaviour of citta. Further on we read about the processes of citta, about details of nāma and rūpa. The translator speaks about the subject of meditation (kammatthana) and this is, according to the subcommentary: "The subject of meditation of the elements (modes or processes) that is according to the method about to be stated with the words 'Within there is no soul' and so forth."

Bending and stretching that the monk should do is explained by way of nāma and rūpa and this is included in clear comprehension of non-delusion. One may read the whole passage about the behaviour of the monk with wrong understanding, as Achan reminded us.

We should keep in mind that life is nāma and rūpa in the ultimate sense.

The explanations about the way of behaviour of the bhikkhu point to realities, to citta, cetasika and rūpa. It is emphasized time and again that mere processes are going on, and that there is no self.

Sampajanna is paññā that is able to understand what appears. There is clear comprehension of purpose if one sees that listening to the Dhamma and understanding the truth of the reality that is appearing is of the highest value in life. Sampajanna is understanding of what is of the highest value for those who are born a human being and have the opportunity to listen to the Dhamma.

Clear comprehension of suitability is listening to true Dhamma. One should not think that a particular place or time is not suitable for awareness. There are seeing, thinking, attachment on account of what is seen at any place, at any time. Awareness and right understanding should be developed in a natural way. If we think that a certain place or situation is not suitable for awareness, one is thinking about oneself. When we are in a difficult situation, we may think of "poor me, why me?" We are bound to forget that this is thinking at that moment, no self who thinks. It is thinking that is preoccupied with the self. If one can be mindful and not forgetful, there can be right understanding of whatever appears and then falls away.

One may truly understand that conditioned realities are impermanent, that nothing can stay. Each reality arises because of the appropriate conditions and then falls away. Clear comprehension of suitability, sappaya sampajanna, is the condition for knowing the truth of what is not permanent. When understanding of what is impermanent, conditioned, has been fully developed it leads to the attainment of what is unconditioned, nibbāna.

We read in the "Sappaya Sutta" (Kindred Sayings IV, Third Fifty, §146, Helpful) that the Buddha said:

"I will teach you, brethren, a way that is helpful for Nibbāna. Do you listen to it. And what, brethren, is that way?

Herein, brethren, a brother regards the eye as impermanent. He regards objects, eye-consciousness, eye-contact, as impermanent. That weal or woe or neutral state experienced, which arises by eye-contact, that also he regards as impermanent."

The same is said with reference to the other sense-doors, the mind-door, the objects experienced through those doorways, the other sense-cognitions, contacts and feelings.

The Buddha spoke about what appears now, at this moment; he spoke about what arises and falls away, what is impermanent, but this is not yet known.

As to clear comprehension of resort, gocara sampajanna, gocara is any object that can be object of right understanding, also akusala. There should be no selection of the object of right understanding; understanding can be developed at this very moment.

Gradually understanding of whatever object appears can develop, so that there will be asammoha sampajanna, clear comprehension of non-delusion. One will know that the truth is at this moment; it is the reality that arises and falls away, but the arising and falling away has not been realized yet. Understanding can become firmer, one begins to have right understanding of the true characteristics of realities. That is asammoha sampajanna. One is not deluded, one has not wrong understanding and clinging to a reality one believes to be permanent.

The four aspects of sampajanna show us the conditions for the arising of clear comprehension. One will have more confidence that it is not "I" who can do anything.

Achan said: "Be patient enough to let dhamma condition dhamma, not 'I' who tries so hard to cause the arising of understanding. The arising of pañña is very natural, as natural as ignorance. There cannot be many moments of understanding, only very, very few. It takes a long, long time to become detached from wanting to experience the truth."

The Buddha explained about realities appearing through the senses and the mind- door, one at a time. We have heard his teaching about realities often, in many suttas, but we can hear his words again and again, they are deep in meaning. He taught about what is really appearing at this very moment: citta, cetasika and rūpa that arise and fall away. When seeing arises and appears, it experiences visible object through the eye-door, not a person or thing. The world experienced through the eye-door is completely different from the world experienced through the ear-door. When hearing arises, it experiences sound through the ear-door. Life exists only in one moment, the present moment.

As Sarah reminded us many times: "All problems in life come down to clinging now. Less clinging means more mettā to those around us, regardless of how we are treated." The following sutta gives us a good illustration of this fact.

We read in the "Kindred Sayings" (IV, Second Fifty, Ch 4, § 88, Punna), that Punna asked the Buddha for a teaching in brief. The Buddha taught him about all the objects appearing through the six doorways. If he would cling to these objects, this would lead to suffering. If he would not cling there would be the end to suffering.

The Buddha explained about realities appearing through the senses and the mind-door, one at a time. We have heard his teaching about realities often, in many suttas, but we should hear his words again and again, they are deep in meaning. He taught about what is really appearing at this very moment: citta, cetasika and rūpa that arise and fall away. When seeing arises and appears, it experiences visible object through the eyedoor, not a person or thing. When hearing arises, it experiences sound through the eardoor. Punna had right understanding of realities, he did not take any reality for self. The Buddha asked him where he would be dwelling. When Punna said that he would dwell in Sunaparanta, the Buddha said:

> "Hot headed, Punna, are the men of Sunaparanta. Fierce, Punna are the men of Sunaparanta. If the men of Sunaparanta abuse and revile you, Punna, how will it be with you?"

Punna answered that they were kind not to smite him a blow with their hands.

The Buddha then asked him how he would feel if they would throw clods of earth.... beat him with a stick... strike him with a sword or slay him. Punna gave in each case a similar answer, he had no aversion. As to being stabbed to death, Punna said that some disciples who are disgusted with body and life stabbed themselves, but he would have come by a stabbing that he never sought. He was not afraid of fierce people, because in reality there are no fierce persons who could cause one to suffer injuries. He did not have any ideas of revenge. Punna had understood that there are no people in reality, only conditioned dhammas. Punna clearly understood what is meant by "living alone" alone with what is experienced through the senses, one at a time. Life is only the experience of one reality at a time.

Experiencing pain or even being killed has nothing to do with people who act. If one is convinced that there is no one there, one has no ill feelings about people. When bodily painful feeling arises, this is vipakacitta, citta that is the result of akusala kamma committed in the past. When one has not heard the Dhamma, one may think about one's afflictions with akusala cittas and blame those who caused injuries to us. Punna had right understanding about cause and result and answered the Buddha with wise attention when the Buddha asked him what he would do if the people of Sunaparanta would afflict him. Even if they would stab him to death he had no fear. No one can control in which circumstances one will die and at which moment. Punna had no attachment, aversion or ignorance and hence he had endless loving kindness and compassion.

We may believe that we notice different realities such as sound, odour or hearing. We may believe that we know the present reality. That is not understanding that knows realities one at time as only a dhamma. When paññā arises there is no need to think: it is just a dhamma. Very, very gradually understanding can become firmer and it realizes sound that appears as just a dhamma that cannot be changed, without having to think about it. What arises does so because of its own conditions. We do not mind if the present reality is envy, conceit or stinginess, they are all conditioned and they are gone immediately.

Achan reminded us many times of the subtlety of the Dhamma: "It is so very difficult to understand that there is not anyone at all. There is only that which impinges on the eyebase and can condition seeing to see it. We have to learn to understand realities one at a time so that it can be understood that there is no self. That which appears has arisen, just to be seen and then it exists no more, it will never arise again."

I am most grateful for all good advice and reminders of the truth about realities of daily life, given by Achan and other friends during our journey. These are real treasures.

Part VIII

Once Upon a Time

44

Preface

In January 2014, a year after my last journey, Acharn[1] Sujin and Sarah had organised another sojourn in Thailand for our Vietnamese friends, including a girl of five years old, and other Dhamma friends from different countries: from Canada, Australia, from the U.S., from Japan and from Italy. In the Hague I had had an accident in the tramway and broken my hip. I was happy to be able to make the journey after several months of hard training with my therapist. A day trip was planned to Bangsai, near Ayuthaya, and shortly after that we would go to Kaeng Krachan, the place where Acharn Sujin and Khun [2] Duangduen regularly stay and then to Suanpheung in the mountains outside Ratchbury. At the end of my stay I went to Chiengmai with my Thai friends.

Our stay in Thailand coincided with political unrest. Those who opposed the government and prime minister Yingluck whose brother Thaksin was ousted, organised demonstrations and blocked roads. How-

---

[1] Acharn is the Thai word for teacher. In Pali: ācariya.
[2] Khun is the Thai word for Mr. or Mrs.

ever, we could make all our planned trips inspite of the political situation.

I received great assistance from all my friends, whenever there was a difficult high step to be taken, or when I had to walk in a dark garden. Khun Noppadom, one of our Thai friends, was asked to look after me. At breakfast in Kaeng Krachan he fetched the food for me all the time and also later on in Chiengmai he saw to it that I would not go hungry. In Suanpheung several Thai friends provided us with an abundance of fruits and sweets whenever we had a break in between the discussions.

In Bangkok I stayed again in Hotel Peninsula where Sarah and Jonothan often stay. I was next door to them which gave me a safe feeling. I listened four times a day to Acharn's radio programs in Thai and heard that one should not be impatient in the development of understanding. One should not have expectations as to its development since we have accumulated such an amount of ignorance. If one is discouraged it shows that one clings to the idea of self. Understanding should be developed with courage and cheerfulness.

Acharn asked me to write a summary of our discussions and she even suggested a title: "Once upon a time". I am very grateful that Acharn explained with great patience that the characteristic of seeing and visible object appearing at this moment should be investigated. If we do not know what seeing is, only a dhamma, a conditioned reality, we shall continue to cling to a self. Everything is dhamma and "there is no one there" she repeated many times. We cannot hear this often enough.

45

Once upon a Time

"Once upon a time..." Stories of the past begin with these words. We do not really know the past. We do not even know what we did and thought yesterday from moment to moment, it is all gone. We do not know who we were in a past life, it is forgotten. We were happy and unhappy but all those experiences are completely gone, never to return. Also in this life it is true that all we find so important is gone immediately. This life will be the past life in the next life.

In reality the past can be as recent as one moment of citta (consciousness). What we call mind is citta that falls away immediately. There are different types of citta and each citta experiences an object: seeing is a citta that knows visible object and hearing is another citta that knows sound. Citta arises, experiences an object and then falls away immediately, never to return. Each citta is accompanied by mental factors, cetasikas, that assist the citta in cognizing the object. The mental factor remembrance or saññā accompanies every citta and it marks and remembers the object that is experienced. That is why we recognize a chair and know that it is for sitting, or we recognize a person who is in

311

the room. Seeing only sees what is visible, it does not see people and things. After seeing has fallen away, there can be thinking of people and things which are remembered by saññā. In reality there is no one there.

During our discussions, Acharn repeated many times: "There is no one there". She said: "Dhamma means: no one there. It is just a characteristic of reality that appears". I am grateful for this reminder, because we are deluded most of the time and we believe that people exist. What we take for a person is in reality only citta (consciousness), cetasika (mental factor accompanying consciousness) and rūpa (physical phenomena) which arise for an extremely short moment and then fall away. When we see, we are immediately attached to seeing and visible object but before we realize it they are completely gone. They are past already, they were present "once upon a time". We may think of a dear person who passed away, but there is only the idea or memory of what is gone completely. Only attachment and ignorance are left, Acharn said. This helps us to begin to understand, at least intellectually, the disadvantage and uselessness of clinging to persons.

We believe that we live with many people, but when we consider the different cittas that arise one at a time and experience different objects through the senses or the mind-door, we can understand what "living alone" means. Life is only the experience of one object at a time such as visible object or sound. When visible object is experienced, there is the world of visible object and when sound is experienced there is the world of sound. Different worlds appear through the senses and the mind-door. They could not appear if there were no citta which experiences them.

Sarah said that this is an encouragement to wake up from our dreams. Understanding of the reality appearing now is the only way to lessen attachment to whatever appears. She also said that we usually live in "once upon a time" stories, but, that just for a moment now, there can be truly living alone with the world that appears. When we appreciate this, we begin to have a sense of urgency, with understanding.

It takes an extremely long time before the truth can be realized. It is realized by paññā, a mental factor that is understanding. This is developed stage by stage, during countless lives. Intellectual understanding of the Buddha's teachings is a foundation for the development of direct understanding. But if we wish for direct understanding we are on the wrong Path. There is clinging instead of understanding. Ignorance and clinging have been accumulated for aeons.

We are heedless and we need many reminders of the truth. Our life is very short and therefore, we should not waste opportunities to listen and consider the Dhamma. Actually, life is as short as one moment of citta. Each moment of seeing or hearing is one moment in the cycle of birth and death. Seeing is only once in a life time and then it falls away. Hearing is only once in a life time and then it falls away. Life is only one moment of citta experiencing an object.

One of the first days of our stay we went to Bangsai. Bangsai is near Ayudhaya. Here Khun Duangduen has a peaceful place, surrounded by fields and near a temple. In the background we could hear the monks preaching, because it was Uposatha day [1].

Acharn asked: "Do you know me? What you see is only visible object, and you do not know visible object yet. It is very difficult to eliminate the idea of self and it can only be achieved by paññā. Is there visible object or are there people around here? It takes a long time to develop the understanding of not me, not anyone, no self, no thing in it. Seeing sees only visible object. It has to be right now, it should be very natural. Understanding begins to develop, there is no 'I' who tries. It is a very long way but one can begin to see that the Buddha knew through his enlightenment whatever reality appears. The development of right understanding has to be the understanding of whatever appears now."

She wanted to remind us that we see only visible object, not a person. She said: "Me or visible object, exactly the same. But you don't know visible object. Understanding has to be developed until there is no one at all, no thing at all in that which can just impinge on the eyesense. Citta arises to see it and then falls away. Visible object cannot be anyone. What is left is only the sign (nimitta) of reality, no matter there is seeing, hearing, thinking. Even intellectual understanding is not easy. Whatever arises is like a flash. Attachment cannot be known by a self, only right understanding can know it."

It is true that persons cannot impinge on the eyesense, only visible object or colour can impinge on it so that it can be seen.

---

[1] Special day of vigilance.

Someone asked whether the "Element of Wind" or motion can be experienced through the bodysense. This is a kind of rūpa (physical phenomenon) that can be experienced as motion or pressure.

Acharn Sujin answered: "You like to experience it, and there is not the understanding of it when it appears. That is the point. Attachment or craving is the second noble Truth [2]. If this is not gradually eliminated, it hinders. Someone may try very hard to make the Element of Wind or motion appear. Right now, many realities have passed without there being understanding of them, including motion, heat or anything. It is not under anyone's control to let it appear. Mindfulness, sati, can be aware of it[3]. Sati is very rapid. Before we can think about it, it is already aware. There is no need to think that one would like to know a particular reality. It is time to accumulate understanding so that there are conditions for having less attachment to experiencing particular realities. Would you like to have satipaṭṭhāna[4] right now?"

Nina: "I would like to."

Acharn: "That is already wrong practice, sīlabbata parāmāsa, clinging to rites and rituals."

Nina: "Already? That is very heavy."

Sarah: "It is very common."

Acharn: "Anything which does not lead to the understanding of reality is sīlabbata parāmāsa."

Nina: "That is so strong. It had not thought of that. Such a strong word."

Acharn: "Only paññā can see reality as it is. Otherwise there is no understanding of anything."

---

[2]The Buddha taught four noble Truths: the Truth of suffering, dukkha. The Truth of the cause of suffering which is craving or attachment. The Truth of the cessation of suffering which is nibbāna. The Truth of the Path leading to the cessation of suffering which is the eightfold Path, the development of right understanding of realities.

[3]Sati, mindfulness or awareness, is non-forgetful of the realities that appear. Usually there is forgetfulness, we are absorbed in thinking of "stories". When kusala citta with sati arises there can be mindfulness of one reality at a time as it appears through one of the senses or the mind-door.

[4]Satipaṭṭhāna is the development of right understanding of mental phenomena and physical phenomena.

Understanding of realities is developed by listening to the Dhamma and carefully considering it. When intellectual understanding has been developed sufficiently, there are conditions for direct understanding of realities. When the mental factor sati is aware of a characteristic of reality, understanding, paññā, can know its true nature. Paññā is another cetasika that may accompany kusala citta (wholesome citta). Cittas may be akusala (unwholesome), kusala, vipākacitta (result of kamma) or kiriyacitta, inoperative citta[5]. Nobody can make a particular citta arise, they arise because of their own conditions.

Realities have each their own characteristic that can be directly experienced. Concepts are not realities, they can only be objects of thought, they do not have characteristics that can be directly experienced. The truth of non-self pertains to realities. Person or chair do not have the characteristic of anattā.

It is important to know the difference between realities and concepts. Seeing and visible object are realities. Seeing sees what is visible, what has impinged on the eyesense. There is no person who sees, only seeing sees. Dhammas that appear one at a time through one of the senses or the mind-door are ultimate realities or paramattha dhammas [6]. Ultimate realities have each their own unalterable characteristic. We may call them by another name but their characteristics cannot be altered. Seeing is always seeing, no matter how we call it. Persons, trees, chairs are not ultimate realities, they are concepts formed up by thinking.

We dream of persons, mountains or trees. These are all stories we think of. When we see someone in our dreams it is not really seeing, but thinking of what is remembered, of what we saw before. It seems so real, it seems that we really see. When we believe that we see a person now, while we are awake, it is exactly the same; this is not seeing of what is visible, it is only thinking.

We read in the "Middle Length Sayings", "Potaliyasutta" (I, 365) that the Buddha used different similes for sense pleasures. The text states:

---

[5]Kiriyacitta performs different functions within a process. The arahat has no more kusala cittas but he has kiriyacittas instead.

[6]Paramattha means the highest sense. In Pali "parama" is highest and "attha" is meaning or sense. Paramattha dhammas are: citta, cetasika, rūpa and nibbāna.

"And, householder, it is as if a man might see in a dream delightful parks, delightful woods, delightful stretches of level
ground and delightful lakes; but on waking up could see
nothing. Even so, householder, an ariyan disciple reflects
thus: 'Pleasures of the senses have been likened by the Lord
to a dream, of much pain, of much tribulation, wherein is
more peril.' And having seen this thus as it really is by means
of perfect wisdom... the material things of the world are
stopped entirely."

It is necessary to consider why we want to study the Dhamma. We
study to have more understanding of what is real, to have more understanding of the fact that there is nobody in what is seen or heard,
nobody who sees or hears. We have accumulated so much ignorance
and wrong view for aeons and aeons and, thus, we cannot expect to get
rid of these soon. Only paññā, wisdom or understanding, can eradicate
ignorance, but it develops only very little at a time. If we think that
we can control or manipulate understanding or make it grow, there will
only be more attachment and wrong view. Thus, there should not be
any expectations as to the growth of paññā, it develops according to its
own conditions. It does not belong to us.

Acharn said: "We talk very often about visible object and seeing.
Otherwise we are always forgetful of realities. We think of a collection of
several realities as 'something'. When sati is aware of a reality it is time
to know that all the stories we think of are useless. They are only the
object of thinking. Without thinking there is no situation. Ignorance
conditions attachment."

During our discussions Acharn emphasized very much the uselessness
of experiencing objects. They are gone immediately, but we are clinging
to objects, life after life. What is the use of clinging to what falls
away immediately? Acharn wanted to remind us that life is dukkha
(suffering), not worth clinging to. But just now we do not see the danger
and disadvantage of all our experiences in life. Only paññā that sees
realities as they are can realize this. Paññā can condition detachment.
There can be a letting go, even of paññā, not wanting it again and
again. There should be no selection of the objects of awareness and
understanding.

Acharn said: "The characteristic of hardness appears as 'no one'. Paññā can see that this is part of the cycle of birth and death (saṃsāra). The cycle is the succession of the arising and falling away of realities. There is no one there."

The English discussions in Bangkok took place in the "Dhamma Study and Support Foundation"[7]. On Sunday I attended Thai sessions the whole day. For luncheon we walked to a restaurant nearby. The widow of Khun Denpong sponsored one of these luncheons. Khun Denpong passed away three years ago and before he died he said to Acharn Sujin: "I would like to live just somewhat longer in order to develop more understanding." I have known him as someone who always had many good questions. His widow said that he was a wise man.

After luncheon Elle helped me to take the difficult, steep steps down from this restaurant on the way back to the Foundation. We talked about the deaths of our husbands and spoke about it how sudden death comes. There is no time to take leave of our dear ones. We were dwelling on stories of the past, "once upon a time". This is thinking and Acharn's words always bring us back to reality now.

I remember what Acharn once said to Khun Weera when his wife, Khun Bong, was about to die:

"Dukkha is heavy, nobody likes it. It is a danger, it causes citta to be sorrowful, troubled. Nobody is freed from it, but we must understand it. When we have more understanding of the Dhamma we shall see that what arises must fall away, this cannot be altered.

Birth is really troublesome. We have to eat to stay alive, we have to see, there is no end to seeing. Seeing is a burden, because of seeing there is attachment. Is seeing beneficial or is it a danger and disadvantage? When there is seeing, there will be clinging to what is seen. We are searching for the things we like, but if we do not search for what we like we live more at ease. From where comes the burden? From seeing and from wanting the things we see. We can come to understand that each citta that arises and falls away is a burden. Everything that arises and falls away is great dukkha. Defilements cannot be eradicated by ignorance, only by understanding. When we listen more and develop understanding more there will be less dukkha. Everyone has to die, this

---

[7]This is the center where all sessions with Acharn Sujin take place each weekend.

cannot be changed. What arises now has to fall away, and then there is nothing left. When a dhamma arises and there is ignorance, one clings and takes it for 'self' or 'mine'."

46

Ignorance

Not knowing conditioned realities which arise and fall away is ignorance. Ignorance, in Pali avijjā or moha, is an akusala cetasika (unwholesome mental factor) that accompanies each akusala citta. It is the root of all that is akusala. We read in the following text ("Sammadiṭṭhi Sutta: The Discourse on Right View", MN 9)[1] that ignorance is not understanding the four noble Truths. We read :

> "Not knowing about suffering, not knowing about the origin of suffering, not knowing about the cessation of suffering, not knowing about the way leading to the cessation of suffering — this is called ignorance."

We have to apply this text to the present moment. The first noble Truth, suffering, dukkha, is the arising and falling away of reality now. Seeing now falls away and it never comes back. All our experiences fall

---

[1] Translated from the Pali by Ñanamoli Thera and Bhikkhu Bodhi. Access to Insight, Legacy Edition, 30 November 2013.

away never to return. What is impermanent is not worth clinging to, clinging only brings sorrow.

The second noble Truth, the origin of suffering, that is craving or attachment. So long as we have attachment there are conditions for realities to arise again and again in new births. Also now we have attachment, attachment to all sense objects, and we often have subtle attachment we do not notice. Whatever we do, whatever we say, whatever we are thinking, the idea of self is there. During our discussions Acharn reminded us time and again of this fact. Even when we engage in kusala, we do this often for the sake of ourselves.

The third noble Truth, the cessation of suffering, is nibbāna[2]. We cannot imagine what it is like but Acharn said that no arising and falling away is to be preferred to arising and falling away, which is the dukkha of life.

The fourth noble Truth, the way leading to cessation, this is the eightfold Path, the development of right understanding of realities[3]. Only paññā, right understanding, can eliminate ignorance. Right understanding can be developed by listening to the Dhamma and carefully considering it. Even one moment of understanding can condition the arising of understanding again later on. Understanding, a cetasika that accompanies kusala citta (wholesome citta), falls away together with the citta, but it is not lost. Cittas arise and fall away in succession, and, thus, understanding is accumulated in the citta from moment to moment so that there are conditions for its arising again. We have accumulated ignorance and wrong understanding for aeons and therefore, they cannot be eliminated immediately. Courage and patience are needed to continue to listen and develop more understanding. That is the reason why Acharn explained time and again about seeing and visible object and all realities of daily life.

---

[2]Nibbāna is the unconditioned dhamma, it does not arise and fall away. It is experienced by lokuttara citta, supramundane citta, when enlightenment is attained and defilements are eradicated. There are four stages of enlightenment and at each stage defilements are eradicated until they are all eradicated at the attainment of arahatship.

[3]The eightfold Path consists of sobhana cetasikas, beautiful cetasikas, of which the foremost is right view or paññā. The factors of the eightfold Path have to develop on and on so that enlightenment can be attained.

We listen to the Dhamma in order to have more understanding of realities. A beginning can be made now: seeing appears now and what is the nature of seeing? Seeing only sees what is visible, seeing is not a person, no "I" who sees. Visible object is a type of rūpa, a physical phenomenon, and it can impinge on the eyesense which is another rūpa. Visible object and eyesense are rūpas, they do not know anything. They are conditions for seeing. Seeing is a type of nāma, a mental phenomenon, a citta that experiences visible object. Cittas arise and fall away in succession very rapidly. It seems that we see immediately the shape and form of persons and things, but in reality there are many different cittas arising and falling away.

It seems that there is one moment of seeing and perceiving people and things all at the same time, but in reality there are many different moments. Seeing arises in a process of several cittas that experience visible object. When that process is over, there is another process of cittas experiencing visible object through the mind-door. Later on other processes of cittas arise that think of shape and form and take this for a person or thing. It seems that there is a long period of seeing people and things, but in reality there are many different cittas succeeding one another.

Seeing does not think, it only sees, but when it has fallen away we think of long stories, forgetting that thinking of stories is conditioned by seeing, hearing and the other sense-cognitions. Acharn said: "After once upon a time, then what? Right now there is past all the time. Even now, it is once upon a time."

Sarah remarked: "Not only when we are asleep, but even now we are always dreaming, building up stories with worry about how to take steps in the dark. Always stories like 'once upon a time', continuing the story again and again."

Citta knows an object, each citta knows or experiences a particular object and the cetasikas that accompany it also experience that object, but while they are doing so, they each have their own function or task while they assist the citta. Citta is the leader in knowing the object and the cetasikas are the assistants of citta. When we read about cetasikas, we should not get lost in names or terms. It is not the name that is important, but the characteristic of cetasika that can be gradually understood. Studying them helps us to see that citta is conditioned by the cetasikas that accompany it. Citta cannot arise without cetasikas and cetasikas cannot arise without citta. The Buddha taught conditions for the dhammas that arise in order to make it clear that they do not belong to us, that they are not "self" or "mine".

Feeling is a cetasika that accompanies each citta, and we find feeling so important. We cling to it all day long. Feeling may be happy, unhappy or indifferent. It is only a conditioned dhamma. Attachment (lobha) and aversion or anger (dosa) are unwholesome cetasikas (akusala cetasikas). We do not have to name them in order to come to understand their characteristics when they appear. When they appear now, at the present moment, their different characteristics can be known very gradually. When there are conditions they arise and nobody can prevent their arising. They can be understood as anattā.

We have to know the difference between intellectual understanding of a reality such as seeing, and the actual, direct understanding of seeing when it sees, just now. That is understanding without words. We usually pay attention only to that which is known, seen or heard, and we forget that without citta there would not be anything that appears, no world. Visible object could not appear if there were no seeing, sound could not appear if there were no hearing. There can be less attachment to citta that experiences and to that which is known by citta. But we should not have any expectations. Understanding cannot arise by wishing or wanting. We can come to know that all the time the idea of self comes in that wishes to know, wishes to observe, and this works counteractive. When there is more understanding of realities it leads to detachment from the idea of self who wants to do something, who is trying to know.

We had planned to go to Kaeng Krachan outside Bangkok and this was on the first day that Bangkok would be "shut down" by those who opposed prime minister Yingluck and the government. Streets would be barricaded. The day before our departure was a Sunday and the Foundation was closed so that people could prepare for the "shut down". This happened to be Acharn's birthday, of which she said that she would rather be without it. However, now people still came with presents on Saturday. We had an opportunity, with Betty's help, to give her presents and appreciate other people's generosity. They smiled and kept on telling her how much they appreciated her teaching. Some people presented her with huge vegetables. In no time the whole room was packed with presents.

We could go on our journey as planned and we stayed four nights in Kaeng Krachan. We stayed in bungalows situated in a large park with flowering trees. Early morning we walked from the bungalow where we stayed through the park to the restaurant for breakfast, outside along a lake. For the discussions we were sitting in the garden at the place where Acharn and Khun Duangduen stayed. The subject of our discussions was mental phenomena and physical phenomena, the many defilements that arise and kamma that brings result. A good deed, kusala kamma or a bad deed, akusala kamma, can produce result later on, even after many lives. The kusala citta or akusala citta that motivates a deed falls away but kusala and akusala are accumulated from one citta to the next citta, from life to life. When it is the right time kamma produces result, vipākacitta, in the form of rebirth-consciousness or the sense-cognitions arising throughout life, such as seeing, hearing, smelling, tasting or body-consciousness experiencing bodily ease or pain. I mentioned that one never knows when kamma will produce result. My accident, when I broke my hip, was completely unexpected; I never thought that it would happen. Acharn reminded me that we always think of people and situations, but that in reality there are eyesense, seeing, earsense, hearing, conditioned dhammas that are only there for an extremely short time. She said: "There is the flux of the elements that arise and fall away, uncontrollable. We should understand them as not 'me'. There is no one there. We do not have precise understanding of a reality that is seen but we keep on thinking in terms of people and situations. The conditions are not sufficient to make us understand what appears now."

She always referred to the present moment since that is the moment a dhamma appearing through the senses or the mind-door can be investigated and understood. They appear one at a time and they each have their own characteristic. When we think about situations, the reality is thinking; it is usually akusala citta that thinks, and the situation is not a reality. Acharn reminded us to develop understanding of this moment, just one moment in the cycle of birth and death.

We were discussing realities, and we can also use the word dhammas or paramattha dhammas. For example, sound is a reality, it can be directly experienced when it appears. We do not have to name it sound, but its characteristic can be directly experienced. Thinking about sound is not the same as the direct experience of it. We can learn that its characteristic cannot be changed into something else. Sound is always sound, it is the object of hearing. Attachment is always attachment, no matter how we call it.

We think of concepts most of the time. It seems that we hear dogs barking, words spoken, that we see persons in the room, mountains or trees. But the difference between concepts and ultimate realities, paramattha dhammas, should be known, at least on the level of intellectual understanding. This can lead to direct understanding. Then we shall know that there is no one there, no person. We shall know that realities are anattā. At this moment anattā is just a word we repeat. But the truth of anattā has to be directly realized.

When we are thinking about realities they have fallen away already. We all try very hard to find out the truth about realities, reasoning about them. That is not the way. What about now, while we ask questions about something or have doubts? Acharn said:

"At the moment of not understanding, what is there? Usually we think without understanding, so it is like a dream. At this moment, what is real? Now, when there is not direct awareness and understanding, it is a dream. Even when talking about paramattha dhammas the object is a concept of paramattha dhammas, they do not appear. When there is direct understanding, you are not thinking of that subject."

Also when we ask questions she reminded us to consider the citta that does so. Instead of wondering or having doubts shouldn't we attend to the present moment, such as seeing right now? We should know what type of citta motivates our questions. Often it is akusala citta.

We had Dhamma discussions in the morning and later in the afternoon, even after dark. In between we went out for luncheons in different places where we had panoramic views of a lake and mountains or we sat along the waterside. When the steps to reach the place were too deep for me I always had support from my friends. Acharn, her sister Khun Jeed and Khun Duangduen offered us a luncheon on the first day and for the other days we took turns in sponsoring them. Even during luncheon Acharn untiringly explained about mental phenomena, nāma, and physical phenomena, rūpa. We were asking about the characteristic of sati, mindfulness. This is a sobhana cetasika, beautiful cetasika, that can only arise when there are conditions. Nobody can cause its arising. We touch many times during the day different things and body-consciousness experiences hardness, but there is no mindfulness of a characteristic of a reality. Body-consciousness is not accompanied by sati, it is vipākacitta that merely experiences tangible object. When sati arises it is mindful of the characteristic of tangible object without thinking of the hardness of "my body" and at the same time paññā, understanding, which is another sobhana cetasika, can investigate that characteristic so that it is known as just a dhamma, not belonging to a self.

Listening and discussing are conditions for awareness but we should not be wishing or wanting to have it.

Acharn explained: "When one is touching and hardness appears it is different from thinking about what is touched. When a characteristic of a reality appears it is not as usual because there is direct awareness[4] of it. You do not have to name it and you do not expect to have it. Understanding knows the difference between the moments of sati and the moments there is no sati. This is the only starting point for the development of awareness. Paññā knows when there is attention with awareness to the characteristic that appears. Attachment or aversion may arise when one does not have awareness as much as one would like to. Sati is only a reality, a dhamma, not different from other realities."

When there is awareness of hardness which is a kind of rūpa, there is not some "thing" in the hardness such as a hand or the table. Only hardness appears and nothing else. It seems that seeing and hearing can arise at the same time, but when awareness arises one knows that realities appear one at a time. Seeing experiences visible object and hearing experiences sound, these cittas cannot experience more than one object. At the moment of awareness just one reality appears at a time and there is nothing else, no world. When this is not realized one knows that understanding has not been accumulated sufficiently. We need to listen again and consider again and again. Since ignorance is deeply rooted we cannot expect that paññā develops rapidly. In each life very little understanding is being accumulated, Acharn said. Now and then just a glimpse of understanding arises. When we have an interest

---

[4]Sati can be translated as mindfulness or awareness.

in the Dhamma now and listen to the Dhamma there are conditions for listening again in a future life. In this way paññā develops gradually from life to life.

I had a conversation with Acharn about awareness:

Acharn: "Is there anyone in visible object which is seen? This is the beginning of seeing the world as it is. Otherwise one is born and dies without any understanding of reality."

Nina: "I have regret when there is no awareness".

Acharn: "One can see clinging, it is always there. Only paññā can lead to detachment."

Nina: "When I ask 'how can I develop paññā... how can I have more detachment...', I know that this indicates clinging."

Acharn: "It is a reminder how much ignorance and clinging are there."

Nina: "We have regret about what is all gone."

Acharn: "If there is no understanding of the present reality there will not be any understanding of the past and the future. There is only thinking. Life is just the arising of different realities. We begin to understand the reality of dhamma, not just the word dhamma. Seeing, for example, is real and there is no need to say that seeing is dhamma. It is the same for hearing. We begin to understand the nature of dhamma: it is arising and falling away and never comes back."

Sati is aware of the reality appearing now, at the present moment. Acharn repeated many times that there is seeing now and that its characteristic can be investigated with awareness. When we think about seeing or talk about it, it is not the same as attending to the characteristic of seeing when it appears at the present moment. We do not know the past since it is gone, nor do we know the future which has not come yet. The reality appearing at the present moment can be investigated.

We read in the "Kindred Sayings" (I, the Devas, Ch I, a Reed, 10, Forest)[5] that the Buddha spoke about the benefit of attending to the present moment:

At Sāvatthi. Standing to one side, that devatā recited this verse in the presence of the Blessed One:

---

[5]Translated by Ven.Bodhi.

"Those who dwell deep in the forest,
Peaceful, leading the holy life,
Eating but a single meal a day:
Why is their complexion so serene?"

The Blessed One:

"They do not sorrow over the past,
Nor do they hanker for the future,
They maintain themselves with what is present:
Hence their complexion is so serene.
Through hankering for the future,
Through sorrowing over the past,
Fools dry up and wither away
Like a green reed cut down."

47

Gradual Development

Understanding of the realities that appear through the eyes, the ears, through the other sense-doors and through the mind-door should be known as they are, as non-self. First there should be intellectual understanding of realities and this can condition later on direct understanding. Intellectual understanding is called in Pali: pariyatti. Pariyatti pertains to the reality at this moment, be it seeing, visible object, body-consciousness or hardness. Pariyatti is not mere theoretical knowledge, it is not different from considering reality appearing at this moment. There cannot be direct awareness and understanding of these realities yet, but one can begin to consider them when they appear. The texts help us to consider the realities that appear now. When we read the teachings we should remember that they pertain to this very moment.

We read, for example, in the "Kindred Sayings" (IV, Third Fifty, 5, §152) that the Buddha said to the monks:

> "Is there, brethren, any method, by following which a brother, apart from belief, apart from inclination, apart from hearsay,

apart from argument as to method, apart from reflection on reasons, apart from delight in speculation, could affirm insight, thus: 'Ended is birth, lived is the righteous life, done is the task, for life in these conditions there is no hereafter'?"

The Buddha then explained that there is such method:

"Herein, brethren, a brother, beholding an object with the eye, either recognizes within him the existence of lust, malice and illusion, thus: 'I have lust, malice and illusion', or recognizes the non-existence of these qualities within him, thus: 'I have not lust, malice and illusion'. Now as to that recognition of their existence or non-existence within him, are these conditions, I ask, to be understood by belief, inclination, or hearsay, or argument as to method, or reflection on reasons, or delight in speculation?"

"Surely not, lord."

"Are not these states to be understood by seeing them with the eye of wisdom?"

"Surely, lord."

The Buddha said that this was the method. He then said the same about the other sense-cognitions. The Buddha spoke time and again about seeing, hearing and the other sense-cognitions. One should know one's defilements when they arise. There should not be mere intellectual understanding; dhammas should be "seen with the eye of wisdom".

We learn that nāma (citta and cetasika) is a reality that experiences an object and that rūpa is a reality that does not experience anything. Hardness which is a rūpa could not appear if there were not a citta that experiences it. We may begin to understand that not a self experiences hardness or any other object. That is understanding of the level of pariyatti. Pariyatti, when it has been sufficiently developed, leads to paṭipatti, awareness and direct understanding of the reality that appears now. Paṭipatti leads to paṭivedha, the direct realization of the truth beginning with the stages of insight-knowledge [1] and leading on

---

[1] Insight, direct understanding of nāma and rūpa, is developed in the course of several stages of insight leading on to enlightenment, when nibbāna is experienced and defilements are eradicated.

to enlightenment. But if one wishes to have direct understanding and clings to it, it will not arise.

Acharn spoke many times about pariyatti, explaining that it is different from just reading the teachings: "It is this moment. It is the same as coming to the Buddha and listening to his teaching. It all pertains to whatever appears now."

We read in the "Mahāparinibbāna Sutta"[2] that the Buddha, before he passed away, exhorted the monks: "Behold now, Bhikkhus, I exhort you: Transient are all the elements of being! Strive with earnestness!"

The commentary explains: "You should accomplish all your duties without allowing mindfulness to lapse!"

We should listen heedfully and learn to understand the present reality, then we follow the Buddha's teachings. Acharn explained that all of the teachings deal with the present reality as non-self. She said several times that we should carefully study each word of the teachings. I remarked that life is so short and that we should not waste opportunities to hear true Dhamma.

Acharn answered: "Understanding of the words 'once upon a time' can condition detachment. There can be more understanding of each moment as just once in a life time."

We think of a whole life that lasts but actually life is only one short moment of citta, such as seeing, hearing or thinking. They are part of the cycle of birth and death which goes on and on so long as there is ignorance and attachment. Each reality that arises falls away and never returns. It occurs only once in a life-time.

We read in the "Mahāniddesa" (I, 42) quoted by the Visuddhimagga (VII, 39):

"Life, person, pleasure, pain- just these alone
Join in one conscious moment that flicks by.
Ceased aggregates of those dead or alive
Are all alike, gone never to return
No world is born if consciousness is not
Produced; when that is present, then it lives;
When consciousness dissolves, the world is dead:

---

[2]Wheel Publication 67-69, Kandy. Ven. Nyanaponika added in a note the explanation of the commentary to this sutta.

The highest sense this concept will
allow."[3]

As we read: "ceased aggregates of those dead or alive, are all alike,
gone never to return." The nāma and rūpa that fall away at this moment
will never return and so it is at the moment of dying. When understanding is developed of the present reality there will be less clinging to a self
who could make realities arise or be master of them.

Acharn explained that when the citta is full of akusala there will
not be much interest in listening to the Dhamma and developing understanding. Akusala has been accumulated in many lives and, thus, very
few moments of kusala citta arise. The good qualities which are the
perfections[4] are supportive to the development of paññā up to the stage
of enlightenment. We should develop them, not because we expect a
result of kusala, but because we see the danger of each kind of akusala.
Our aim is the eradication of defilements and eventually to reach the
end of the cycle of birth and death.

Kusala citta can arise with paññā or without it. Kusala is not a
perfection when it is not accompanied by paññā, but paññā does not
arise very often. Acharn spoke about "pre-pāramīs", indicating that
kusala, even without understanding, can precede the arising of the perfections. At the moment of kusala citta there is no opportunity for the
arising of akusala citta, and, thus, there is no accumulation of akusala.
It depends on conditions what type of kusala citta arises. If we try very
hard to make kusala citta with paññā arise, we are clinging to the idea
of self who can exert control over realities. We need the perfection of
truthfulness so that we do not mislead ourselves, believing that there
is kusala citta whereas in reality there is the wrong view of self. We
need patience and courage so that we are not discouraged and paññā
continues to investigate the characteristic of the present reality.

---

[3]As to the word "the highest sense this concept will allow", the commentary
to the "Visuddhi-magga" explains: "the ultimate sense will allow this concept of
continuity, which is what the expression of common usage "Tissa lives, Phussa lives"
refers to, and which is based on consciousness (momentarily) existing along with a
physical support; this belongs to the ultimate sense here, since, as they say, "It is
not the name and surname that lives" (Paramattha-mañjūsā 242, 801).

[4]The perfections or pāramīs are: generosity, morality, renunciation, wisdom, energy, patience, truthfulness, determination, loving kindness, equanimity. The Buddha developed these for aeons in order to become the Sammāsambuddha.

The present reality is nāma or rūpa. Nāma, citta and cetasika, experiences an object, whereas rūpa does not experience anything. There are twentyeight classes of rūpa, but seven rūpas appear all the time in daily life. These are: visible object appearing through the eye-door, sound appearing through the ear-door, odour appearing through the nose-door, flavour appearing through the tongue-door, and the three tangibles of solidity (the Earth Element), temperature (the Fire Element) and motion (the Wind Element) to be experienced through the bodysense. Solidity appears as hardness or softness, temperature appears as heat or cold, and motion appears as motion (oscillation) or pressure.

Rūpas do not arise solely, they arise in groups. The four Great Elements which are the Element of Earth or solidity, of Water or cohesion, of Fire or temperature, and of Wind or motion, always arise with each group of rūpas, they are the foundation for each group. The Element of Water or cohesion cannot be experienced through the bodysense, only through the mind-door. Visible object is always accompanied by the four Great Elements. The four Great Elements arise in different combinations with visible object and that is why they condition visible object to be seen as different colours. For example, the Element of Earth or solidity that accompanies visible object may have different degrees of hardness or softness, the Element of Fire or temperature that accompanies it may have different degrees of heat or cold. There are many varieties in these Elements.

A rūpa such as visible object is not only experienced by seeing, it is experienced by several cittas arising in a process. Rūpa does not fall away as rapidly as nāma[5]. One rūpa such as visible object can be experienced by several cittas arising in a process. Only seeing sees visible object, and the other cittas of that process do not see, but they perform other functions while they experience visible object. When visible object, sound or another sense object has been experienced by cittas arising in a sense-door process, it is experienced by cittas arising in a mind-door process. Thus, rūpa can be experienced through a sense-door and after the sense-door process is over, it is experienced through the mind-door. Nāma is only experienced through the mind-door. We

---

[5]Rūpa lasts as long as seventeen moments of citta.

should not try to find out when there is a sense-door process and when a mind-door process. Cittas arise and fall away in different processes extremely rapidly and only when the first stage of insight arises will we know what a mind-door process is.

Acharn said that we discuss seeing and visible object, hearing and sound so that there are conditions for the arising of awareness. Without intellectual understanding the arising of awareness is not possible. She said about the experience of hardness: "When hearing again and again that there is no one in hardness, no arms, no legs, that it is only hardness, there can be conditions for understanding the characteristic of hardness. It just appears and there is no need to name it. Usually it does not appear. There is touching and then other things are experienced immediately. But when sati arises hardness appears, even if it is very short. It is different from the moment when it does not appear to sati, there is just a slight difference. When there is more attention to that characteristic with the understanding that there is no one in it, paññā develops. Because of conditions one does not pay attention to other things at that moment. Paññā begins to understand that characteristic as not 'me' or 'I'. Hardness appears to the reality that is aware. There is no idea of 'I am aware.' One can understand the anattāness of reality. It arises unexpectedly."

Our discussions about nāma and rūpa were held in different places. The location was changed, but the subject of discussion was always about realities appearing now. Nāma and rūpa appear, wherever we are. We went to Hotel Toscana, outside Bangkok and this was a resort in the mountainous region of Suanpheung past Ratchbury. Our hostesses were Khun Luk and Khun Ten. They were very concerned about my handicap and arranged things in such a way that I would stay in their bungalow, in a room near Sarah and Jonothan so that I would be more comfortable. All discussions were in a new building where Acharn and her sister Khun Jeed stayed. The place was hilly with a large orchard. Our hostesses supported me whenever I had to take big steps to enter the bungalow or to go out. We took turns to sponsor the luncheons which were nearby in woods or near waterfalls. All around we had a panoramic view of the mountains.

At that time there was a cold period for a few days, and in the morning even frost was on the grass. Maeve became ill and had to go to hospital where two of our friends, Elle and Azita, were allowed to stay overnight with her. They discussed different cittas that arise in such situations. Kusala cittas arise when helping, but there were many akusala vipākacittas when unpleasant odours were experienced. Elle and Azita, while walking, saw a picture and each of them was taken in by what she saw according to her different accumulations. Elle who is always engaged with flowers and who arranges the flowers at the Foundation in Bangkok, saw immediately flowers on that picture. Whereas Azita, who is a nurse, saw on the same picture a mother nursing her child. We all follow our different accumulations in life. It is due to the different accumulations as to what is interpreted and imagined on account of the visible object which is seen.

Awareness of nāma and rūpa should be very natural so that paññā comes to know accumulations. When lobha, attachment, arises, paññā can come to know it. If it is ignored, paññā will never know it. I said that when I find the akusala that arises very ugly, I do not want to know it, I rather suppress it. Acharn explained that if one tries not to have akusala with an idea of self who is trying there is wrong practice. Awareness should be very natural. Natural is the way of anattā, she said. I thought before that the natural way of development is easy, but now I see that it is not easy. The natural way is difficult when defilements are in the way. When paññā becomes stronger it is a condition for the natural way of development. There can be awareness and understanding of whatever dhamma appears, pleasant or unpleasant, wholesome or unwholesome. This is the way to know our accumulations. The perfection of truthfulness is necessary, so that we do not delude ourselves into thinking that we have a great deal of kusala.

48

The hidden Self

So long as we are not a sotāpanna[1] who has eradicated the wrong view of self we are not free from clinging to the idea of self. Acharn helped us to realize that clinging to the idea of self happens more often than we ever thought. I had a conversation with Acharn about wrong view. I thought that there was just ignorance, not clinging to the idea of self.

Nina: "I am not thinking all the time that this is my eye or that I am seeing. So, there is just ignorance."

Acharn: "What is there?"

Nina: "Ignorance."[2]

Acharn: "But the idea of 'I see' is there. Not the other person sees, it is 'I see',".

Nina: "Where is it when I do not think 'It is I?' "

---

[1] The sotāpanna or "streamwinner" is the person who has attained the first stage of enlightenment. He has eradicated wrong view, but he still has defilements. There are four stages and at each stage different defilements are eradicated. The stage of the arahat, when all defilements are eradicated, is the fourth stage.

[2] Rūpa lasts as long as seventeen moments of citta.

337

Acharn: "If there would be no I at the moment of seeing it would be completely eradicated."

Nina: "We usually think of concepts like a table or a person who is sitting here."

Acharn: "At the moment of seeing, who is seeing? The other person? Not the other person is seeing."

Nina: "I, I who is seeing".

So long as it is not directly understood that seeing sees, we are bound to take seeing for self, even if it is not apparent. That is why Acharn spoke about seeing and visible object every day. It seems that there is no wrong view but it is there. She also reminded us that when we read or study, this may be with the idea of self. One may think: "O, I have read this, I understand better" and that is reading with the idea of "I want to have more understanding". Paññā has to become keener and keener to see when the idea of self is there, no matter how large or slight it is. It seems that we have understanding of words like nāma and rūpa, or of dhamma, but these are just words and there is no understanding of a characteristic of reality that appears. If one would never consider what appears now it means that there is no understanding. Acharn repeated again: "Dhamma means 'no one there' in reality."

We were talking about accumulated inclinations and I mentioned that I like to appreciate what is wholesome in others, that I am inclined to "anumodana dāna"[3]. Acharn mentioned that there may be attachment at such moments: one likes to have such thoughts and one may be clinging to the idea of self at those moments. It is true, most often one clings to a self, a self which is thought to be kusala. This is not known most of the time.

We may want to have more understanding than we actually have at this moment, and that is clinging to a self, that is wrong. Whatever we say or think, mostly it is done with the idea of self. There may be clinging to the idea of self even when we do not think, that it is "I" or "mine". Clinging is a yoke, it is like the thread of a spider's web, very fine but strong and hard to cut through.

Seeing sees visible object. When sati arises one can begin to know that it is not "I" who sees. Seeing is different from visible object. Only

---

[3] Anumodana means gratefulness, and dāna is generosity. It is the appreciation of someone else's kusala.

very little at a time can be understood. Visible object may appear, but we should not try to make ourselves experience visible object with nobody in it. When we learn more about nāma and rūpa there will be conditions for awareness of them.

Very shortly after seeing, hearing or the other sense-cognitions akusala citta with clinging arises already. Acharn said that it is not easy to understand that there is clinging to seeing right now. It sees. When asked "who sees?" we would answer that it is "me". She explained that the more understanding develops, the more it realizes how difficult and subtle the Path is. As understanding develops, it has to understand more and more subtle defilements and other dhammas as not self. Paññā can see how complex it is to have more understanding of each reality. If there is no understanding latent tendencies cannot be eradicated. When I remarked that we would have less problems when there is more understanding, she answered: "Right, but paññā goes deeper, deeper than we can imagine. Paññā has to become very keen and develop, otherwise it cannot understand realities as not self. Paññā has to see lobha in order to let go of taking lobha for 'me'. Energy or effort (viriya cetasika) encourages one to continue all the way."

Clinging can be so subtle that it is not noticed. That is why the Buddha taught us the akusala cetasikas which are āsavas, intoxicants or cankers.

There are four āsavas (Dhammasangani §1096-1100):

1. the canker of sensuous desire (kāmāsava),

2. the canker of becoming (bhavāsava),

3. the canker of wrong view (diṭṭhāsava),

4. the canker of ignorance (avijjāsava).

The āsavas keep on flowing from birth to death, they are also flowing at this moment. Are we not attached to what we see? Then there is the canker of sensuous desire, kāmāsava. We are attached to visible object, sound, odour, flavour and tangible object. We are infatuated with the objects we experience through the senses and we wish to go on experiencing them. One of the cankers is clinging to becoming. Every

one clings to becoming, to being alive. We want to experience all objects
through the sense-doors.

Another group of defilements is the group of the Floods or Oghas
(Dhammasangani §1151). There are four floods which are the same defilements as the cankers, but the classification as floods shows a different
aspect. The "floods" submerge a person again and again in the cycle of
birth and death.

Another group of defilements are the Yoghas or Yokes. They are the
same defilements as the cankers and the floods. The yoghas or yokes
are stronger than the āsavas, they tie us to the cycle of birth and death.

We often ask questions with an idea of self, and it is unknown when
we cling to the idea of self at such a moment. Acharn would remind us
all the time: "There is a yoke." When I answered that I would not say
anything any more, she said "Yoke again". We cannot escape the yokes
but they are there to be known. We have to develop understanding,
only paññā can know realities precisely.

Acharn said: "Does one mind about having kusala or akusala? When
one minds it is 'me', the yoke is there. If one tries to stop akusala, how
can one know one's accumulations? The idea of 'self' is so strong. There
is no understanding that it is there, while one is wishing. Many people
just want to be good and they do not know their defilements at this moment. Right mindfulness can arise before you can think about wanting
to have it, or waiting for its arising. In the same way as seeing arises.
This is the understanding of its nature of anattā. Paññā understands
when there is a moment with sati and when without sati. Otherwise
sati cannot develop. It does not develop with desire and this is very difficult. Usually there is attachment but paññā can begin to understand
attachment. One is trapped all day."

Seeing only sees what is visible object and after it has gone we think
of many stories on account of what was seen. Seeing arises only for one
moment and at that moment people and things do not appear. After
that many moments of thinking arise. Every reality arises only once,
"once upon a time", and then it is gone completely. Acharn asked
several times: "Is it worth clinging to what is completely gone, each
moment?" We think of what is past, once upon a time, and then we
live in a dream. Without awareness and direct understanding life is like
a dream. Even when we talk about ultimate realities we are dreaming,

we are not mindful of them. When direct understanding arises we are awake just for a moment. At the moment of direct understanding no words are needed and as soon as we use a word we are thinking. At that moment the reality has gone completely.

We learn from the texts that kamma produces result, vipāka, in the form of rebirth-consciousness and of sense-cognitions throughout life, such as seeing or hearing. Without understanding of the characteristic of seeing, we cannot know what vipākacitta is. "It is still me, not vipāka", Acharn said. In the beginning it is not possible to understand seeing as vipāka. Seeing has to be known as a reality, as a dhamma. Seeing is nāma, it has no shape and form; it arises because of conditions and it sees now. It is different from thinking. We do not have to name it vipāka or think of vipāka. No one can prevent seeing from arising. It is uppatti (origin, coming forth). It just appears for a moment, but we believe we see people and think of many stories, and that is nibbatti (generation, resulted) [4]. There are five pairs of the sense-cognitions of seeing, hearing, smelling, tasting and the experience of tangible object through the bodysense, and of each pair, one is kusala vipākacitta, the result of kusala kamma, and one is akusala vipākacitta, the result of akusala kamma. These cittas directly experience a sense object as it arises at the appropriate sense-base.

We can come to know the difference between seeing that directly sees visible object and the other cittas that follow. Even the citta that succeeds seeing and that, though it does not see, still experiences visible object, needs the cetasika vitakka, thinking, in order to be able to experience visible object. Vitakka is translated as thinking, but it is not thinking in conventional sense. It "strikes" or touches the object so that citta can experience it. Afterwards in that sense-door process kusala cittas or akusala cittas arise in a series of seven and they experience visible object in a wholesome way or unwholesome way. In the following mind-door process kusala cittas or akusala cittas arise, and after that mind-door processes of cittas arise that think about the object. Thus, the vipākacittas that are the sense-cognitions of seeing, hearing,

---

[4]These terms occur in the "Visuddhimagga" XXI, 37, 38, under "appearance as terror". "Herein, arising (uppādo) is appearance here in this becoming with previous kamma as condition (purimakammapaccayā idha uppatti)... Generation (nibbatti) is the generating of aggregates (the khandhas)".

smelling, tasting and the experience of tangible object directly experience the relevant sense object and they do not need vitakka. They are completely different from all following cittas. In order to distinguish them from the following cittas they are called "uppatti". Whereas the following cittas are called "nibbatti".

Throughout our discussions Acharn emphasized time and again the difference between uppatti and nibbatti. Uppatti, such as seeing or hearing, is what appears now. One moment of seeing or hearing is quite different from the following moments of citta when we think of what was seen or heard, when we think of stories that are not real, when we live in a dream. It reminds us of the fact that seeing arises and falls away very rapidly and that after they have fallen away we are thinking on account of what is seen for a long time. We believe that the stories we think of are true. We like what has already fallen away. We continue to live in the past, in what is "once upon a time". Thinking is conditioned and we should not try not to think but it can be understood as a reality different from seeing. It is beyond control. The notions of uppatti and nibbatti remind us of the nature of anattā of realities. The Buddha explained time again about the sense-cognitions and the objects experienced by them. After the sense-cognitions kusala cittas or akusala cittas may arise. When there are mindfulness and understanding, ignorance will be eliminated and even arahatship may be attained.

In the "Bāhiyasutta" ("Minor Anthologies", Khuddaka Patha, the "Verses of Uplift" Udāna, I, 10) we read that Bāhiya Dārucīriya thought of himself as an arahat. A deva advised him to visit the Buddha at Sāvatthī. He asked the Buddha to give him a teaching but the Buddha refused this two times. The commentary[5] explained that the reason for this was that Bāhiya was too excited to listen. When Bāhiya asked for a teaching the third time, the Buddha said:

> "Then, Bāhiya, thus must you train yourself: In the seen there will be just the seen, in the heard just the heard, in the imagined just the imagined, in the cognized just the cognized. Thus you will have no 'thereby'. That is how you must train yourself. Now, Bāhiya, when in the seen there will be to you just the seen, in the heard just the heard,

---

[5]Translated by Peter Masefield, Volume I. PTS.

in the imagined just the imagined, in the cognized just the cognized, then, Bāhiya, as you will have no 'thereby', you will have no 'therein'. As you, Bāhiya, will have no 'therein', it follows that you will have no 'here' or 'beyond' or 'midway between'. That is just the end of Ill."

We read that Bāhiya attained arahatship. Not long after the departure of the Exalted One, Bāhiya was attacked by a cow and gored to death.

We read in the commentary as to "with respect to the seen... merely the seen...": "It is of the extent seen (ditthamattaṃ) since it has the extent seen (ditthā mattā), meaning, the thought process will be of the same extent as eye-consciousness. This is what is said: 'Just as eye-consciousness is not excited, is not blemished, is not deluded with respect to the form that has gone into its range, so will there be for me an impulsion of the same extent as eye-consciousness in which lust and so on are absent, I will set up an impulsion of the same measure as eye-consciousness.'"

Seeing-consciousness is vipākacitta which is not accompanied by the unwholesome roots of attachment, aversion and ignorance. It merely sees visible object. Usually akusala cittas with attachment and ignorance follow upon seeing, but when there is awareness and right understanding instead they do not arise. Bāhiya could not have reached arahatship without realizing nāma and rūpa as mere dhammas. We read further on in the commentary about visible object and seeing:"... occurring (as they do) in accordance with conditions, being solely and merely dhammas; there is, in this connection, neither a doer nor one who causes things to be done, as a result of which, since (the seen) is impermanent in the sense of being oppressed by way of rise and fall, not-self in the sense of proceeding uncontrolled, whence the opportunity for excitement and so on with respect thereto on the part of one who is wise?"

The same is said with respect to the other objects experienced by the sense-cognitions through the relevant doorways.

It will take a long time to know seeing as it is, as a mere dhamma. Sometimes a moment of understanding may arise and after that ignorance arises again and covers up the truth. As Acharn said, we should not mind, because that is the way it is. If we long for more understanding we are yoked again.

49

Thinking of the Past

We think of death as the end of a lifespan but in reality there is at each moment death of citta that falls away. There are three kinds of deaths[1]: momentary death, khaṇika maraṇa, which is the arising and falling away of all conditioned dhammas; conventional death, sammuti maraṇa, which is dying at the end of a lifespan; final death, samuccheda maraṇa, which is parinibbāna, the final passing away of the arahat who does not have to be reborn.

Life goes on without understanding the truth. Seeing sees visible object and because of our delusion we think that we see people who seem to be already there. It also seems that seeing can stay, that we are seeing all the time. Ignorance covers up the truth. Seeing falls away immediately, but since dhammas arise and fall away so rapidly it seems that the different moments of seeing that arise again and again are one period of time that lasts for a while. Understanding can be developed

---

[1] "Dispeller of Delusion," Commentary to the Book of Analysis, Classification of the Truths, 101.

of the characteristic of seeing and there is no need to pinpoint in what process it has arisen.

Seeing falls away but the sign (in Pali: nimitta) of seeing remains. Even so visible object falls away but the sign or nimitta of visible object remains. The nimitta covers up the truth of realities which arise and fall away very rapidly in succession. No one can really directly experience one particular reality, because there are so many realities arising and falling away. The rapid succession of dhammas, such as visible object, leads to the experience or impression of shape and form and to the idea of people and things. A simile can be used to explain this: when we take a torch that we swing around we notice a circle of light. In fact what we take for a circle of light consists of many moments, but it seems to be a continuous whole. There is a reality that can be seen and paññā begins to understand that what is seen cannot be any one at all. Only memory and thinking condition the idea of someone or something.

The term saṅkhāra nimitta, the sign of conditioned dhammas [2] pertains to the fact that each of the five khandhas[3] which arise and fall away has a nimitta: rūpa-nimitta, vedanā-nimitta (feeling), saññā-nimitta (remembrance), saṅkhāra-nimitta (the other fifty cetasikas apart from feeling and saññā)[4] and viññāṇa-nimitta (citta). Since nibbāna does not arise and fall away it is without nimitta, it is animitta.

Conditioned dhamma falls away but the nimitta remains. It is a sign or nimitta of the reality that arises and falls away, but we do not realize the arising and falling away. We mislead ourselves, taking for permanent what is impermanent. We take for self what is beyond control. There is no need to think all the time: "it is a nimitta" or, "the reality has fallen away". Characteristics are appearing and they can be investigated. Saṅkhāra nimitta denotes a nimitta of a reality appearing right now. The reality and its nimitta can be compared to a sound and its echo. We should remember what Acharn said: "The reality and the nimitta

---

[2]The "Path of Discrimination" ("Patisambhidhamagga"), I, 438 speaks about seeing as terror the signs of each of the five khandhas, whereas nibbāna is animitta, without sign. Saṅkhāra nimitta also occurs in the Visuddhimagga XXI, 38.

[3]All conditioned dhammas, saṅkhāra dhammas, can be classified as five different khandhas or aggregates. One khandha is rūpa, and four are nāma.

[4]In this context saṅkhāra refers to saṅkhārakkhandha. The term saṅkhāra dhammas refers to all conditioned dhammas, to all khandhas. Saṅkhārakkhandha refers to one khandha, the khandha of "formations".

of it appear like sound and its echo, who knows which is which? Instead of finding out whether nimitta is a paramattha dhamma, know that it is now. No one can pinpoint a moment of experiencing an object or the object itself."

We learn to be aware of characteristics of dhammas that appear but knowing about nimitta makes it clearer that dhammas fall away so fast. It helps to understand their nature of anattā, they are beyond control. What has arisen is gone already before we realize it. "Once upon a time" can be seen as an extremely short moment ago. We can remember what Acharn said long ago: "We have dear people, people who are close to us, but dhamma arises and then falls away. Seeing has fallen away and there is nothing left. Thinking and all dhammas fall away completely. This is not different from the moment a dear person dies. We are thinking about a dear person but thinking falls away completely."

The colour that appears through the eyes is the nimitta, the sign referring to the visible object that is accompanied by the four Great Elements of Earth (solidity), Water (cohesion), Fire (temperature) and Wind (motion). There is a great variety of the four Great Elements, and since they have different degrees of hardness, softness, heat or cold, it is a condition for the nimittas to be varied. Whenever visible object appears or seeing appears, there is the sign of the rapidly arising and falling away of realities. A single moment of seeing cannot be experienced.

The succession of the arising and falling away of visible object leads to an idea of continuity, the perceiving of shape and form. Acharn explained: "Memory just marks and forms up the idea of a particular shape and form of this or that person. It is all that can be seen. Close your eyes and there is no more that which can be seen... Without reality there is no nimitta but the arising and falling away is so rapid that it cannot be directly experienced."

Because of wrong remembrance of self, attā-saññā, the nimitta is taken for something. Concepts are thought of because of different nimittas. Sarah also gave some more explanations: "Thinking has an idea of shape and form and that leads to the idea of eyebrows, people and things. Without experiencing visible object many times there could not be the sign of visible object and without that sign there could not be thinking about the outward appearance and details of things. One thinks of concepts of people and things on account of what is seen."

When we have no understanding there are just concepts about realities as permanent phenomena which don't arise and fall away instantly.
When we have more understanding of nimitta, we see that whatever we
experience arises for a moment and is then completely gone. We cannot
hold on to it. Acharn said:

"That is life. No matter how happy or unhappy we are, all these
moments are gone. What we take for so very important in life is gone.
Such moments are just objects of ignorance and attachment. What is the
use of experiencing all these realities at this moment? Understanding
this is the beginning of seeing dukkha, which is the arising and falling
away of realities. Each conditioned reality is dukkha. It just arises and
falls away and it cannot be controlled. It is time to eat, to sleep, to
move, to think, but we have an idea that 'I will do this'. We can come
to understand the paññā of the Buddha and his compassion to teach,
to let others understand whatever appears."

At the end of my stay in Thailand a short visit to Chiengmai was
planned and I wanted to join this. We took the plane and stayed one
night, but there were two full days of Dhamma discussions. I had been
to Chiengmai before and, thus, it was a happy meeting again with old
friends. We had lunch in the cultural center where we were offered
traditional Northern dishes, like bamboo filled with pork and a great
variety of vegetables. The sessions were in an auditorium in the hotel
where we stayed overnight. I had to climb a podium with very steep
steps, but people assisted me from all sides.

Acharn explained about nimitta that when seeing, there is clinging
to the nimitta as something or somebody. The impingement of visible
object on the eyesense is a condition for seeing that arises and falls
away very rapidly. Because of the arising and falling away again and
again a nimitta or sign of continuity appears. She said: "There is a
nimitta of different shapes and forms. Saññā remembers them wrongly
as something that stays. There is wrong remembrance of self, attā-
saññā. Concepts are known because of different nimittas. Because of a
concept we know what something is. Because of thinking of nimitta we
know when and where there is food. If there is no reality, there is no
nimitta and no shape and form."

We have to know the extent of our understanding and if we try to
find out more than we can understand, we are clinging again. When

understanding develops we can let go of clinging very gradually. We have possessions in our house but do we have them now? We are only thinking of them. When we return home, they may not be there anymore. We should develop understanding with courage and cheerfulness. People mostly follow their own ideas and do not study the teachings with respect. Therefore, the teachings will dwindle and disappear.

The last afternoon, before our departure, one of our friends sang a song in honour of Acharn. She praised her wisdom in explaining the Dhamma to all of us. The song was very charming with a melody in the Northern style of music. When we were at the airport on our way back we waited in the VIP room where we had a Dhamma discussion for another hour. People showed a great interest and had many questions. Acharn reminded us again of the Buddha's last words, saying that we should not be neglectful, also with regard to listening to the Dhamma. There are dhammas all the time but we do not know that they are dhammas. Their different characteristics should be investigated.

The Buddha taught the four noble Truths: the Truth of dukkha, the Truth of the origin of dukkha, the Truth of the cessation of dukkha and the Truth of the Path leading to the cessation of dukkha.

Dukkha is the arising and falling away of dhammas. What arises and falls away is not worth clinging to, it is unsatisfactory. The origin or cause of dukkha is craving, because of craving we have to reborn and that means the arising and falling away of nāma and rūpa again and again. The cessation of dukkha is nibbāna and the Path leading thereto is the eightfold Path.

Paññā has to be developed on and on for aeons before the four noble Truths can be penetrated. The Buddha showed in his first sermon[5] that there are three phases in the development of understanding and these pertain to each of the four noble Truths.

There are three "rounds" or inter-twining phases of the understanding of the four noble Truths. They are: understanding of the truth, sacca ñāṇa, knowledge of the task to be performed, kicca ñāṇa, which is the development of understanding of realities, and knowledge of the task that has been done, kata ñāṇa, which is the direct realization of the truth.

---

[5]Kindred Sayings, V, 420. The Foundation of the Kingdom of the Norm.

Acharn referred very often to these three "rounds" or phases and explained that without the first phase, sacca ñāṇa, the firm understanding of what the four noble Truths are, there cannot be the second phase, kicca ñāṇa, the performing of the task, that is, satipaṭṭhāna, nor the third phase, kata ñāṇa, the fruit of the practice, that is, the penetration of the true nature of realities.

With regard to the first phase, she said that there should be the firm intellectual understanding of the first noble Truth, and that means understanding that there is dhamma at this moment, that everything that appears is dhamma. Acharn said that it must be the firm understanding that seeing arises and falls away, and that we should not be ignorant of seeing. All dhammas should be known, otherwise the idea of self cannot be eradicated. She said:

"Who sees? When anattā is understood it is the beginning of the right Path." When we listen to the Dhamma and consider what we hear the intellectual understanding of realities, that is, the first phase, sacca ñāṇa, gradually develops and then it can condition the arising of satipaṭṭhāna. This means that the second phase, knowledge of the task, kicca ñāṇa, begins to develop. The practice, paṭipatti, is actually knowledge of the task that has to be performed.

The second noble Truth is craving or attachment. Craving or clinging in daily life should be understood. The clinging to self has been deeply accumulated and we should consider this more. We cling to satipaṭṭhāna and this can induce wrong practice. We should learn at what moment this occurs, the test is always at this moment. Understanding of what appears at the present moment through one of the six doorways leads eventually to the abandonment of craving. Seeing, for example appears now and it can be known as only a conditioned dhamma, no self who sees. However, attachment takes us away from the present object, time and again, so that we are forgetful of seeing that appears now. Also attachment can be known as a dhamma.

The ceasing of dukkha, namely nibbāna, is the third noble Truth. Also with regard to the third noble Truth there are three phases: understanding what the ceasing of dukkha is, sacca ñāṇa. Paññā can come to see the danger and disadvantage of the arising and falling away of conditioned dhammas and it will see the unconditioned dhamma that does not arise and fall away as freedom from dukkha. We should have the firm understanding that detachment and the eradication of defilements is the goal. We should be convinced that it is possible to attain this goal only if we follow the right Path. Understanding of the task in order to reach this goal is kicca ñāṇa. At the moment of enlightenment nibbāna is experienced and defilements are eradicated. Understanding of the task which has been performed, the realization of nibbāna, is kata ñāṇa.

The way leading to the ceasing of dukkha, namely the eightfold Path, is the fourth noble Truth. Also with regard to the fourth noble Truth there are three phases or rounds. The first round is understanding what the development of this Path is, sacca ñāṇa. This is not theoretical understanding, but it pertains to the development of understanding of the dhamma appearing at this moment. Nāma and rūpa, paramattha dhammas, are the objects of which understanding should be developed. These are different from concepts, from the image of a 'whole' of a person, of the body, of a thing. When there is firm understanding of what the Path is, we shall not deviate from it. The teaching of the three phases shows us that the development of paññā is bound to be an age-long process. We need to develop it with courage and patience.

Acharn was invited to speak at the "World Fellowship of Buddhists". I went to their center with Jonothan. It was a long taxi drive because at that time several streets were blocked during anti-government demonstrations. We had to walk through a park to reach the place.

Acharn said:

"Reality is very daily. It should be studied, otherwise we never know the truth. Does anything belong to you? Even seeing does not belong to you. Right understanding, when it arises, begins to see realities as no being. Seeing is seeing. At the moment of hearing there is no seeing. Is sound real? It has its own characteristic. Nobody can change the characteristics of realities. When one has not heard the Dhamma one thinks: 'I see a person'. Visible object is a reality that is seen and after that one thinks of shape and form because of saññā. Each moment is conditioned. Understanding is conditioned."

Several people showed a real interest and asked questions. We discussed the fact that it is not by chance that someone comes to a particular place at a particular time to listen to the Dhamma. It must be because there was an interest in the past and this has been accumulated so that there are conditions to listen again, to consider again. In this way understanding can grow.

The Buddha taught anattā all the time. Anattā of what? Of realities or dhammas. We should not think so much about names and terms, but understand the reality represented by a name. We may stare at the texts but it may happen that the meaning escapes us. Then we may go all the wrong way, and this is very dangerous.

When reading suttas it may seem that the Buddha spoke about impermanence of concepts, such as persons or possessions, but this was the method of teaching to certain people who needed first conventional truth until they were ready to accept ultimate truth (paramattha sacca). So, he often spoke about people in different situations. When reading about conventional truth we can consider the deeper meaning, the truth of realities.

When people had deep sorrow about the loss of dear ones, they needed at first a gentle approach by way of situations and persons. Not everybody is ready to accept the truth that each reality falls away very rapidly, never to come back, and that there is nothing left. When we read in the suttas about death we can be reminded of momentary death. At each moment dhammas arise and then fall away never to return. If we believe that people stay or that possessions are there all the time, we live in a dream.

We read in the "Sutta Nipāta", the Group of Discourses, the Chapter of The Eights No.6[6]:

> " Truly this life is short; one dies less than one hundred years old. Even if anyone lives beyond (one hundred years), then he dies because of old age.

> People grieve for their cherished things, for no possessions are permanent. Seeing that this separation truly exists, one should not live the household life.

> Whatever a man thinks of as 'mine', that too disappears with his death. Knowing thus indeed, a wise man, one of my followers, would not incline to possessiveness.

---

[6]Translated by K.R. Norman, PTS 1992.

Just as a man, awakened, does not see whatever he met with in a dream, even so one does not see beloved people when they are dead and gone.

Those people are seen and heard of, whose name is 'so and so'. When he has departed, only a person's name will remain to be pronounced. Those who are greedy for cherished things do not abandon grief, lamentation and avarice. Therefore the sages, seeing security, have wandered forth, abandoning possessions. Of a bhikkhu who lives in a withdrawn manner, resorting to a secluded residence, of him they say it is agreeable that he should not show himself in any dwelling.

Not being dependent upon anything, a sage holds nothing as being pleasant or unpleasant. Lamentation and avarice do not cling to him, as water does not cling to a (lotus)-leaf.

Just as a drop of water does not cling to a lotus(-leaf), as water does not cling to a lotus, so a sage does not cling to what is seen or heard or thought.

Therefore a purified one does not think that purity is by means of what is seen, heard or thought, nor does he wish for purity by anything else. He is neither empassioned nor dispassioned."

The commentary explains as to the words "a bhikkhu who lives in a withdrawn manner", that he practises so that the citta becomes detached. The word bhikkhu refers to the "excellent worldling" (kalyāṇa putthujana) or the "trainer" (sekha puggala, the ariyan who is not arahat). As to not showing himself in any dwelling, this means that the wise person is free from dying, he does not have to be reborn.

The development of understanding of whatever reality appears now leads to detachment. As we read: "A sage does not cling to what is seen or heard or thought". He understands realities as they are.

50

Courage

The world with all the people is quite different from what we used to think, before we heard the Dhamma. Even though we listened for a long time we have not penetrated the truth of realities. We may repeat the word "There is no one there. Everything is dhamma", but as we listen more to Acharn we come to realize how little we know. This is beneficial, we have to continue to listen and consider the Dhamma with courage and cheerfulness.

The world seems so large, but there is only one citta that experiences an object and then falls away. Acharn reminded us many times that we are not together with another person but with citta that experiences visible object and with citta that thinks, with citta that experiences sound and with citta that thinks, with citta that smells odour and with citta that thinks. We are alone in our own world. We think of another person but there is only citta that thinks and then falls away.

Acharn said: "Paññā can arise and it can accumulate. It is not a matter of 'doing something' but of understanding. Everyone would like to have paññā, but the moment of understanding is paññā. When a

355

reality appears paññā can know the truth. Do not try to have it. At this moment it can be known to what extent paññā has developed."

We have to understand seeing and visible object. Time and again seeing arises and, thus, we should not be forgetful of the present reality. Some people may find seeing too ordinary to consider, not interesting enough. But it arises because of the coming together of different factors. Visible object and eye-base are rūpas that have not fallen away yet. Rūpa does not fall away as rapidly as nāma. There are conditions for them to associate exactly at the time they have not fallen away yet, so that kamma, a deed committed in the past, can produce seeing. We always took seeing for granted, but actually, it is amazing that seeing arises.

Seeing experiences visible object and only for that extremely short moment the world is bright. When seeing has fallen away other cittas succeed seeing in the eye-door process which, although they do not see, still experience visible object, but the world is no longer bright. It seems that when we notice persons on account of what has been seen, that the world is still bright, but this is not so. We are thinking and, although our eyes are open, the world is dark. Thinking and other experiences are interspersed with moments of seeing visible object very rapidly, and it seems that we are seeing all the time. However, the moment of seeing is extremely short, it arises and falls away. Thus, in reality only one short moment is bright and all other moments are dark.

Because of our ignorance we take phenomena for permanent and self. It seems that we see people and things and that whatever we see was there already for a long time and that the world keeps on being bright.

In the beginning the momentary arising and falling away of realities, one at a time, cannot be realized. Understanding has to be developed further so that impermanence can be directly penetrated.

We read in the "Kindred Sayings" (IV, First Fifty, Ch 3, § 23, Helpful), that the Buddha said:

> " 'I will show you a way, brethren, that is helpful for the uprooting of all conceits. Do you listen to it. And what, brethren is that way?
>
> Now what think you, brethren? Is the eye permanent or impermanent?'

'Impermanent, lord.'

'What is impermanent, is that weal or woe?'

'Woe, lord.'

'Now what is impermanent, woeful, by nature changeable, –
is it fitting to regard that as: This is mine. This am I. This
is myself?'

'Surely not, lord.' "

The Buddha then explained the same about the other sense-doors,
the objects experienced through them, and the cittas that experience
these objects. He said that the person who realizes the truth attains
arahatship and eradicates conceit.

The Buddha draws our attention to realities such as the senses, all
the objects that can be experienced and all the cittas that experience
these objects. The Dhamma is very precise. We do not even know what
hearing is. It seems that we hear words that are spoken, or that we hear
dogs barking, but only sound is heard. We have to get used to realities
one at a time. It will take very long before the arising and falling away
of precisely this or that reality is directly known. In this sutta we see
that the Buddha mentions realities (dhammas) and not concepts, no
collection of things. In this sutta he truly teaches Abhidhamma, higher
dhamma or dhamma in detail. Or in other words, paramattha dhamma,
dhamma in the highest sense. The Buddha asked after each reality he
mentioned whether it was permanent or impermanent. He wanted the
listeners to consider the truth with respect to each reality, one at a time,
right at that very moment. It is only dhamma at this moment that can
be investigated.

A collection of things does not exist. Where is a person? Is it
seeing, hearing or thinking? Only one citta arises at a time. Once we
understand this, we know the difference between reality and concept.

The Great Disciples at the Buddha's time could after only a few
words realize the truth of impermanence: the arising and falling away
of seeing that appeared at that moment, of visible object and of the
other realities that appeared at that moment. But we are beginners.
Impermanence is not realized by thinking, it is by direct understanding

and no words are needed. It is not thinking: "everything comes to an end". Anybody could come to this conclusion.

We read and repeat: "all conditioned dhammas are impermanent", but these are only words to us. What arises and falls away at this moment: a nāma or a rūpa? Citta with understanding and mindfulness can take only one object at a time. Does seeing fall away now, or visible object? This has to be known very precisely.

There are specific characteristics (visesa lakkhaṇa) and general characteristics (samañña lakkhaṇa). The general characteristics are: impermanence, dukkha, anattā. These general characteristics cannot be realized immediately. First it has to be known precisely what seeing is as different from visible object. The specific characteristics have to be known first. So long as we join realities together we take them for some "thing", for a self, for permanent. Seeing is different from thinking, different from attachment, these are different realities, each with their own specific characteristics. That is the reason why Acharn always stressed: you have to know realities first as only a dhamma, and that at the present moment, now.

The Buddha taught for forty-five years so that people would have conditions for direct awareness and understanding. The Buddha had immeasurable compassion to teach so that others could understand whatever reality appears at this moment. Without him we would be in complete darkness, the darkness of ignorance. We would not know what is real and what is not real. We would not know our attachment and all other vices, we would not know how to develop kusala. We should study what the Buddha taught with genuine respect. Every word he said is important.

We should begin to learn what dhamma is from this very moment. In the beginning one does not know anything at all about dhamma, the reality that is appearing now. When we listen we can begin to see that what arises and appears at this moment is dhamma; we can understand it as dhamma. We can understand the characteristic of dhamma instead of thinking about the "story" of dhamma.

We read in the "Path of Discrimination" (Patisambhidamagga, Treatise on Knowledge I, Ch 71, the Great Compassion) that Enlightened Ones when seeing all the dangers and disadvantages of worldly life, have great compassion for beings. We read at the end:

"Upon the Enlightened Ones, the Blessed Ones, who see
thus, 'I have crossed over and the world has not crossed over;
I am liberated and the world is not liberated; I am controlled
and the world is uncontrolled; I am at peace and the world
is not at peace; I am comforted and the world is comfort-
less; I am extinguished and the world is unextinguished; I,
having crossed over, can bring across; I, being liberated, can
liberate; I, being controlled, can teach control; I, being at
peace, can pacify; I, being comforted, can comfort; I, being
extinguished, can teach extinguishment,' there descends the
Great Compassion. This is the Perfect Ones knowledge of
the attainment of the Great Compassion."

It was the Buddha's great compassion to teach in such a way that
people who listened could develop their own understanding.

Many conditions are necessary for right understanding to develop.
Acharn often reminded us that there is not a self who is trying to develop
paññā, but that saṅkhāra-kkhandha is operating. Saṅkhārakkhandha
(the khandha of formations) includes all cetasikas apart from feeling and
remembrance. All sobhana cetasikas (beautiful cetasikas) are included
such as sati, paññā and other wholesome qualities. She explained that
the development of right understanding is understanding of whatever
appears. This is conditioned by listening and considering the Dhamma.
She said: "Leave it to saṅkhārakkhandha. They are working on and
on, all by themselves." When we really consider this we shall be less
inclined to think that we have to "do" something special in order to
have more understanding.

All wholesome qualities, such as the "perfections" have to be developed together with right understanding. Paññā is very weak, it needs
the support of all kinds of kusala so that the 'other shore' can be reached.
This shore is the shore of defilements and the 'other shore' is enlightenment, when defilements are eradicated. We need courage, viriya, so as
not to become downhearted but continue on the right way of development. We need dāna, generosity, so that we are not self-centered all the
time, thinking of our own pleasure. We need determination (adiṭṭhāna)
to continue on and on considering the reality appearing now, whatever
difficult situations we have to face, since we see the benefit of right un-

derstanding. We need truthfulness, sincerity: to what extent is there paññā and to what extent still ignorance. We do not want to be deluded about the truth of realities and be blinded. We should not mistakenly believe that we have understood what we are still ignorant of. With sincerity we have to develop all kinds of kusala. We need patience, to listen and carefully consider each word of the teachings. We see that many conditions are necessary for the development of paññā.

Sarah spoke about difficulties many people face with anxiety and depression. She said: "We learn that these are kinds of aversion, not liking, not accepting life now as it is. No one likes such states because of the unpleasant feelings, but no one minds about the attachment and pleasant feelings which lead to the anxieties and depressions. So often, we find ourselves lost in the stories about past and future and just forget that now, the realities are simply the seeing of what is visual, the hearing of sounds and thinking about such experiences. The ideas thought about in our imagination are not real. This is why we look at the actual realities more and more."

This is true, the more we listen, the more we come to see the importance of understanding the present dhamma. In our daily life we are absorbed in many different events that take place, or in what we read in the newspaper. At the hotel in the small pool that I use for my early morning swim, a huge snake was found, just ten minutes before I would enter the pool. On account of this it is natural that we think of many stories of what could have happened. At this time it was Chinese New Year, the Year of the Horse. Children were dressed and performed a dance mimicking a lion's movement. One could throw money inside his wide-open mouth and then the lion would bow and thank the giver. Only visible object is seen, but on account of visible object we go on thinking for a long time. Gradually we can come to see the difference between thinking of stories, of concepts and the experience of seeing and other ultimate realities.

At our last session in the "Foundation" Acharn stressed all the time: not the words are important, but what is understood right now at the present moment. What about seeing now? We do not need any words, we have to attend to its characterisic when it appears now. The present moment cannot be emphasized enough. It is very helpful that Acharn stressed the difference between textbook knowledge and understanding without naming realities, by attending to their characterstics. We are likely to call seeing vipāka (result of kamma) and clinging to visible object akusala but we can learn that their characteristics are different when they appear. Gradually we can learn that seeing is quite different from attachment, without calling them by name.

Acharn spoke about "seeing now" every day. Once we have some understanding of it as only a conditioned dhamma we will come to know what a reality is as different from a concept. Acharn often explained that what has fallen away never comes back and that this is the meaning of dukkha: the reality that just appears and disappears and never comes back. What was experienced in the morning is not now and what will be experienced in the evening is not now. Each moment is past and there is just the idea of self, of "I", all the time. What from head to toe could be "I"?

During our sessions clinging to the "self" became more apparent, even when we do not think expressively: "it is mine". We may believe that hardness is known as only hardness, but when it appears at some location in the body it shows that we cannot let go of the idea of body, it is always "somewhere in my body". Seeing appears but when it appears at some location, namely at the eye-base, there is still an idea of my eye. It takes a long time before there is detachment from the idea of "self" or "mine". Direct understanding of a dhamma is without words. Even when we talk about ultimate realities we are thinking of concepts, concepts of realities. During our discussions this became clearer.

Usually there is no understanding, and, thus, we live in a dream. Now, when there is not direct understanding and awareness, we are dreaming. Even when we are talking about ultimate realities, we are dreaming. But when direct understanding arises we are not merely thinking, we are awake just for one moment. It takes a long time to realize the true nature of realities. Acharn explained with endless patience that "there is no one there". To remind me of the truth she said: "Where is Lodewijk? He is no more, but also when he was still alive there was no Lodewijk. No Lodewijk, no Nina". Her remark helped me to see that the Dhamma has to be applied in daily life, at this moment. She often asked whether seeing, hearing or thinking is a person. It is not a person, because each moment is gone completely. It is hard to accept, but it all depends on paññā: is it sufficiently developed? We

need more listening and considering so that paññā can grow. In theory
we know that person is a concept, not a reality. But right now we cling
to concepts, to persons, as if they are real. It is beneficial to know what
one does not know yet. I am very grateful to Acharn that she untiringly, with great compassion, explained that this moment is dhamma,
not "us". She said "this moment", because only what is present can be
investigated, it arises only once and immediately it is past: "once upon
a time".

Part IX

The Cycle of Birth and Death

51

Preface

In Memory of Lodewijk

Soon after Lodewijk's passing away I decided to undertake alone a journey to Thailand. In January 2013 Acharn[1] Sujin, Sarah and other friends had organized a three weeks sejourn in Thailand for a group of Vietnamese friends and other friends from different countries whom I have known for a long time. There were three different trips outside Bangkok: to Hua Hin which is near the sea, to Wang Nam Khiao or Korat, in the North East, and to Kaeng Krachan, a place where Acharn Sujin and Khun [2] Duangduen regularly stay and where we often had visited them before.

I had never thought that I would come to Thailand again, but it all happened according to conditions. Thanks to Sarah's encouragement I could undertake this journey, and I am most grateful for the kind concern and moral support of Sarah, Jonothan and the other friends.

---

[1]Acharn is the Thai word for teacher. In Pali: ācariya.
[2]Khun is the Thai word for Mr. or Mrs.

365

I was surrounded by a group of sympathetic friends who were always ready to give me assistance.

When I was young and I married my beloved one I did not think that there must be an ending too. That seemed so far away. When the end comes it is so hard to accept the unavoidable. We keep on thinking of stories, beautiful ones and sad ones. Thinking is a reality, it arises for a moment and then falls away. The stories we think of are not realities, they are imaginations.

Throughout our journey Acharn Sujin was never tired of explaining again and again the true nature of what appears right now, at this moment, like seeing, visible object, hearing, sound or thinking. I am very grateful to her that she time and again reminded us of the present moment, the reality appearing now. That is the only moment the true nature of a reality can be investigated. This helped me to understand that the truth in the ultimate sense (in Pali: paramattha dhamma) is quite different from concepts and stories which are made up by our imagination and which we find so important.

We may think for a long time about what happened in the past, about other people, what they did and said, but such moments are different from developing understanding of realities that appear now, one at a time. The whole of the Buddha's teachings deal with the present moment.

It is beneficial to constantly hear about seeing, visible object, hearing or thinking that can be directly known when they appear. Otherwise we forget what is reality and what is not and we spend our days dreaming about what is not reality. A great lesson I learnt while in Thailand. These constant reminders were most helpful to me.

52

What is Life?

In the "Kindred Sayings", II, 180 (Nidāna, Ch XV, § 4, Tears) we read that the Buddha said at Sāvatthī:

> "Incalculable is the beginning, brethren, of this faring on. The earliest point is not revealed of the running on, faring on, of beings cloakedd in ignorance, tied to craving.

> As to that, what think you, brethren? Which is greater:- the flood of tears shed by you crying and weeping as you fare on, run on this long while, united as you have been with the undesirable, sundered as you have been from the desirable, or the waters in the four seas?"

> "As we allow, lord, that we have been taught by the Exalted One, it is this that is greater: the flood of tears shed by us crying and weeping as we fare on, run on this long while, united as we have been with the undesirable, sundered as we have been from the desirable- not the waters in the four seas."

"Well said! Well said, brethren! Well do you allow that so has been the doctrine been taught by me. Truly the flood of tears is greater...

For many a long day, brethren, have you experienced the death of mother, of son, of daughter, have you experienced the ruin of kinsfolk, of wealth, the calamity of disease...

Why is that? Incalculable is the beginning, brethren, of this faring on. The earliest point is not revealed of the running on, faring on, of beings cloakedd in ignorance, tied to craving.

Thus far enough is there, brethren, for you to be repelled by all the things of this world, enough to lose all passion for them, enought to be delivered therefrom."

We are born, we die and then we are born again, this goes on and on so long as we are in the cycle of birth and death. Each life is very short, before we ralize it it comes to an end. When we are reborn we do not remember our life as it is at present, just as at this moment we do not remember our past life. What has fallen away never comes back and this is true of each moment of consciousness, and each physical reality. Each moment will be immediately past, but we are deluded and take mental phenomena and physical phenomena for permanent and self. The Buddha taught about realities in detail so that they can be understood as non-self (in Pali: anattā).

For a few days I stayed in the same hotel as my friends Sarah and Jonothan, the Peninsula hotel in Bangkok. I spent a happy time in their company and throughout my journey they gave me kind advice when I was in trouble. From my window I looked across the river to the Oriental Hotel where Lodewijk and I had enjoyed many pleasant days. These belong to the past now.

The next day I heard that a good friend, Ivan Walsh, had died suddenly. We went to the temple where rituals were performed and where later on the cremation would take place. Here Acharn Sujin and several friends were present. In the morning Acharn's sister, Khun Sujid, and Khun Sujid's daughter had still seen Ivan on the street, and now he is another person. It can all happen so suddenly.

The departing from this life is similar to the departing from last life. When we passed away from last life and we were born into this life, all that happened in the past is forgotten. It is difficult to accept this because of our clinging. We do not like the idea of being forgotten by our beloved one who passed away to another life.

Acharn explained to me that it is also difficult to accept the truth of this moment: "Whom do you see? There is always someone, even now." In reality there is no person, there is no one who can stay. What we take for a person is consciousness (in Pali:citta), mental factor arising with consciousness (in Pali: cetasika) and physical phenomena (in Pali: rūpa). These are only fleeting mental phenomena and physical phenomena which arise and then fall away immediately.

Seeing-consciousness is a moment of consciousness, a citta, that sees only what is visible, visible object, which is a physical phenomenon, a rūpa. It sees visible object just for an extremely short moment, and then it falls away. After the seeing has fallen away we think with attachment about things and persons we believe we see. It seems that we see them, but in reality we do not see them, seeing has fallen away already. Because of remembrance, saññā, a cetasika (mental factor) arising with each citta, we think of persons and things and we believe that they stay. In reality seeing, visible object or thinking arise for a very short moment and then fall away. They are mere elements and nobody can change their nature. Acharn said: "What has fallen away never comes back again, never, never."

I said that it is so sorrowful when I think about Lodewijk, that he never comes back. Acharn answered:

"Think of yesterday. Where were you yesterday? And think of this morning, where were you? There is no one at all, just this moment. We have to be very courageous to know that this is true. Even when there is unpleasant feeling, it is just a moment. It has arisen, and if it had not arisen it could not be here right now."

Nina: "Right understanding is so weak."

Acharn: "Yes, because of the self, because of you. But when it is not you it is only the nature of an element. So, we do not mind how many lives will come because we cannot force the ending of the cycle without conditions. It has to be like this. But paññā (understanding of realities) develops and develops. That is why the Buddha taught us the

Jātakas, the stories of his previous lives as a Bodhisatta. Each reality has gone, sound, sight, nothing is left. Is one attached to someone in one's thoughts? But actually there are only seeing, thinking, visible object."

The Buddha, during countless previous lives as a Bodhisatta, developed wisdom, right understanding, so that in his last life he could become the omniscient Buddha. He developed right understanding again and again of seeing, visible object, hearing, sound, attachment, generosity, of all realities of daily life. We also have to develop right understanding of realities life after life so that eventually enlightenment [1] can be attained and defilements eradicated.

Seeing is a reality, it arises and experiences just what is visible, and then it falls away. It arises because of conditions: eyesense and visible object are conditions for seeing, and it is a citta that is the result of kamma, vipākacitta. It only sees visible object, but we believe that we see a person or thing. That is thinking, arising on account of what is seen. Thinking is not vipākacitta. When we think, the citta may be wholesome citta (kusala citta) or unwholesome citta (akusala citta). It seems that we can see and think at the same time, but only one citta can arise at a time and experience one object. Cittas arise and fall away succeeding one another extremely rapidly and that is why we are deluded about the truth.

Thinking is usually motivated by akusala (unwholesomeness), and this is the case when we are not intent on what is wholesome, such as generosity, helping others or developing understanding. Citta can think of reality or of what is not a reality, but a concept. When we are living in a dream world all day, thinking of what is not real, we are deluded and the citta is akusala. We should remember that there is no one in the visible object, no person or thing. Visible object is only a kind of rūpa that impinges on the eyesense and that can be seen. We have an idea of "I see", but there is no self who sees, only seeing sees.

Acharn explained: "When thinking of Lodewijk or Ivan, there is attachment and it hinders, it hinders the understanding of seeing, but

---

[1] Enlightenment, in the context of the Buddhist teachings, is highly developed paññā that eradicates defilements and experiences the unconditioned dhamma, nibbāna. There are different stages of enlightenment.

it takes a long time to really understand this. The Path is very subtle, but very effective, paññā really knows what hinders.

Now we do not know what hinders. We cry and we think a lot about the situation we are in. When paññā sees what is a hindrance it cannot hinder any more, because it is understood."

Sarah remarked: "People often say that they found it so difficult in the case of separation through death that they did not have a chance to say farewell, but actually, it is just clinging to one's own thought, one's own idea."

Acharn Sujin said: "Even that moment is gone, not to be thought about again. It is past and past and past, all the time. Nothing is left, only thinking and memory. Nothing can belong to anyone at all."

This was a good lesson reminding us not to attach too much importance to the stories which are objects of our thinking. Thinking arises, it is conditioned and we cannot prevent it, but we can remember that what really matters is learning the truth of the reality appearing right now.

Ivan's body was laid in state in the temple with one hand stretched out so that we could sprinkle water over it and remember his good deeds. Ivan had always encouraged me to keep on writing about the Dhamma. I was disinclined to use a computer but he had persuaded me to start writing on the computer, so that I could share what I wrote with many people.

Acharn remarked: "So, I smile to Ivan, and may he appreciate all my good deeds. The Buddha did not teach anyone to cry, because that is akusala. At the moment of kusala there is no aversion (dosa), no crying, but appreciation."

When I said that there are conditions for aversion and sadness, she said:

"When there is understanding one can see that paññā is the best of all conditioned realities, that it is a precious thing in one's life. Everything is past in one's life, all the time. It passes away never to come back."

I remarked that intellectual understanding does not really help. It helps for a while and then it is gone and sadness arises again.

Acharn answered: "The accumulation of right understanding can become stronger, better than other accumulations. Without intellectual understanding how could there be stronger understanding? We have to go step by step, like climbing a mountain. We cannot reach the top immediately. Each step leads to more right understanding."

We have accumulated such an amount of attachment, ignorance and wrong view. Acharn explained that it has to be eradicated little by little, very, very little at a time, but that this is better than none at all. We have to be courageous and patient to develop understanding of one reality at a time.

Elle, Ivan's wife, asked Acharn how to cope with sadness and loneliness. She found it so very difficult to be alone in the house. Acharn explained that one is not alone when one studies the word of the Buddha; one is in his presence, he is addressing his words to us. This is true, but we have to listen again and again until there is more understanding of whatever appears at the present moment.

Acharn said: "As to thinking about living alone, as soon as it is known it is gone, as fast as that. Thinking follows and it seems permanent, but as soon as it is known it is gone."

During this journey I began to see that dwelling in the past, in stories about Lodewijk's sickbed, his last days, his suffering, is quite different from studying and considering what is real in the ultimate sense and appearing at this very moment, like seeing and visible object. We discussed about paramattha dhammas (ultimate realities) for hours, day after day. There is a great contrast between the world of concepts and imaginations and the world of realities. This helped me not to be completely absorbed in what is not real.

Ivan's body was laid down in a case and then the monks chanted texts. Acharn spoke about Ivan's life, and this is also the life of all of us:

"He was born and he died. What did he get from his whole life? Everything arises and passes away in splitseconds, all the time, from day to day, from moment to moment. Nothing belonged to him because there is no him. The rūpa-elements and the nāma-elements arise and fall away by conditions and never come back. Everyone's life is like this because there is no self. That is why we listen to the truth of whatever appears now, to understand it as truth. To understand seeing as seeing; no one sees and it does not belong to anyone because it is gone completely, never to come back. How can it be my seeing? It is only a moment of experiencing an object. Who can prevent seeing from arising? There are conditions for its arising, and, thus, it arises."

Life is only the experiencing of an object through one of the six doorways of the senses and the mind. Only one citta arises at a time, experiences an object and then falls away. At the moment of seeing just what is visible, there cannot be the experience of sound, these are different cittas, experiencing different objects. The citta which thinks, thinks of persons or situations. In the ultimate sense a person is mere elements that arise and fall away. We can learn that one is born alone, sees alone, thinks alone and dies alone. After passing away from this life there is no return of the same individual.

53

Living alone

Acharn Sujin repeated many times that what is now today, will be yesterday tomorrow. This reminds us that all we find so important now will be past in no time. Right understanding of realities that arise and fall away will lead to detachment. We find it very important to be in the company of friends, but Acharn reminded us that in a short while we shall not know each other anymore. In a next life we shall have new friendships. She spoke about an example in the Tipiṭaka about seven friends who in their last life did not remember that they were friends before. They attained arahatship.

Acharn said: "When we listen more there will be more understanding of seeing. There must be that which sees and that which is seen, only that. There is no other world, no one there. Cittas arise just one at a time, there is no hearing, no sound, no idea about the object that is seen and no thinking.

If nothing arises at all there is no world. Whatever arises, even just one reality, that is the world. It is the arising and falling away of different realities. The meaning of arising and falling away is: it never

375

comes back. No one is there, only different cittas, different cetasikas, different realities. Understanding is not developed by anyone. It is developed by listening, considering; no one can do anything because there is no self.

A moment of understanding is like a drop of water in the ocean of ignorance."

Understanding is not developed by anyone because there is no person, no self who develops it. Understanding itself develops when there are the right conditions for it. There is such a great deal of ignorance, but the Dhamma is like an island in the ocean of concepts, the ocean of defilements.

Seeing is one citta and when it arises there cannot be hearing at the same time. Seeing experiences visible object. Hearing is another citta that experiences sound. It may seem that we can see and hear at the same time, but this is a delusion. Each citta can experience only one object at a time, and it falls away immediately. After it has fallen away we think of what has been seen and heard, and then we live in the world of concepts.

What we take for a person are mere elements arising and falling away. We read in the "Visuddhimagga" (XI, 30):

> "What is meant? Just as the butcher, while feeding the cow, bringing it to the shambles, keeping it tied up after bringing it there, slaughtering it, and seeing it slaughtered and dead, does not lose the perception 'cow' so long as he has not carved it up and divided it into parts; but when he has divided it up and is sitting there, he loses the perception 'cow' and the perception 'meat' occurs; he does not think 'I am selling cow' or 'They are carrying cow away', but rather he thinks 'I am selling meat' or 'They are carrying meat away'; so too this bhikkhu, while still a foolish ordinary person–both formerly as a layman and as one gone forth into homelessness–does not lose the perception 'living being' or 'man' or 'person' so long as he does not, by resolution of the compact into elements, review this body, however placed, however disposed, as consisting of elements. But when he does review it as consisting of elements, he loses

the perception 'living being' and his mind establishes itself
upon elements."

We think of people as "this man" or "that woman" and we are not
used to seeing what we take for a person as different elements. We might
find it crude to think of a body which is carved up and divided up into
parts, just as a cow is carved up by a butcher. When a cow is peeled
and carved up and then covered again by the skin we may believe that
there is a cow, but in reality there is no cow at all. Evenso we may
believe that a person exists, but there isn't any person, there are only
elements devoid of "self".

We should consider again and again that what we take for a lasting
person are actually mental phenomena (in Pali: nāma) and physical phenomena (in Pali: rūpa) that arise and fall away. Consciousness, citta, is
nāma. There is only one citta arising at a time, but each citta is accompanied by several mental factors, cetasikas, which each perform their
own function while they assist the citta in knowing the object. One can
think of something with aversion, with pleasant feeling or with wisdom.
Aversion, feeling and wisdom are mental phenomena which are not citta;
they are cetasikas which accompany different cittas. Thus, both citta
and cetasika are nāma, they experience an object, whereas rūpa such
as sound or eyesense do not experience anything. Some cetasikas such
as feeling or remembrance, saññā, accompany each citta, whereas other
types of cetasikas accompany only particular types of citta. Attachment,
lobha, aversion, dosa, and ignorance, moha, are akusala cetasikas which
accompany only akusala cittas. Non-attachment, alobha, non-aversion,
adosa, and wisdom, amoha or paññā, are sobhana cetasikas, beautiful
cetasikas, which can accompany only sobhana cittas.

When we lose dear people through death we are bound to feel lonely.
I had the following conversation about this subject:

Nina: "When feeling lonely it is difficult to be aware of one reality at
a time. But if we try to escape this situation there is lobha (attachment)
again."

Acharn Sujin: "That does not work. We have to be courageous,
brave enough to see that there is actually no one, not even you at that
moment. This is the best cure."

Sarah: "Even when we are with people, we are seeing alone, hearing alone."

Nina: "Akusala cetasikas are bad friends and they are gone."

Sarah: "When feeling sorry, there are bad friends."

Nina: "They come again and again and again."

Acharn: "There is only citta with such realities. It cannot stay, it will go away. Is it good to have it?"

Nina: "It is not good to have it."

Acharn: "So, it is better to have understanding."

Nina: "This is not possible on command."

Acharn: "At the moment of understanding there is no regret. One is freed from being enslaved, and this was never realized before because one enjoyed being enslaved.

When there is more understanding of Dhamma there is no wish for anything at all. This is the beginning of understanding. It has conditions for its arising and nobody can do anything at all. We can learn to see realities, one at a time. Like now, there is seeing and at other moments there are hearing or thinking, unknown all the time. But if there is a moment of understanding of a reality, it can arise again and go on to other realities."

Citta experiences one object, and it is actually alone. At the moment of seeing visible object there is no one else, seeing is alone. At the moment of seeing no hearing or thinking arise. Seeing experiences the object alone. When realities are taken as a mass, a collection, there is the world of many people. Cittas arise and fall away in succession very rapidly, they are like a flash. That is why we have a concept or idea of what appears as something permanent. Acharn said that we have to be brave in order to understand that what appears is just a reality. We need courage to let go of wrong view that clings to the idea of person or "self". Right understanding leads to detachment, but our nature is attachment.

While we were in Huahin we went to the sea where Ivan's ashes and bones were to be let down into the water. We went out on a boat that belonged to the Water Police. While we were waiting for the boat in the harbour and also while we were on the boat Acharn kept on speaking about the true nature of the reality appearing at the present moment. We considered realities instead of dwelling too much on situations, on sad events. A monk who always listened to Acharn's radio program was present and after he recited some texts, the ashes were let down into the water. The boat went three times around this place and we kept on throwing flowers into the water. In the end there was a circle of flowers around the place where the ashes went down. Acharn said: this is like the cycle of birth and death.

It is good to be reminded of the cycle of birth and death. The last citta of this life, the dying-consciousness (cuti-citta), is succeeded immediately by the rebirth-consciousness (paṭisandhi-citta) of the following life. Our life is an unbroken series of cittas. Wholesome qualities and unwholesome qualities which arose in the past can condition the arising of such qualities at present. Since our life is an unbroken series of cittas, succeeding one another, wholesome qualities and unwholesome qualities can be accumulated from one moment to the next moment, and, thus, there are conditions for their arising at the present time. When we listen to the Dhamma and we have a little more understanding, this is never lost. Understanding is accumulated and it can grow from life to life.

Each day we had one session of two hours in the morning and one session of two hours later in the afternoon. In Huahin the sessions were in a large lounge of a bungalow where Jonothan and Sarah had one room and where I had another room. After the afternoon session, Thai friends arranged for fruits, cookies and different snacks. There was such an abundance of food that there was no need to go out for supper anymore. Our friends were most attentive to all our needs and looked after us all the time. We went out for lunch to different places and even while we were having lunch Acharn would speak about paramattha dhammas appearing right now. The whole atmosphere was most pleasant while we enjoyed each other's company, the beautiful panorama and the great variety of dishes.

We had the following conversation about understanding realities:

Acharn: "Visible object can be understood but memory takes it for a person or a thing. There should be the development of all realities, even of thinking. One can begin to see the difference between right understanding and wrong thinking about people and things. Do not have the idea that there should not be thinking, but understand thinking as just a reality."

Nina: "Trying not to think is forced."

Acharn: "It is not natural. Paññā cannot grow when it is not natural.

It arises by conditions and it can become stronger and stronger."

Sarah: "When it is time for thinking, time for sadness, it is conditioned like that. No one can change it or stop it."

Nina: "We should not select, but just be aware of any reality."

Acharn: "The self is trying. When there is trying it shows that the understanding of anattā (non-self) is not firm, not well established.

But no matter whether there is a day without awareness, it is by conditions. When awareness arises by its own conditions it is much better than trying the whole day with the idea of self. The idea of self is building up at that very moment. When awareness arises for only a moment the difference can be seen between unawareness the whole day and a moment of understanding of a reality. Only paññā can see when lobha does not arise and when it arises all the time, after seeing, hearing, at the moments of trying. Lobha is like a big boss."

Several times Acharn reminded us of the power of lobha, attachment. It is dangerous that it is mostly unknown. Only paññā can see when lobha arises and leads one astray. One may wish to have more understanding but at such a moment one clings to the idea of self.

After our sejourn in Huahin, we stayed for the weekend in Bangkok. On Saturday Khun Duangduen offered us a lunch in her garden which is a pleasant, restful place. On Sunday there were sessions in Thai in the building of the "Dhamma Study and Support Foundation"[1]. It was Acharn's birthday and it was inspiring to see many people who came with gifts and paid respect to Acharn. We could watch the great generosity of the Thais. The little room Acharn uses to meet people privately was full of flowers, fruits and other gifts.

During the session we had conversations about life in conventional sense and life in the sense of paramattha dhammas. It was stressed that it is important to know the difference between concept and reality. When we think of people we live in the world of concepts and when understanding is developed of reality as it appears through one of the six doors, one at a time, we come to know the world of paramattha dhammas.

---

[1]This is the center where all sessions with Acharn Sujin take place each weekend.

We had lunch in the Foundation building at a long table with Acharn and other friends. We were enjoying the food offered by a couple who sponsored the meal. Husband and wife served us with such great concern and affection, taking care all the time to see if anybody needed anything. Their children entered the room and paid respect to Acharn. I found it a special experience to be back again in the Foundation. All my Thai friends welcomed me with great cordiality and they kept smiling, radiating kindness. When everyone around us is smiling with sincere kindness, we just have to smile too and it is impossible to be sad and depressed.

Our second trip outside Bangkok was to the North East, to Wang Nam Khiao, also called Korat. On the way we visited a museum of a petrified forest. It was an exposition of the geological history of the region and one could see many rare examples of petrified trees. It was crowded with school children so that we had to wait a long time and since our visit took many hours we arrived rather late in Wang Nam Khiao. This is a mountainous region where we went out for walks in the morning before breakfast. We stayed in peaceful bungalows with a balcony situated at the waterside. We had to walk from our bungalow to the restaurant for breakfast. For lunch we went out to a variety of places. The lunch tables were outside in the garden of the restaurant so that it seemed that we were in the middle of a forest. One of our outings was to the best restaurant in the region where very refined food was served and which, as healthy air was concerned, had the seventh place in the world. This made me think of Kuru where the outward conditions and the climate were most favorable for the development of the understanding of Dhamma.

I was sitting next to Acharn in the car and I enjoyed the mountainous landscape. Meanwhile we had a most beneficial Dhamma conversation.

Acharn: "Sometimes there is very strong lobha or very strong dosa (aversion), who can condition that? The nature of attachment is different from the nature of aversion. Who can control them? There must be conditions, no matter kusala or akusala arises. The truth can appear little by little as not permanent. At this moment there can be a little understanding of what appears as uncontrollable; it does not belong to anyone. Can that which arises and falls away and never comes back be anyone? Not at all. That is the way paññā develops from pariyatti (intellectual understanding), to paṭipatti (development of direct understanding), to pativedha (direct realization of the truth).

Next life one is a different person, suddenly. But past accumulations go on. That is why people have different characters, different likes and dislikes."

Nina: "I experience a very pleasant object with pleasant feeling, such as the mountains."

Acharn: "It is a reality, it is conditioned. It falls away before we know what it is. As soon as it is an object that is experienced, it is gone. Then another object appears and paññā can understand that. The intellectual understanding conditions detachment from clinging when time comes. But it is not as effective as direct understanding. The difference between the two can be seen."

Nina: "It is not so easy to know direct understanding."

Acharn: "When awareness arises it can be seen that it is quite different. Intellectual understanding can condition direct understanding, and it keeps on going by conditions. Otherwise it is always, how, how can 'I' understand."

Often we ask questions with "how can I... " and true, this is motivated by attachment, lobha. We were reminded by Acharn to keep in mind that all dhammas are non-self, anattā, and that we, in that way, never will be lost by our own thinking or by wrong understanding. We cling to having progress in understanding and this is not effective. As Acharn often said, we cannot do anything. Realities arise because of their own conditions and nobody can cause their arising. Seeing arises when there are the appropriate conditions for its arising. Visible object and eyesense are rūpas that condition seeing. Visible object impinges on the eyesense and then there are conditions for seeing. Seeing is caused by kamma, it is vipākacitta.

Some cittas are results of akusala kamma and kusala kamma, they are vipākacittas. Kamma is intention or volition. Unwholesome volition can motivate an unwholesome deed which can bring an unpleasant result later on, and wholesome volition can motivate a wholesome deed which can bring a pleasant result later on. Akusala kamma and kusala kamma are accumulated from one moment of citta to the next moment, and, thus, they can produce results later on. Kamma produces result in the form of rebirth-consciousness, or, in the course of life, in the form of seeing, hearing, smelling, tasting and the experience of tangible object through the bodysense. Vipākacittas experience pleasant objects or unpleasant objects, depending on the kamma which produces them.

Kamma also produces rūpas such as eyesense, earsense and the other sense organs. Without eyesense and without visible object there could not be seeing.

There are several conditions for each dhamma that arises and this shows the nature of anattā of dhammas. We cannot cause their arising.

Evenso, nobody can cause the arising of sati, mindfulness, and paññā, understanding, however much we wish for their arising. They can only arise when there are the appropriate conditions. They are sobhana (beautiful) cetasikas that can only arise with sobhana citta and there are many levels of them. When we listen to the Dhamma and we learn about the realities that can be experienced through the six doorways, one at a time, and when we consider again and again what we hear, gradually intellectual understanding can develop. If the conditions are right, direct awareness of realities can sometimes arise so that direct understanding can develop. But this does not occur so long as we are wishing for it.

Acharn reminded us all the time of clinging to sati and paññā that is deeply rooted and hard to detect. We tend to forget that sati and paññā are non-self, anattā. The development of understanding leads to detachment, detachment from the idea of self.

54

No Return

We read in the "Sutta Nipata" (vs. 547-590) [1]:

"Unindicated and unknown is the length of life of those subject to death. Life is difficult and brief and bound up with suffering. There is no means by which those who are born will not die. Having reached old age, there is death. This is the natural course for a living being. With ripe fruits there is the constant danger that they will fall. In the same way, for those born and subject to death, there is always the fear of dying. Just as the pots made by a potter all end by being broken, so death is (the breaking up) of life.

The young and old, the foolish and the wise, all are stopped short by the power of death, all finally end in death. Of those overcome by death and passing toanother world, a father cannot hold back his son, nor relatives a relation.

---

[1] Translated by John D. Ireland (Kandy: Buddhist Publication Society, 1983).

See! While the relatives are looking on and weeping, one by one each mortal is ledaway like an ox to slaughter.

In this manner the world is afflicted by death and decay. But the wise do not grieve, having realized the nature of the world. You do not know the path by which they came or departed. Not seeing either end you lament in vain. If any benefit is gained by lamenting, the wise would do it. Only a fool would harm himself. Yet through weeping and sorrowing the mind does not become calm, but still more suffering is produced, the body is harmed and one becomes lean and pale, one merely hurts oneself. One cannot protect a departed one (peta) by that means. To grieve is in vain."

As we read, we do not know the path by which a person came into this world or departed from it. We do not know his past life nor his future life. We are in this world for a very short time and since we still have the opportunity to hear the Dhamma and to develop right understanding of all that appears through the senses and the mind-door, we should not waste our life away. The understanding of Dhamma makes our life worth living. Understanding is more precious than any kind of possession.

Visible object, sound and the other sense objects that appear are present only for an extremely short while. As soon as they have been experienced they are gone already, never to return. Visible object falls away and then a different visible object arises and falls away again. It seems as if visible object can stay for a while. We cling to shape and form and we are taken in by the outward appearance of things. It seems that we see people and things, but this is a delusion.

Visible object is that which is seen. It could not appear without the citta which sees, seeing-consciousness. Seeing-consciousness is an element that cognizes or experiences, it is nāma, whereas visible object is rūpa, it does not know anything. Rūpas do not arise alone, they arise and fall away in groups or units of rūpas. Each group consists of several kinds of rūpas which always include four kinds of rūpas which are called the four Great Elements. These are the following rūpas:

the Element of Earth or solidity

the Element of Water or cohesion

the Element of Fire or heat

the Element of Wind (air) or motion

The Element of Earth appears as hardness or softness, the Element of Fire as heat or cold, and the Element of Wind as motion or pressure. These are tangible object, they can be directly experienced through the body-consciousness when they appear. The Element of Water is not tangible object, it cannot be experienced by body-consciousness. When we touch what we call water it may be softness, heat or cold which are experienced. The function of the Element of Water or cohesion is holding together the accompanying rūpas in one group, so that they do not fall apart.

These four Great Elements that arise with all other rūpas are their foundation, they support them. Thus, when visible object appears, there have to be these four Great Elements together with visible object in one group, but they are not seen. Only visible object is seen at that moment. The "Visuddhimagga" (XI, 100) states that the four Great Elements are "deceivers":

"And just as the great creatures known as female spirits (yakkhinī) conceal their own fearfulness with a pleasing colour, shape and gesture to deceive beings, so too, these elements conceal each their own characteristics and function classed as hardness, etc., by means of a pleasing skin colour of women's and men's bodies, etc., and pleasing shapes of limbs and pleasing gestures of fingers, toes and eyebrows, and they deceive simple people by concealing their own functions and characteristics beginning with hardness and do not allow their individual essences to be seen. Thus they are great primaries (mahā-bhūta) in being equal to the great creatures (mahā-bhūta), the female spirits, since they are deceivers."

Realities are not what they appear to be. Because of saññā, the cetasika remembrance that arises with every citta, we remember shape and form and immediately we cling to what we believe are things and persons.

One may be infatuated by the beauty of men and women, but what one takes for a beautiful body are mere rūpa-elements.

The "Visuddhimagga" (XI, 98) states that the four Great Elements are like the great creatures of a magician who "turns water that is not crystal into crystal, and turns a clod that is not gold into gold..." We are attached to crystal and gold, we are deceived by the outward appearance of things. When we touch crystal or gold, only hardness or cold is experienced. There is no crystal or gold in the ultimate sense, only rūpas which arise and then fall away.

We cling to our body, but in reality what we take for our body are only different elements that arise and then fall away immediately. We can ask ourselves: "where is our body?" It is nowhere to be found.

We learn about the different rūpas of our body, but intellectual understanding of what the Buddha taught is not sufficient. Acharn reminded us all the time to pay attention and investigate the reality appearing right now. What is past has gone already and the future has not come yet. Learning the characteristic of what appears at this moment is the only way to penetrate the truth of realities.

Hardness appears and we immediately have an idea of "my hand" or "my leg", it is not understood yet as just a reality, just a dhamma. When we think of my hand or my leg, we think of a collection of things, of a "whole", and that is a concept, not a paramattha dhamma. Hardness impinges on the rūpa that is bodysense, and then it is experienced by the citta that is body-consciousness. This is a vipākacitta arising in a process of cittas. Cittas which experience objects through the six doors arise in a process of cittas. When, for example, body-consciousness arises, it occurs within a series or process of cittas, all of which experience tangible object while they each perform their own function. Body-consciousness is vipākacitta, it merely experiences tangible object, it neither likes it nor dislikes it. After body-consciousness has fallen away there are, within that process, akusala cittas or kusala cittas which experience the tangible object with unwholesomeness or with wholesomeness. There are processes of cittas experiencing an object through the eye-door, the ear-door, the nose-door, the tongue-door, the body-door and the mind-door. There is a great variety of cittas: they can be kusala, akusala, vipāka or kiriya, which is "inoperative". Kiriyacitta is neither kusala citta nor akusala citta nor vipākacitta [2]. After the cittas of a sense-door process have fallen away, the object is experienced by cittas arising in a mind-door process, and after that process has been completed other mind-door processes of cittas may arise which think of concepts. We may think of hardness with attachment or wrong view. We take the hardness for a hand or leg that belongs to us.

The teaching about the different processes of cittas helps us to understand that cittas arise and fall away in succession extremely rapidly. The processes take their course according to conditions and we cannot do anything about them and this shows their nature of non-self (in Pali: anattā).

When we listen again and again to the explanation of nāma and rūpa which are conditioned dhammas, non-self, there may be conditions for the arising of sati that is mindful, for example, of the characteristic of hardness. At that moment paññā can begin to investigate that reality so that it will be understood as only a dhamma.

Acharn explained that when hardness appears and there can be awareness of it, it is not the ordinary experience of it by body-consciousness. The object is the same, but it appears more clearly. At that moment there is not vipākacitta but kusala citta accompanied by sati. When direct awareness of a reality arises there is no thinking about it. When we are thinking about realities there usually is an idea of self, we take that reality for something or someone. We can learn the difference between the moments with sati and without sati. When sati arises paññā can begin to know its characteristic, it can understand it as only a reality that does not belong to anyone. When hardness appears we tend to think that it can stay, but it arises and falls away.

We may say that there is no self, but what is it that is non-self? We may use the names nāma and rūpa, but more important is knowing their characteristics when they appear at the present moment. We can learn that what experiences and that what is experienced are different characteristics, without naming them nāma and rūpa. Knowing a characteristic is more important than knowing the name of a reality.

I had a beneficial conversation with Acharn about concepts we are dreaming of and the understanding of realities.

---

[2] Kiriyacitta performs different functions within a process. The arahat has no more kusala cittas but he has kiriyacittas instead.

Nina: "I am absorbed in stories, thinking, O, I would have liked to share this experience with Lodewijk. He would have liked this so much. Now I cannot share this with Lodewijk."

Acharn: "There is no Lodewijk after his death and not even while he was alive."

Nina: "I am thinking in that way because it is conditioned."

Acharn: "Then you are not living alone. In the lone world there is no one."

Nina: "When he was alive I tried to remember that there was no Lodewijk. There is a great deal of thinking, clinging to concepts and dreaming about them."

Acharn: "How rare it is to just be aware of a reality. That can happen when there is more intellctual understanding, sufficient to be a condition for right awareness. By developing more understanding one will let go of the idea of trying to know.

One may be thinking of the self and trying to understand what does not appear."

Nina: "When people have worries or dreams you will always point to the present reality. That is the only solution to our problems."

Acharn: "You want to have the solution with the idea of self and that cannot be a solution at all."

Nina: "That is quite true, we cling to an idea of how I can solve this problem while having dreams all the time, sadness all the time."

Acharn: "Actually, whose problem?"

Nina: "Self, self."

It was most beneficial that Acharn reminded us to what extent we cling to a self. We do not want sadness which is akusala and we try to find methods not to have it. There is no method. When it appears it can be understood as just a conditioned dhamma. We should not try to change the reality that appears already because of conditions. Ignorance of realities can be eliminated, but courage and patience are needed to continue developing understanding of realities.

We tend to hold on to thoughts about the past, but then we should remember that what we find so important today will be yesterday tomorrow. It is completely gone. We have no idea who we were in the past life. All realities we take for a person arise and fall away never to come back. I had a conversation with Acharn about this subject:

Acharn: "It is not I, only the way elements are, different all the time. No one can manage them or have them at will."

Nina: "I can accept this, but it is difficult for me."

Acharn: "That is because of clinging to the self. This will decrease only when there is understanding of a reality as a reality. Otherwise we are always living in a dream. Reality does not appear as it is. Today will be yesterday tomorrow, completely gone, of no importance. No matter what it is. It experiences something and then it falls away."

Nina: "The second day I was In Thailand I heard that Ivan had died and we all went to the temple. I never thought that this would happen."

Acharn: "Today will be yesterday tomorrow and then you do not think much about it. Just let it go.

You see visible object and then it is gone, like yesterday. Remembering this helps to understand anattā. There are no conditions to choose, realities have arisen already. Understanding this is the best in life, otherwise there is only akusala."

Nina: "It was a very long, tiring day to come here, to Wang Nam Khiao."

Acharn: "One can be very patient because of understanding. Everything is just temporary, it is conditioned. Why worry about it. Right understanding saves one from akusala."

It is helpful to be reminded that sad events that happened the day before are all gone. When a dear person is gone for good and will never return we should remember that whatever reality appears now falls away and will never return. Seeing that appears now falls away and will never return. What we take for a person is only citta, cetasika and rupa, elements that are beyond control. When Acharn says that we should understand a dhamma that appears as just a dhamma, it means that we should not take it for self or a person. Instead of thinking of a person who will never return we should remember that each citta and each rūpa that arises now falls away never to return again. Instead of holding on to the world of concepts and situations, to our dreamworld, we can develop understanding of realities so that we will see them as elements that are beyond control. Even when we think of sad events, the thinking is only a citta that arises because of conditions, there is not a person who thinks.

55

Understanding the Present Moment

In the " Mughapakkha Jātaka" (no. 538) we read about the life of the Bodhisatta as prince Temiya who pretended to be cripple, deaf and dumb. He did not want to become a king so that he would be in a situation to commit akusala kamma. The King wanted to find out whether he was really cripple, deaf and dumb and let him undergo all kinds of trials and tribulations.

Finally the King was advised to bury him alive. When the charioteer was digging the hole for his grave, Temiya was adorned by Sakka[1] with heavenly ornaments. He became an ascetic and preached to his parents about impermanence:

> "It is death who smites this world, old age who watches at
>   our gate,
> And it is the nights which pass and win their purpose soon
>   or late.
> As when the lady at her loom sits weaving all the day,

---
[1] King of the Devas.

Her task grows ever less and less- so waste our lives away.
As speeds the hurrying river's course on, with no backward
flow,
So in its course the life of men does ever forward go;
And as the river sweeps away trees from its banks upturn,
So are we men carried along by age and death in headlong
ruin."

He explained to his father that he did not want the kingdom, stating that wealth, youth, wife and children and all other joys do not last. He said:

"Do what you have to do today,
Who can ensure the morrow's sun?
Death is the Master-general
Who gives his guarantee to none."

Lodewijk and I often spoke about the lady sitting at her loom and weaving until her task is done. A life comes to its end so soon.

The text can remind us not to put off our task of developing right understanding of any reality which appears now. The Bodhisatta was unshakable in his resolution to develop right understanding. Also when he was put to severe tests, he did not prefer anything else to the development of wisdom. We are likely to be forgetful of what is really worthwhile in our life. Wisdom is more precious than any kind of possession, honour or praise.

We have learnt that what we take for a person or self are nāma and rūpa. We were often reminded by Acharn that we may say that there are nāma and rūpa, but that their characteristics can be known only right at the moment they appear. Then we do not need the words nāma and rūpa, we do not have to think about them. There is a reality that experiences and a reality that is experienced. We pay attention mostly to the object that is experienced but we should remember that if there is no reality that experiences, nothing can appear, there is no world.

Acharn wanted to help us to understand the characteristic that appears right now instead of thinking about it. When we think about seeing and visible object we only know concepts of realities. Acharn said:

"We do not have to say that seeing is nāma, visible object is rūpa. There is no need to say this because that is only remembrance of the terms one has heard many times and thought about. But what about this moment of seeing? It is so real, because whatever is seen, is seen now and that which is seen is not that which experiences or that which sees it. We do not have to say: 'It is nāma which sees and rūpa which is seen.' This is not necessary. That is not the way to understand it. The way to understand it is knowing that when there is seeing right now that this is seeing. What does it see, what is seen? The thing that is seen is not the seeing. So, there is the beginning of understanding the nature of a reality which can be seen as just that which can be seen, not: that which can be heard."

Acharn kept on reminding us, saying: "There is seeing right now, seeing sees visible object." We immediately think of shape and form of things and we do not know the distinction between seeing and thinking about what is seen. Cittas arise and fall away in succession so rapidly that it seems that cittas such as seeing and perceiving shape and form occur at the same time, but in reality different types of citta arise in different processes. Many citttas arise and pass away between seeing and preceiving the shape and form of something, thinking of things and of persons we believe we see. When the rūpa that is visible object or colour associates with the rūpa that is eyesense, just for a short moment, there are conditions for seeing. Acharn said:

"Without the reality that experiences an object, nothing can appear. One just pays attention to what is experienced and not to that which experiences. That which experiences can be understood as a reality. Without it there is no world, nothing can appear. By understanding this little by little one can know that at the moment of seeing, seeing is not visible object but that it sees a reality, no shape and form. Now it sees. It is very difficult to understand this because we have accumulated a lot of ignorance. We learnt only about concepts. We can come to understand what is meant by right understanding, paññā. It has to be right understanding of whatever appears now. Otherwise it is not paññā, it cannot understand the true nature of the reality which appears. It is only thinking, dreaming about different things. We can have theoretical understanding when we say: 'what is seen is visible object and then there is thinking of a concept'. And now? It is time to understand the distinction between that which is seen and that which is the object of thinking, taking it for something. Thinking of shape and form is not thinking in words. Thinking is not always thinking in words."

It may seem very simple to know that seeing is the experience of visible object and visible object is that which is seen. But this may be only theoretical understanding. Understanding the theory is quite different from the direct understanding of what appears at the present moment. Acharn said: "And now?" The different characteristics of dhammas have to be realized one at a time at the moment they appear, right now. Penetrating characteristics of realities that appear is more important than remembering their names. Whatever appears has to be realized as just a dhamma, so that we shall really be convinced of the fact that in reality there are only dhammas, no person or thing. Dhammas do not stay, they are only present for an extremely short time. No one can condition anything.

When we returned from Korat to Bangkok, we stopped on the way back at Toscana Village for a Dhamma discussion and a lunch. The hilly landscape is somewhat similar to Toscane in the North of Italy. The area was laid out by way of terraces and there was an abundance of flowering trees. After the Dhamma discussion we enjoyed an Italian style lunch. When looking at the gardens, listening to the Dhamma discussions or tasting the food, different sense objects impinged on the doorways of the senses and the mind-door. We are constantly interpreting what we see, hear or experience through the other sense-doors. This can be compared with reading. When we are reading a book, visible object is seen, we see black and white and then we perceive letters and interprete their meaning. Evenso, there is just seeing, hearing, smelling, tasting and body-consciousness and aferwards we are thinking on account of what is experienced. This is our life: seeing and interpreting what is seen, hearing and interpreting what is heard.

We have to carefully consider and understand each word of the teachings, even one word, for example, the word "dhamma". Dhamma is reality which has its own characteristic and which cannot be changed into something else. When we cling to concepts which are denoted by conventional terms such as "tree" or "chair", we do not experience any characteristic of reality. What is real when we look at a tree? What can be directly experienced? Visible object is a paramattha dhamma, a reality; it is a kind of rūpa which can be directly experienced through the eyes. Through touch hardness can be experienced; this is a kind of rūpa which can be directly experienced through the bodysense, it is real. Visible object and hardness are paramattha dhammas, they have their own characteristics which can be directly experienced. We may give them another name, but their characteristics cannot be altered. They appear only for one moment and then they fall away. They are uncontrollable. "Tree" is a concept or idea we can think of, but it is not a paramattha dhamma, not a reality which has its own unalterable characteristic, which arises and then falls away. Ultimate realities should be clearly distinguished from concepts or ideas which are objects of thinking.

Intellectual understanding of the teachings is necessary but it is not enough. It is an introduction to direct understanding. What the Buddha taught pertains to the present moment. Only the present reality can be really understood, not what is past or what is future. That is why Acharn emphasized seeing now, visible object now all the time. These have characteristics that appear and can be attended to without thinking of their names. There can be a beginning of considering whatever appears at this moment even though it cannot be precise.

Visible object which is experienced by seeing-consciousness does not fall away when seeing-consciousness falls away, because it is rūpa; rūpa does not fall away as rapidly as nāma. When an object is experienced through one of the six doors, there is not merely one citta experiencing that object, but there is a series or process of cittas succeeding one another, which share the same object. When seeing-consciousness has fallen away it is succeeded by other vipākacittas and after these cittas have fallen away kusala cittas or akusala cittas arise. Kusala cittas or akusala cittas arise because of conditions: kusala and akusala that arose in the past and that have been accumulated from one citta to the next citta conditions the arising of kusala and akusala at present. We cannot do anything, cittas arise because of their own conditions, but paññā can come to understand the true nature of realities and their conditions.

After the cittas of a sense-door process have fallen away a mind-door process of cittas follows which experience visible object through the mind-door. After that there are other mind-door processes of cittas may think of concepts. The Buddha taught about cittas arising in processes according to a certain order so that people could see that they are beyond control, that nobody can change this order.

Acharn said: "When seeing arises who knows that it is vipāka, and when thinking arises who knows whether it is kusala or akusala? Their characteristics are different, one can see the difference, by not naming them. There can be understanding that seeing is different from kusala or akusala. Just like now: seeing sees and thinking thinks. There can be a beginning to understand that they are so different from each other. Understanding can grow by considering. One can know that kusala is different from ignorance, that attachment is different from non-attachment. There is no rule that 'I' should do this or that in order to have more kusala."

Before the characteristics of kusala and akusala can be known precisely, they should be understood as "just a dhamma". As Acharn pointed out, the different characteristics of realities can be known by not naming them. When we are naming them we are merely thinking about them instead of penetrating their true characteristics.

We should have no expectations as to the arising of kusala and paññā, that is attachment. When there is understanding that all cittas are conditioned it helps to have less clinging to realities as self. The Buddha taught us realities so that we can develop our own understanding instead of blindly following what he taught.

When we were back in Bangkok we had for a whole day Dhamma discussions on a boat. A friend of Pinna had kindly offered us this boat trip and also the lunch that was included. We passed the Temple of Dawn (Wat Arun) and enjoyed the familiar view of the buildings and bridges, but now from a distance, from the waterside. After a delicious meal we climbed off the boat to have a walk and we looked at the dazzling colours of the shops. When we noticed all these colours we were thinking, thinking without words. Even when we do not think in words, the object of the citta can still be a concept. Some of the shops gave lively presentations of walking toy animals. This conditioned our imagination: there could be thinking of a whole story, of a real animal who was walking. Thinking was leading us away from reality. We were offered samples of herbal tea in small cups and it was explained that these herbs could cure all sorts of ailments. Acharn was also walking and then she stood still explaining for quite a while about realities appearing right now, she was never tired.

Some of us had to take a smaller boat to return to the Peninsula Hotel. The captain of that boat looked with approval at what was written on the back of our shirts: "Do good and study the Dhamma". He had been a monk, even an abbot, for ten years and he spoke about meditation. I tried to explain about studying with awareness realities, no matter where one is. There is no need for a quiet place, the realities to be studied are within us and around us. This boat was noisy, not quiet, but we could still discuss Dhamma, discuss about visible object appearing through the eyes, sound appearing through the ears, many realities. It was a good ending of the day.

56

Momentary death

We read in the Kindred Sayings (V, Mahā-vagga, Book XII, Kindred Sayings about the Truths, chapter V, §6, Gross darkness) that the Buddha said to the monks:

> "Monks, there is a darkness of interstellar space, impenetrable gloom, such a murk of darkness as cannot enjoy the splendour of this moon and sun, though they be of such mighty magic power and majesty."

At these words a certain monk said to the Exalted One:

> "Lord, that must be a mighty darkness, a mighty darkness indeed! Pray, lord, is there any other darkness greater and more fearsome than that?"

> "There is indeed, monk, another darkness, greater and more fearsome. And what is that other darkness?

> Monk, whatsoever recluses or brahmins understand not, as it really is, the meaning of: This is dukkha, this is the arising

of dukkha, this is the ceasing of dukkha, this is the practice
that leads to the ceasing of dukkha, such take delight in the
activities which conduce to rebirth. Thus taking delight they
compose a compound of activities which conduce to rebirth.
Thus composing a compound of activities they fall down
into the darkness of rebirth, into the darkness of old age and
death, of sorrow, grief, woe, lamentation and despair. They
are not released from birth, old age and death, from sorrow,
grief, woe, lamentation and despair. They are not released
from dukkha, I declare.

But, monk, those recluses or brahmins who do understand
as it really is, the meaning of: This is dukkha, this is the
arising of dukkha, this is the ceasing of dukkha, this is the
practice that leads to the ceasing of dukkha, such take not
delight in the activities which conduce to rebirth... They
are released from dukkha, I declare.

Wherefore, monk, an effort must be made to realize: This is
dukkha. This is the arising of dukkha. This is the ceasing
of dukkha. This is the practice that leads to the ceasing of
dukkha."

Lodewijk found this text always very awesome and he was highly
impressed by it. So long as we have ignorance there will be no end to
being in the cycle of birth and death. The Buddha showed the danger
of ignorance and exhorted the monks to develop right understanding so
as to realize the four noble Truths.

When we were having breakfast Acharn would usually join us and
speak about Dhamma. During one of our breakfasts, she reminded us
of the four kinds of right effort (samma-padhānas): the effort to avoid
akusala, to overcome akusala, to develop what is kusala, namely the
enlightenment factors [1], and to maintain what is kusala. With regard
to the first right effort, she exhorted us not to have ignorance anymore,
to avoid ignorance which has not yet arisen. There is no self who can
prevent ignorance, but seeing its danger can condition the development

---

[1] Wholesome factors leading to enlightenment, including the Applications of Mindfulness, confidence, energy, mindfulness, concentration, wisdom and many others.

of understanding. There can be a little more understanding each day. Ignorance is not understanding whatever appears. Not understanding is like dreaming, Acharn said. When there is seeing, there is no one in the seeing. We have to consider this again and again so that there will be detachment from the idea of self or person.

Acharn reminded us that when we feel lonely, we are lonely with ignorance, but when we understand the lone world, the world without self or person, we can be cheerful, without problems. Then there are just seeing, hearing and the other realities arising and falling away.

She gave us a precious reminder, saying that when one is sad and depressed one is preoccupied with "self", one thinks of oneself. Such moments can be understood as conditioned realities which arise and fall away. When one is more attentive to the welfare of others, one will think less of oneself.

When people would say that the development of the understanding of realities is so difficult, Acharn would answer: "Now you are praising the Buddha's wisdom." This is true, he accumulated paññā for countless aeons, and he developed the perfections, such as dāna, sīla, mettā or patience. He was determined to develop them in order to reach Buddhahood, out of compassion for all of us. Had he not become an omniscient Buddha who could teach us all realities today, we would be ignorant and we would be enslaved, clinging forever to sights, sounds and all sense objects. We should also be patient and courageous to develop paññā and all good qualities with determination. There can be a beginning now and we should not mind how long the development of the Path will take. We cannot expect to get rid of defilements on command, they are anattā.

Sometimes people asked what the conditions are for sati of the level of satipaṭṭhāna, thus, for sati which is mindful of nāma and rūpa. We read in the Visuddhimagga" (Ch XIV, 141) that its proximate cause is strong remembrance (thirasaññā) or the four "Applications of Mindfulness"[2]. Firm remembrance of the reality right now conditions satipaṭṭhāna. If we forget that there are now only realities there are no conditions for the arising of satipaṭṭhana. There is not sufficient understanding of anattā to condition right awareness now.

---

[2]As explained in the "Satipaṭṭhāna Sutta", they are: mindfulness of body, of feeling, of citta and of dhammas.

The four "Applications of Mindfulness" include all nāmas and rūpas that can be the objects of mindfulness. When they have become the objects of sati they are a proximate cause of mindfulness. Nāma and rūpa occurring in daily life are the objects of mindfulness. There can be awareness of nāma and rūpa no matter whether we are walking, standing, sitting of lying down. Also when akusala citta arises it can be object of mindfulness, it is classified under the "Application of Mindfulness of Citta". One should learn not to take akusala citta for self.

Several times Acharn reminded us that the lack of awareness was caused because there was not firm remembrance (thirasaññā) of what we heard. When one listens to the Dhamma and considers it again and again there can be firm remembrance of what one has heard, and, thus, there are conditions for the arising of sati which is mindful of the nāma or rūpa appearing at the present moment. Thus, we see the value of listening. We listen but we often forget what we heard. We ought to listen more, it never is enough.

Acharn's reminder that today will be yesterday tomorrow is an exhortation not to waste away our short time in this world as humans where we can still listen to the Dhamma and develop understanding. How fast time goes, before we realize it there will be the dying-consciousness, and we do not know our future.

Knowing the theory of the Dhamma is completely different from attending to the reality that presents itself now. Time and again Acharn reminded us of this fact. For example, we have learnt about different feelings: pleasant feeling, unpleasant feeling and indifferent feeling. In each process of citta kusala cittas and akusala cittas arise and these are called in Pali "javana-cittas". Seven javana-cittas usually arise in each process. When we consider the accompanying feeling, we have learnt that pleasant feeling can arise with kusala citta and with akusala citta rooted in attachment, lobha. Unpleasant feeling invariably arises with the citta rooted in aversion, thus, with akusala citta. Indifferent feeling can arise with kusala citta and also with akusala citta, namely, with citta rooted in attachment and citta rooted in ignorance. We have learnt all this in theory, but feelings are realities arising all the time in daily life. We cling to feeling and take them for mine. We could ask ourselves: is there feeling now? It seems, when there is indifferent feeling, that the citta is not akusala, that we do not harm anyone. However, when our objective is not dāna, generosity, sīla, morality, or bhāvanā, mental development, we act, speak or think with akusala citta. Even when we listen to the Dhamma and consider it, thus, when we apply ourselves to mental development, kusala cittas do not arise all the time. They alternate with akusala cittas. We can see that the teachings help us to know the extent of our defilements that arise because of conditions, because they were accumulated for aeons, from moment to moment, from life to life. We can understand somewhat more the nature of anattā of the dhammas that arise. We cannot control the dhammas that arise, but understanding of them can be developed.

Before we heard the Dhamma we had no understanding of realities, no understanding of defilements. We accumulated more ignorance and clinging from day to day. We should be grateful to have listened to the Dhamma and to be able to begin developing understanding of our life, of the truth. We learn that there are many different types of conditions for whatever reality arises.

We find it difficult to accept that a dear person who has died will never return. However, we should realize that each nāma or rūpa that arises falls away and can never return. There is dying at each moment: seeing arises and then falls away for good, and it is the same with hearing, with the other sense-cognitions and with thinking. We shall have more understanding of what the world is: only one moment of experiencing one object at a time, and then gone for good. Even a person who is alive is actually citta, cetasika and rūpa which arise because of conditions and then fall away, which are very temporary.

Seeing dies, hearing dies at this moment, so, where are people, where is a person? Where is a person who dies? In reality there is no person. A moment of seeing cannot be a person, it arises and falls away. We think that there is a permanent person who sees, who hears, but actually, seeing is a conditioned reality that arises and falls away immediately.

Is there any difference between living in the world of concepts and living in the world of absolute realities? What is the difference? It is actually: living in the world of ignorance and living in the world of right understanding. The world of concepts consists of cup, table, person, things. But in the absolute sense, can whatever appears be someone or something permanent? They seem to be permanent because realities arise and fall away so rapidly. It seems as if there is no arising and falling away of anything at all. Even the arising of seeing does not appear and, thus, the falling away of it cannot appear. Whatever is experienced is gone as soon as it is experienced.

From birth to death there are cittas arising in processes, vīthi-cittas, that experience objects through the doors of eye, ear, nose, tongue, bodysense and mind. Vīthi-cittas are alternated by bhavanga-cittas, life-continuum, which arise in between the processes of cittas. The bhavanga-citta which does not experience sense-objects through the sense-doors experiences the same object as the rebirth-consciousness. The rebirth-consciousness, paṭisandhi-citta, is vipākacitta conditioned by kamma and this citta experiences the same object as the object experienced by the last javana-cittas that arose shortly before dying. The dying-consciousness, cuti-citta, experiences the same object as the rebirth-consciousness and all bhavanga-cittas in one lifespan. The rebirth-consciousness, the bhavanga-citta and the dying-consciousness in one lifespan are the same type of citta. The dying-consciousness is immediately followed by the rebirth-consciousness of the next life and then one is no longer the same individual. However, all accumulated kusala and akusala go on to the next life, they go on from life to life. Thus, the cycle of birth and death goes on until the dying-consciousness of the arahat. Then the end of the cycle has been reached.

Acharn reminded us of three kinds of citta: The first citta (in Pali: paṭhama citta) is the bhavangacitta before anything appears. When something appears, such as seeing, hearing, there is the second citta (in Pali: dutiya citta). Finally there is the dying-consciousness, cuti-citta, of the arahat (in Pali: pacchima citta, the last citta). Each life is like this: the rebirth-consciousness arises and then bhavangacittas arise and the object is unknown, nothing appears. When something appears there are process cittas, the second kind of citta. In this way life keeps going on from moment to moment, from birth to death, again and again, until the last moment of the arahat.

At this moment we are in the cycle of birth and death, saṁsara. Yesterday there were seeing and thinking, hearing and thinking, and today it is the same, and so it will be in the future. We are absorbed in the objects we experience, time and again, and this is the cycle of birth and death.

Acharn said:

"What has disappeared does not return again. Realities arise and fall away, arise and fall away. Should one cling? Then one would cling to what has fallen away and is no more. Where should we find it? There is clinging because one does not know the truth. There are only realities that arise and fall away in succession and this does not stop. This is the cycle of birth and death, saṁsara. There is an opportunity to begin to understand this."

So long as ignorance and clinging have not been eradicated we continue being in saṁsara. If we do not develop insight, vipassanā, the number of rebirths will be endless. It was out of compassion that the Buddha spoke about the dangers of rebirth; he wanted to encourage people to develop right understanding of the reality appearing at this moment.

Acharn was emphasizing all the time the value of understanding this moment of seeing, hearing, thinking and all realities that appear. This helped me to see the disadvantage of being absorbed in sad events that happened in the past and of clinging to what has fallen away and will never return. Such ways of thinking are conditioned and instead of trying to avoid thinking we can learn that also the thinking that arises can be understood in order to know it as not "mine", as only a dhamma.

The contrast between living in a dreamworld while clinging to the past and beginning to understand the world of paramattha dhammas became more obvious to me than before. The difference between those two worlds is actually most striking. I am very grateful to Acharn for pointing this out time and again, in many different ways.

We listen to the Dhamma in order to have more understanding of the present moment. During this journey it became clearer to me that listening to the Dhamma is the most precious in life.

57
Pāli Glossary

akusala unwholesome, unskilful

anattā non self

anumodanā thanksgiving, appreciation of someone else's kusala

arahat noble person who has attained the fourth and last stage of enlightenment

Buddha a fully enlightened person who has discovered the truth all by himself, without the aid of a teacher

citta consciousness the reality which knows or cognizes an object

dhamma reality, truth, the teaching

dukkha suffering, unsatisfactoriness of conditioned realities

jhāna absorption which can be attained through the development of calm

kamma intention or volition; deed motivated by volition

kasiṇa disk, used as an object for the development of calm

khandhas aggregates of conditioned realities classified as five groups: physical phenomena, feelings, perception or remembrance, activities or formations (cetasikas other than feeling or perception), consciousness.

kusala wholesome, skilful

lokuttara citta supramundane citta which experiences nibbāna

nāma mental phenomena,including those which are conditioned and also the unconditioned nāma which is nibbāna.

nibbāna unconditioned reality, the reality which does not arise and fall away. The destruction of lust, hatred and delusion. The deathless. The end of suffering

rūpa physical phenomena, realities which do not experience anything

samatha the development of calm

satipaṭṭhāna applicatioms of mindfulness. It can mean the cetasika sati which is aware of realities or the objects of mindfulness which are classified as four applications of mindfulness: Body, Feeling Citta, Dhamma. Or it can mean the development of direct understanding of realities through awareness.

sīla morality in action or speech, virtue

Tathāgata literally "thus gone", epithet of the Buddha

Tipiṭaka the teachings of the Buddha

vipassanā wisdom which sees realities as they are

A

Books by Nina van Gorkom

Buddhism in Daily Life A general introduction to the main ideas of Theravada Buddhism.The purpose of this book is to help the reader gain insight into the Buddhist scriptures and the way in which the teachings can be used to benefit both ourselves and others in everyday life.

Abhidhamma in Daily Life is an exposition of absolute realities in detail. Abhidhamma means higher doctrine and the book's purpose is to encourage the right application of Buddhism in order to eradicate wrong view and eventually all defilements.

Cetasikas. Cetasika means 'belonging to the mind'. It is a mental factor which accompanies consciousness (citta) and experiences an object. There are 52 cetasikas. This book gives an outline of each of these 52 cetasikas and shows the relationship they have with each other.

The Buddhist Teaching on Physical Phenomena A general introduction
to physical phenomena and the way they are related to each other
and to mental phenomena. The purpose of this book is to show
that the study of both mental phenomena and physical phenomena
is indispensable for the development of the eightfold Path.

The Conditionality of Life This book is an introduction to the seventh book of the Abhidhamma, that deals with the conditionality
of life. It explains the deep underlying motives for all actions
through body, speech and mind and shows that these are dependent on conditions and cannot be controlled by a 'self'. This book
is suitable for those who have already made a study of the Buddha's teachings.

Survey of Paramattha Dhammas A Survey of Paramattha Dhammas
is a guide to the development of the Buddha's path of wisdom,
covering all aspects of human life and human behaviour, good and
bad. This study explains that right understanding is indispensable
for mental development, the development of calm as well as the
development of insight. Author Sujin Boriharnwanaket translated
by Nina van Gorkom.

The Perfections Leading to Enlightenment The Perfections is a study of
the ten good qualities: generosity, morality, renunciation, wisdom,
energy, patience, truthfulness, determination, loving-kindness, and
equanimity. Author Sujin Boriharnwanaket translated by Nina
van Gorkom.

Letters on Vipassanā, author Nina van Gorkom. A compilation of
letters discussing the development of vipassanā, the understanding
of the present moment, in daily life. Contains over 40 quotes from
the original scriptures and commentaries.

Introduction to the Buddhist Scriptures, author Nina van Gorkom. An
Introduction to the Buddhist scriptures with the aim to encourage
the reader to study the texts themselves. The book has a particular emphasis to help with the development of right understanding
of all phenomena of life, at the present moment. It is a follow-up
to Nina van Gorkom 's book "The Buddha's Path".

The Buddha's Path, author Nina van Gorkom. An introduction to the doctrine of Theravada Buddhism and the development of understanding and mindfulness through the Buddhist tradition.